MASTERING EXCEL MACROS
LESSONS 1 -10

MARK MOORE

Copyright © 2016 by Mark Moore. All rights reserved worldwide. No part of this publication may be replicated, redistributed, or given away in any form without the prior written consent of the author/publisher or the terms relayed to you herein.

Icons by Icons8 (https://icons8.com/)

Contents

Lessons 1: Introduction 6
    The Workbooks...7
    Who this book is for 7
    What are macros? Why should you learn them?..7
    A Short Section on Programing Theory 8
    Object Method/Property..9
    Finding Macros in Excel 10
    Recording a Macro 11
    Optional...20
    Saving a Macro 20
    Opening a Macro Enabled Workbook 21
    Recording Another Macro 21
    Testing 23
    How to Organize Your Macros..25
    Modules vs. Subroutines 26
    Variables 27
    Declaring Variables...28
    Passing Variables 29
    Using Excel Formulas in Macros 33
    WorksheetFunction 33
    Advanced Formula Use 34
    Conclusion 37
    Online Excel School 37

Lesson:2 Debugging...39
    Developer Ribbon..40
    The VBA Editor 46
    Debugging a Macro...50
    What's Next?..57

Lesson:3 Beginning to Code..58
    Introduction...59
    Figuring Out Macros 59
    Recording Your Actions 59
    Use Google 62
    Use VBA Help..62
    Use Intellisense 63
    Structure of a Macro 64
    Comments 65
    Beginning to Code...66

Lesson:4 If Statements 75
    OFFSET 76

    ActiveCell 77
    IF Statements 78
    ORs and ANDs 85

Lesson:5 Looping 87
    Collections 88
    Stopping a Running Macro 89
    For Each Loop 89
    Looping through a range of cells 93
    For Loop 94
    Do Until Loop 94
    Do While Loop 98
    More Practice 98
    Acknowledgements 99

Lesson:6 Object Variables 100
    Declaring Variables 101
    What is an Object Variable Anyway? 102
    Code Without Object Variables 102
    Code With Object Variables 103
    Debugging 109
    Invoice Creator 114
    Optional Enhancement 121
    Last Word 122
    Acknowledgements 122

Lesson:7 PowerPoint Automation 123
    Intended Audience and Prerequisites 124
    A Quick Note about Spacing 124
    Background 124
    References 125
    PowerPoint 127
    Miscellaneous Topics 136
    Summary 138

Lesson:8 File System Object 140
    Intended Audience and Prerequisites 141
    Background 141
    References 142
    Create Folder 143
    Create Text Files 148
    List Folders 150
    List Files 152
    Modular Programming 155
    FSO Object Reference 161
    Summary 162

Lesson:9 VBA Forms and Events 163
    Data Forms 164
    Built-in Dialogs 167

MsgBox 167
InputBox 171
GetOpenFilename 173
GetSaveAsFilename 175
ActiveX Controls 176
VBA Forms 189
Worksheet Events 200
Lesson:10 Arrays 203
    Introduction 204
    Arrays 204
    Types of Arrays 205
    Array Dimensionality 205
    Declaring Arrays 206
    Data Types 206
    Dynamic Arrays 212
    Yet Another Way to Loop 217
    Two-Dimensional Arrays 218
    Collections 221
    Using Keys in Collections 226
    Lesson Summary 234
    Other Lessons 234

Lessons 1: Introduction

The Workbooks

Before you get started (and if you are new to my lessons) please go to my website and download all the follow along workbooks for the lessons. Each lesson has one or more workbooks that you can use as you read. Practice will reinforce the topics.

When you go to my website you will receive a few emails. The first one is to confirm that you signed up. I have to do this to prevent spam and well, it's the law here in the US. After you confirm, you will receive a second email with a zip file. Detach that and unzip it. There will have all the workbooks for each lesson.

The page on my website to get the follow along workbooks is:

http://markmoorebooks.com/excel-macro-bundle-lessons-1-10/

Who this book is for

This book is intended for normal Excel users who have always been interested in macros but have never found a good resource to learn them. Yes, macros can be intimidating. They can be very difficult, but they don't have to be. If you have always been interested in Excel programming or have thought of a few projects you would like to do, then this is the series for you.

Notice that I said it was a series. This is the first book in the series. Programming is a HUGE topic and if I tried to put everything in one book, it would be huge tome. Now be honest with yourself, if you saw a book on Excel programming that was 1,000 pages, would you really read it? Unless you're in school, most people won't sit down and slog through a huge, dry topic. At best, you'll get through a few chapters, forget most of the material and then stop trying. There's nothing wrong with you, it's just that it a tough topic and it has a lot of stuff in it; it's both broad and deep.

Instead of a huge dry book, I will have several short, to the point lessons covering just one topic. I think this will make the material easier to absorb, less intimidating and if you buy several lessons, it will be easier to open up a specific lesson and review just that one topic.

The goal is not to make you a star Excel programmer. If you want to be that, go for it! This is a good starting point. What you will learn here is intended to be extremely practical. I will give you some best practices here and there but I am going to break many programming 'rules' because, you're not a programmer, you just need to write an Excel macro to help you get your work done. That's it.

Finally, I am going to try my best to make this stuff entertaining. Maybe if I entertain you as we go through this stuff, you'll stick with it and become the office Excel guru? I may fail miserably at entertaining you, you might hate it but then again you just might like it and learn a ton of stuff. That's means I will get a bit 'chatty' in these lessons; just trying to liven things up. Take heart, the lessons are short!

The only way to learn is to break things, to experiment. I wholeheartedly encourage you to change the code I present. Play with it, then come back to the lesson. Learning to program is like learning English (or any other language). There are many ways to write a sentence that conveys the same meaning. If you don't like the way I coded something, and you think you figured out a better way. Go right ahead and use it.

If all this sounds good to you, let's start, if not, go ahead and return the lesson, I won't be offended.

What are macros? Why should you learn them?

Macros are the programming language of Excel. The programming language is called VBA, which stands for Visual Basic for Applications. Don't confuse this with another programming language called Visual Basic (VB).

Visual Basic is a 'true' programming language in that you can use it to build programs that anyone can use. It creates files called executables (exe) that a person can launch from Windows.

Visual Basic for Applications is a bit different. It can't create standalone programs. You have to run it from inside a Microsoft Office program (yup, not just Excel but also PowerPoint, Word, Access). Think of VBA as VB's little brother. They look really similar, they can do almost the same thing, except one has to be run inside of Office.

VBA is very accessible, if you have Excel, you can learn VBA. VBA is a type of programming language called a fourth-generation language (4GL). Every programming generation is further away from using unrecognizable, confusing symbols. 4GL languages are much easier to understand. For example, look at this code:

Selection.Font.Bold = True

Even without knowing how to program, you can see what this does. It makes your selection bold. Yeah, it's a bit weird, but you can understand it.

Just for fun, look at this line from a C++ program (C++ is not a 4GL language, it's super powerful but very tough to learn).

printf("%d:%od:%d\n",tmp->tm_hour,tmp->tm_min,tmp->tm_sec);

You can't really make sense of that can you? Let's all be grateful for 4GL languages!

Why learn VBA?

- It is a good starting programming language
- It is very practical. Most companies use Excel and Microsoft Office.
- It looks great on your resume
- It will make tedious tasks in Excel easy to do
- You just may end up as the office Excel guru!

A Short Section on Programing Theory

This section is not absolutely necessary to learn macros but I wanted to include this just so you can have a clue as to what's going on behind the scenes. Additionally, you will hear/see some of these terms when you continue to learn about macros. I promise this will be painless.

VBA is a programming language that follows a methodology called Object Oriented Programing (OOP). This programming makes building software much easier and is very powerful. The way it works is that programmers build objects (technical term: classes) that do stuff. This object is a template of sorts, when you need a new object you use the template to build one item (technical term: instance). Here's where it gets interesting. Objects can do stuff (technical term: methods) and have characteristics (technical term: properties). Think of methods as verbs and properties as nouns. Objects can also have other objects inside of them. The objects inside inherit the properties of the parent.

OK, one example will clear this up.

There is an Excel file workbook class (a class is a template). When you click 'New' in Excel, you are building a new instance of the Excel file object. That Excel file object has properties (file name, file create date, file size, file creator) and methods (file delete, file move).

The Excel file object has other objects inside it. It has the worksheet object inside and that has the worksheet name property, tab color property, move method, delete method. Note that although the delete method is called the same it does different things. When used on the file object, it deletes the entire file. When used on the worksheet object, it deletes the worksheet, not the file.

Why does this matter when recording a macro?

Because when you write a macro you are basically manipulating methods and properties. Yes, basically that's all you are doing. We refer to the methods and properties using something called the dot notation. Macros use a period (.) to identify the method or property. The syntax (way to write the code)

Object Method/Property

Look at this method:

$$Rows("7:7").Delete$$

Rows ("7:7") is the object. Delete is the method. Remember methods are actions, so you are deleting row #7.
Now look at this property:

$$Range("A10").Value = "text"$$

Properties don't 'do' anything. Objects just 'have' them. For example, a bicycle has the color property. The bicycle doesn't 'do' red, it 'is' red. Same thing for cell A10 (in VBA we call cells ranges). The cell has the word 'text' inside it. You have to set the property = "text".

In summary, objects have methods (they do stuff) and properties (they have characteristics). You can use the methods to do stuff to the object or you can set properties to change the characteristic.

Finding Macros in Excel

Before you can get started writing macros, we need to add the macro interface into Excel. It is there, but the interface is not activated by default.

Let's activate it.

1. Open Excel
2. Click on File
3. Click on Options
4. In the left pane, click on Customize Ribbon
5. In the far right pane, check the box next to Developer

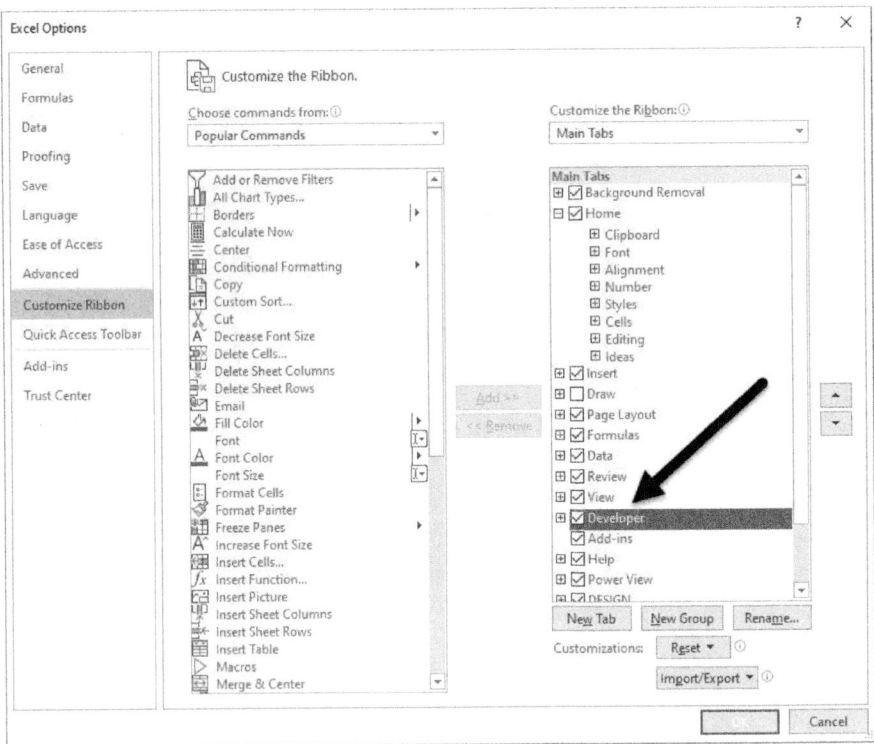

6. Click OK

You now have a new Developer tab in Excel.

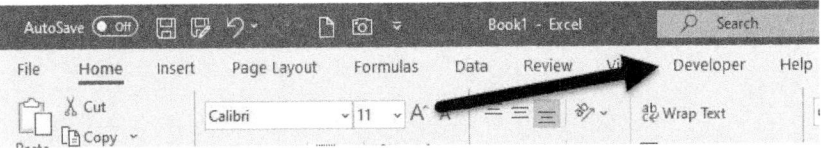

Note: Here's an additional Excel tip. In the Customize Ribbon window you were just in, you can add and remove items from the standard Excel ribbon. If there's a command you use frequently, go ahead and put it where you want it.

Recording a Macro

The best way to learn macros is to let Excel show you how they work. You can record a macro in Excel. Basically, you hit the record button and Excel will literally record every action you make. When you are done, you can hit replay and Excel will repeat all the steps you recorded.

After you record a macro, take some time to look at what was recorded. Change the command around, add or delete some stuff, play with it and you will definitely get the hang of how they work. That's how I began to learn. However, there are tons of things you can't record. That's the major limitation of recoding a macro. It's a good starting point but for anything other than the simplest actions, it falls short.

That being said, that's how we are going to start learning. Let's record a simple macro and then find it.

Before we start, make sure you have added the Developer tab in Excel. If you do not have it yet, please return to the previous section and add it.

Let's record a very simple macro and then examine the generated code.

1. Open a new Excel workbook
2. In the bottom left corner of excel, you will see this icon. The indicated button is one way to start recording a macro.
3. Click that button once

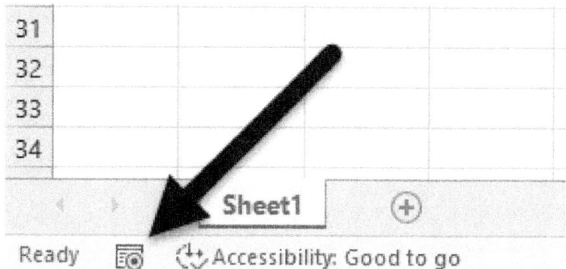

This window will appear:

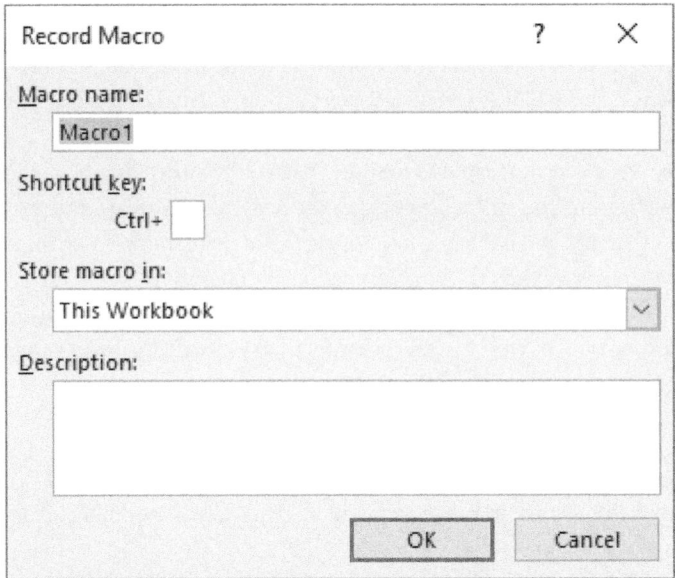

In this window you can set a descriptive name for the macro (no spaces are allowed), a shortcut key, change the location where the macro is stored and add a description. We aren't going to do any of those things for now.

4. Keep all the default values and click OK.
5. Click on cell A1
6. Type in Salesperson
7. Press Enter
8. Click on cell A2
9. Type in Lisa
10. Press Enter
11. Type in Robin
12. Press Enter

If you make a mistake, don't worry about it. Just fix it and continue.

13. Click the Stop Recording button

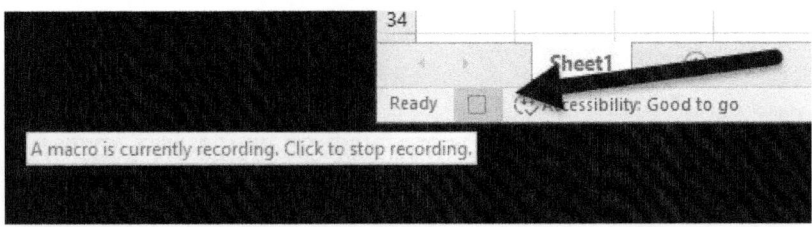

Now let's check out the macro code.

14. Click on the Developer tab
15. Click on the first button. The one that says Visual Basic.

Now an entire new window will show up. This is the Excel VBA editor. I'm not sure what your particular settings are so you might see something a little different than my image. This is what I see.

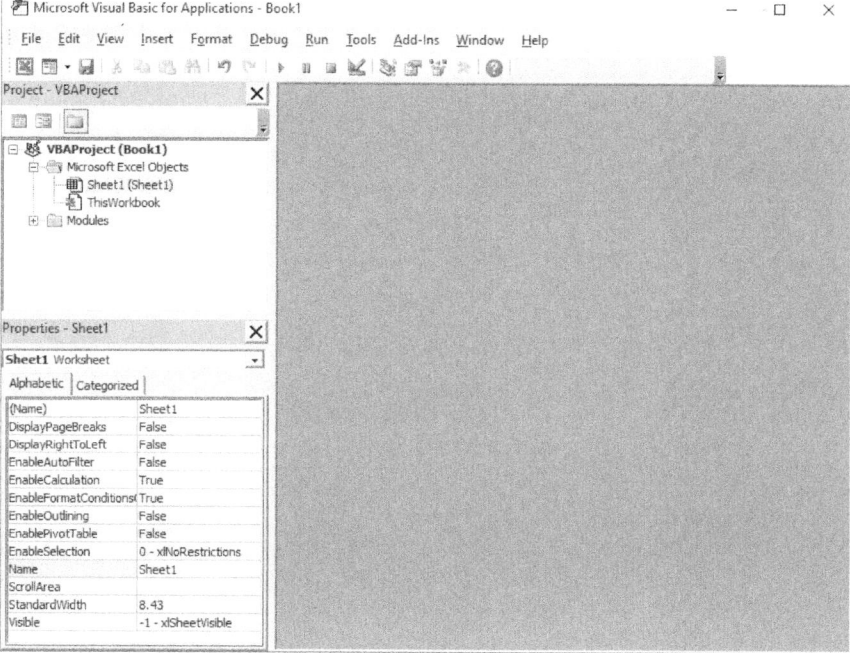

My initial view does not show the macro. The macro is definitely in there, I just have to display it. Before we do that though, let me explain what we are seeing.

The top left pane is the Project window. Here you can see all the worksheets in the workbook and all the modules. What are modules? Modules are where the macros are stored.

The bottom left pane is the Properties pane. This shows the properties of the object selected in the Project window. In the above example, Sheet1 (Sheet1) is selected. It should also be selected in your workbook. If it is not, select it. The properties pane shows the properties for Sheet 1(Sheet1).

The right pane in gray, is the code window. This is where the macro will appear.

Excel trick

I'm going to go on a little tangent to show you a sneaky Excel trick you can do in the Developer window, no programming involved.

Most Excel users understand that a worksheet can be visible or hidden. Hidden worksheets, are obviously, hidden from view. However, there is another state a worksheet can be in...*VeryHidden*.

An exercise will how you how this works.

If you only have one worksheet in your workbook, like I have, you are going to need to insert two more. You'll want three worksheets in the workbook. (Click the + sign next to the worksheet name to insert a new worksheet)

You should have three sheets and your Developer window will show all three:

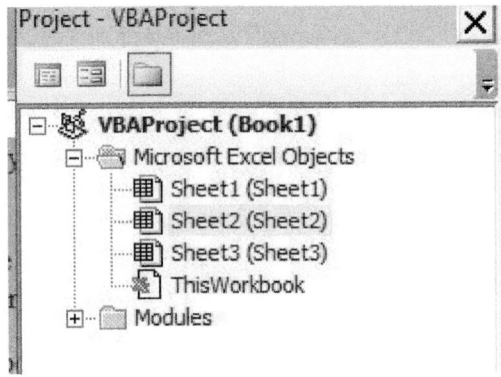

1. In the Developer tab, click on Sheet2 so that it is highlighted like the previous image.

The Properties tab will display the properties for the selected sheet.

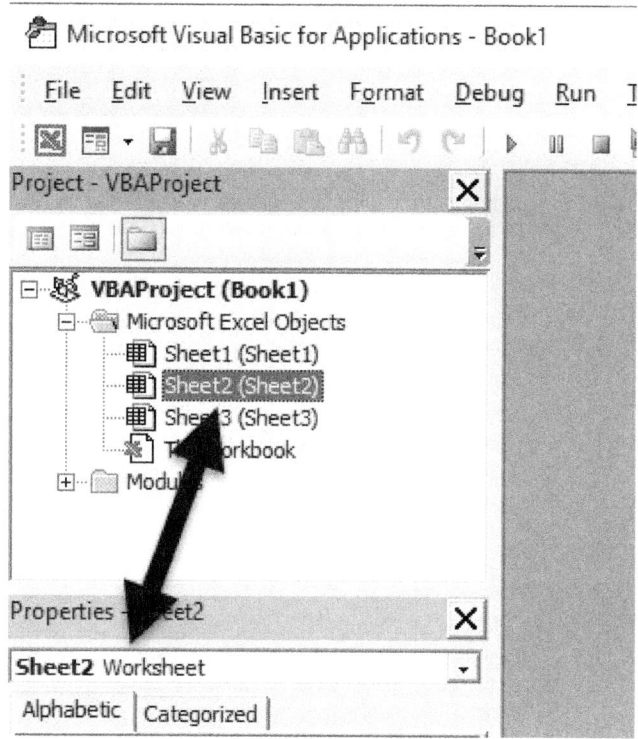

2. Change the last property, the Visible property to Hidden

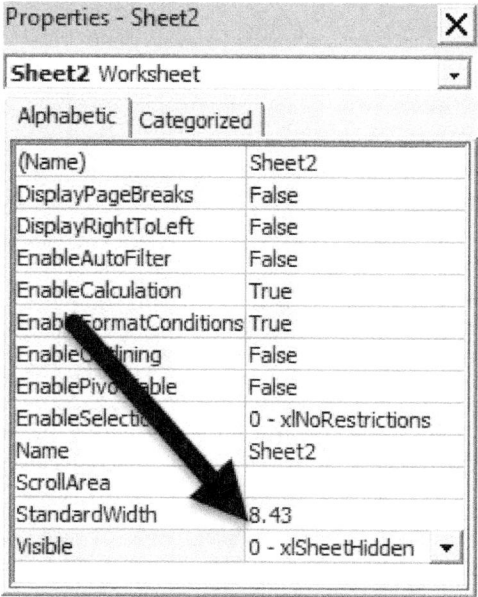

Notice how Sheet 2 is now hidden in Excel.

3. Click on Sheet3 in the VBAProject window to select it

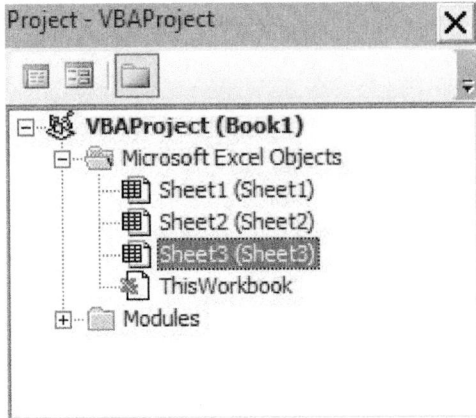

4. Change the visible property of Sheet3 to xlSheetVeryHidden.

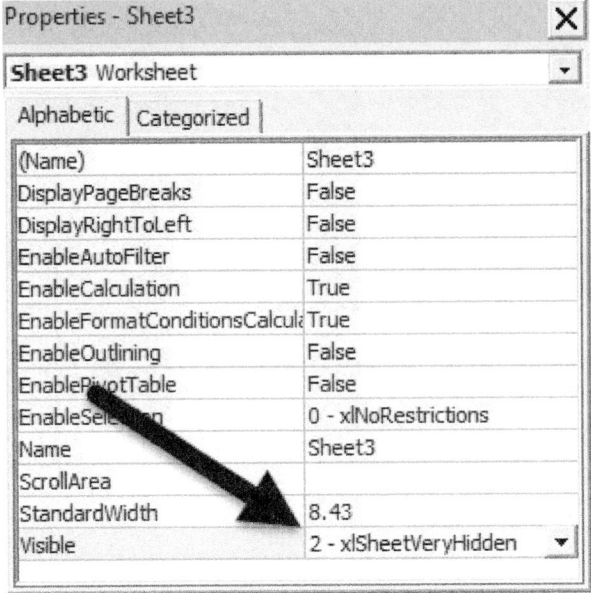

Notice how Sheet3 is now hidden in Excel.
Both sheets are hidden? What's the difference? Let's see.

5. Go back to Excel
6. Right click on Sheet1 and select Unhide

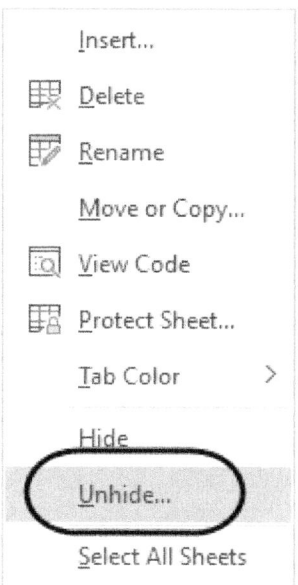

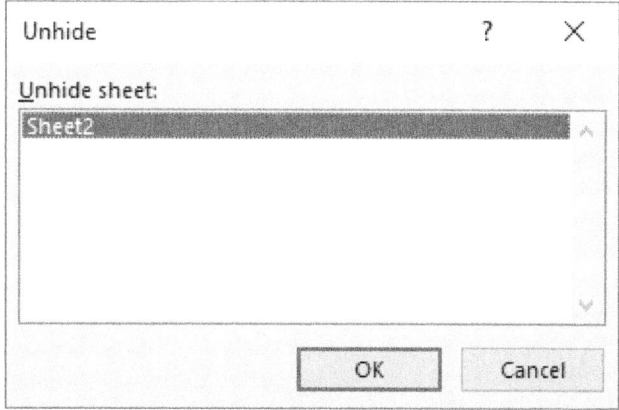

Where is sheet3? Not there. **The Unhide window only shows Hidden sheets, never VeryHidden sheets.**

If you want to add another level of security to your workbooks, you can set worksheets to Hidden to prevent Excel novices from seeing them. You can set worksheets to VeryHidden, to prevent more experienced users from seeing them. You can then set sheets to VeryHidden **and** set a workbook password to prevent most Excel users from accessing the worksheet.

It's not infallible though. Even with VeryHidden and passwords, expert Excel users can get to the worksheet. Use with caution when dealing with sensitive information. Excel is not secure. The best way to keep something secret in Excel is to not have it in the workbook at all.

I hope this was a useful trick. Let's get back to macros.

End of Excel trick

ዳ!

16. Go back to the Developer window
17. Expand Modules in the Project window
18. You will see Module1
19. Double click on Module 1 to display the macro

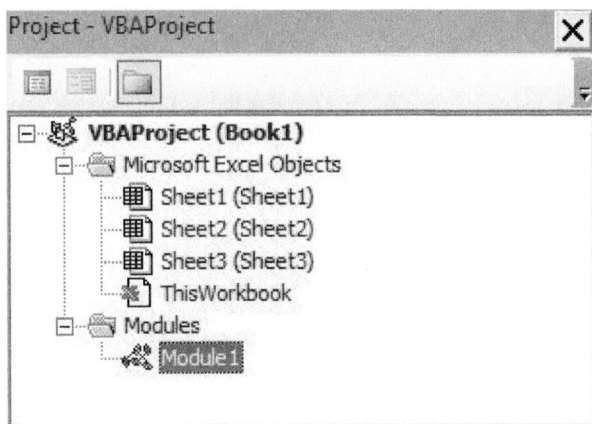

The macro that I have is below. If you followed the steps and didn't make any mistakes, you should have something very similar.

```
Sub Macro1()
'
' Macro1 Macro
'

'
    Range("A1").Select
    ActiveCell.FormulaR1C1 = "Salesperson"
    Range("A2").Select
    ActiveCell.FormulaR1C1 = "Lisa"
    Range("A3").Select
    ActiveCell.FormulaR1C1 = "Robin"
End Sub
```

Based on the brief background we covered before, you can see that Excel selects a cell using the Select method, then it sets the FormulaR1C1 property to the value after the =. Whenever you want to put text in a cell, you must enclose it in quotations like this "This is text".

The macro runs from top to bottom executing every line that does not have a quote ' as the first character.

Here are a few tips on the macro structure:

- Every macro starts with Sub then followed by the macro name (no spaces allowed). (Sub is short for subroutine). The parenthesis after the macro are how different macros communicate with one another. We will cover this in a later lesson.

- Every macro ends with End Sub
- A quote ' means that everything after the ' is treated as a comment. Excel will not execute it. This is a great way to inactivate lines and test the code without deleting them.
- When writing macros (even when recording them) make sure you add several lines of comments (wherever you need to, they can be anywhere not just at the top of the code) explaining what you are doing. You know what you are doing **now** but 7 months from now, if you have to change it or something breaks, you might not remember what the code is trying to do. Comments help you remember.
- The macro code pane is just a text editor. You can change it by typing over it.

Let's run the macro.

1. Go back to the Excel worksheet
2. Delete everything in column A
3. Click on the Developer tab
4. Click on Macros

5. This window will appear. It shows all the macros in the workbook.

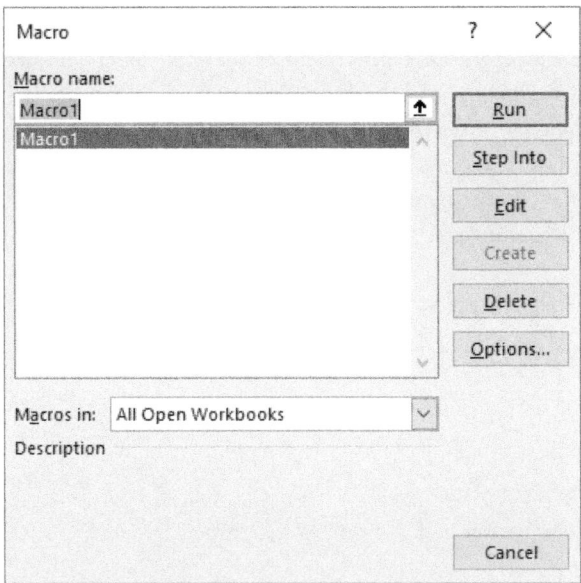

6. Select Macro1 (the macro we just recorded)
7. Click Run

The macro will run and the data in column A will reappear.

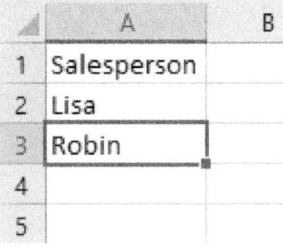

That's it! You have just recorded and replayed a macro.

Optional

If you are feeling extra daring, go ahead and change the Salesperson names in the macro. You don't have to clear out the worksheet to re-run the macro. After changing the names, replay it to see how Excel will use the new names you changed.

Saving a Macro

Macros are part of the Excel workbook. They are saved when you save the workbook. However, you must save the workbook as file type xlsm if you want to save the macro. If you choose xlsx as the file type, Excel will warn you with this message:

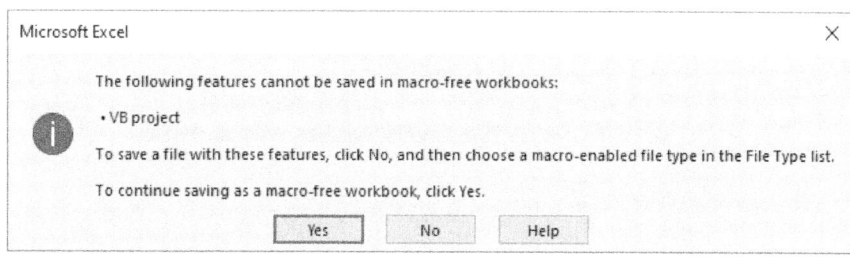

This is telling you that if you click 'Yes' you will save the workbook as xlsx and you will lose the macro. **You cannot recover a macro that has been lost this way.** Save as xlsm.

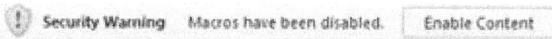

Opening a Macro Enabled Workbook

When you try to open a macro enabled workbook, you will see this warning:

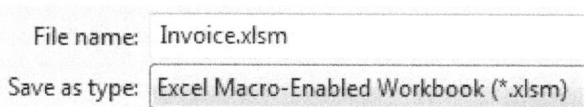

You will need to click Enable Content in order to use the macros in the workbook. Why does Excel do this? For security reasons. There are macros that can be written so they run automatically when a workbook is opened (we will cover those in a later lesson). If there was no warning, people could write computer viruses in Excel that would run without you knowing it.

Recording Another Macro

That first macro was ok for our first try but it's not really that useful. Let's use the follow along workbook to record a macro.

Here is the situation: You receive this invoice every week and the system that creates it does not have formulas. It creates the invoice as text. Sometimes, users change the prices or quantities and they forget to update the Extended Price. You need to create a macro that will input these formulas.

1. Open the Invoice.xlsx workbook (you can download this follow along workbook from my website at http://markmoorebooks.com/macros-introduction/)
2. Save the workbook to a folder you will remember. However, save it as Invoice.xlsm

File name: Invoice.xlsm
Save as type: Excel Macro-Enabled Workbook (*.xlsm)

Extended price is Quantity * Unit Price. We are going to record a macro that does this calculation for each line in the invoice.

3. Start recording the macro by clicking the Record Macro button

4. Name the Macro FixFormulas

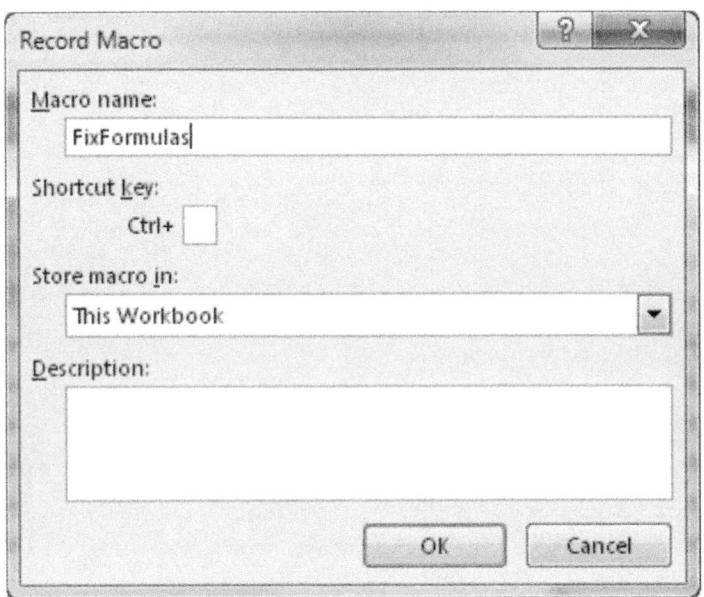

5. Click OK
6. Click on cell F13
7. Input the formula =D13*E13
8. Press Enter
9. Right click on cell F13
10. Click on Copy

11. Select cells F14 through F16
12. Right click and click Paste
    You'll notice that the results changed. Yes, there were errors in the original file.
13. Click on stop recording
14. Save the workbook (we don't want to lose the macro we just recorded)

Testing

Test, test, always test! Writing macros is a process of writing something, running it and then fixing it. You **will** make mistakes. It's ok. That's the natural process of figuring stuff out. That's why you should test constantly.

The correct subtotal is $3,200.00. Let's remove the formulas and rerun the macro. If we did it right, we should see $3,200.00 in cell F23 after we run the macro.

1. Delete the formulas in cells F13 through F16
2. Click the Developer tab
3. Click on Macros

4. Click on FixFormulas

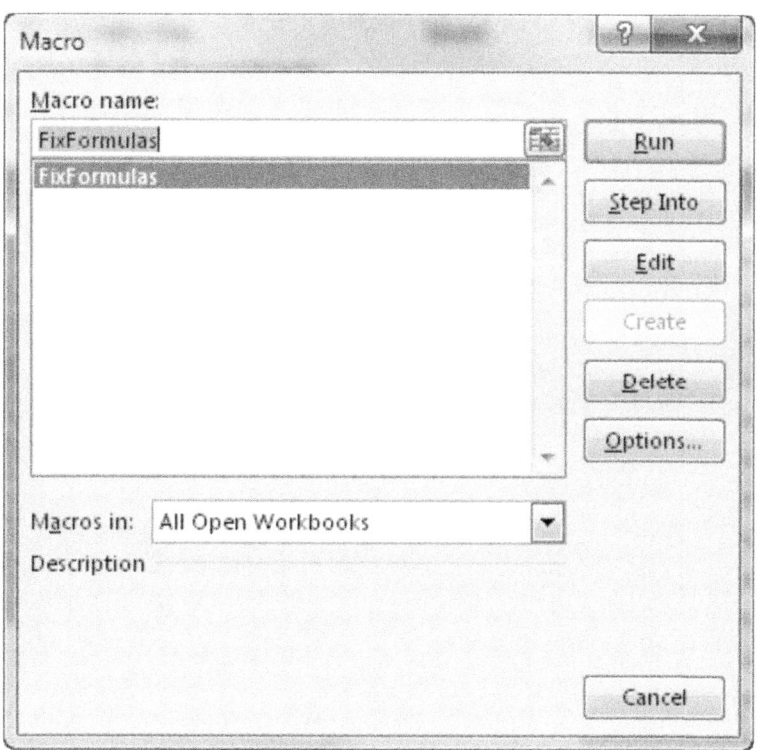

5. Click on Run

You should now see this as the new invoice:

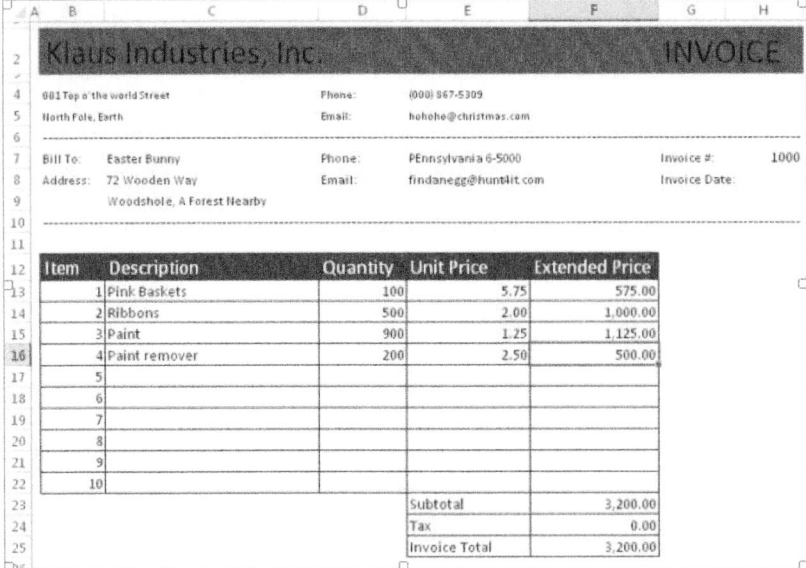

To see the macro

1. Click on the Developer tab
2. Click on Visual Basic

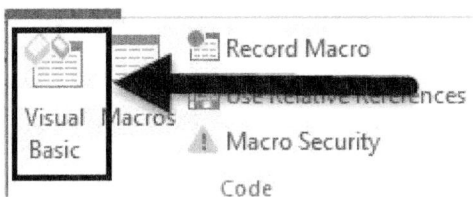

3. Expand Modules and click on Module1

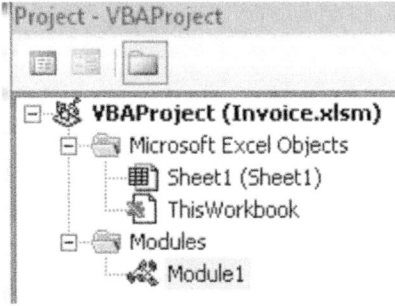

4. The macro will appear in the right pane.

Don't worry if you don't understand all of it. It works, that's all we care about right now. We will get into specific commands in later lessons.

If your macro looks different, don't worry about it. Your Excel settings may be different, maybe you used the keyboard to copy/paste, etc., just focus on getting the right totals of $3,200.00.

```
Sub FixFormulas()

'
' FixFormulas Macro
'



    Range("F13").Select
    ActiveCell.FormulaR1C1 = "=RC[-2]*RC[-1]"
    Selection.Copy
    Range("F14:F16").Select
    ActiveSheet.Paste
End Sub
```

How to Organize Your Macros

Now that you know how to record and make simple alterations to a recorded macro, I am sure that this opens up a world of possibilities for you. Are you thinking of all the things that you could automate? ☺

Let's talk about organization before you start building your macro empire.

The one thing you **should not do**, is have one huge macro that does everything related to a particular task. That is a quick way into a macro nightmare. It is much preferable to have small, single purpose macros that you chain together.

Why is this better?

If you have a 40 page macro and something goes wrong (and trust me, things will *always* go wrong), Excel will tell you which line caused the error. That's the easy part, however, you won't know what *caused* the error. When Excel says, 'error on line 435', you will need to go back 435 lines to figure out what generated the error.

Even more insidious, think about this. The macro ran perfectly, no errors. You look at the results and they are incorrect. There were no syntax errors (the 'error on line 435' message) but you had logical errors. Where is the logical error? Now, you have to go through 40 pages of macro code to figure that out.

I propose that you chain your smaller, individually purposed macros together in a special way. Not one after the other, but one to many.

Suppose you have to build a macro that calculates Revenue for your region. You record and edit several macros that are named like so:

- FindRegion
- FindInvoices
- FindUnitPrice
- CalculateSalesTax

Based on these fictitious names, you can tell what each macro does. What I propose is that you create a new macro. You can call it anything you like; I tend to call it main.

Inside main, I call the other macros in the correct order. Main would look something like this:

```
Sub main()

    Call FindRegion
    Call FindInvoices
    Call FindUnitPrice
    Call CalculateSalesTax

    ThisWorkbook.Save

End Sub
```

Main would call all the other macros and do any other calculations (in this case, save the workbook).

If something goes awry in the macro. I will have an easier time figuring out where the error is. Can't find the Invoice, go straight to 'FindInvoices' and start looking for the issue. SalesTax is wrong? Start at CalculateSalesTax. You don't have to go through the entire macro to start debugging, you can start at a smaller chunk of the code.

Additionally, this adds to the portability of your macros. Suppose next month you are working on a different project and you need a macro that find a region. You can come back to this workbook, copy the FindRegion macro and alter it (if necessary) for the new project.

Modules vs. Subroutines

In addition to organizing your code into smaller, single purpose units, you can also separate them into different modules. So far, we have been working exclusively in Module1.

If you right click on Modules and select Insert, Module you can insert a second module.

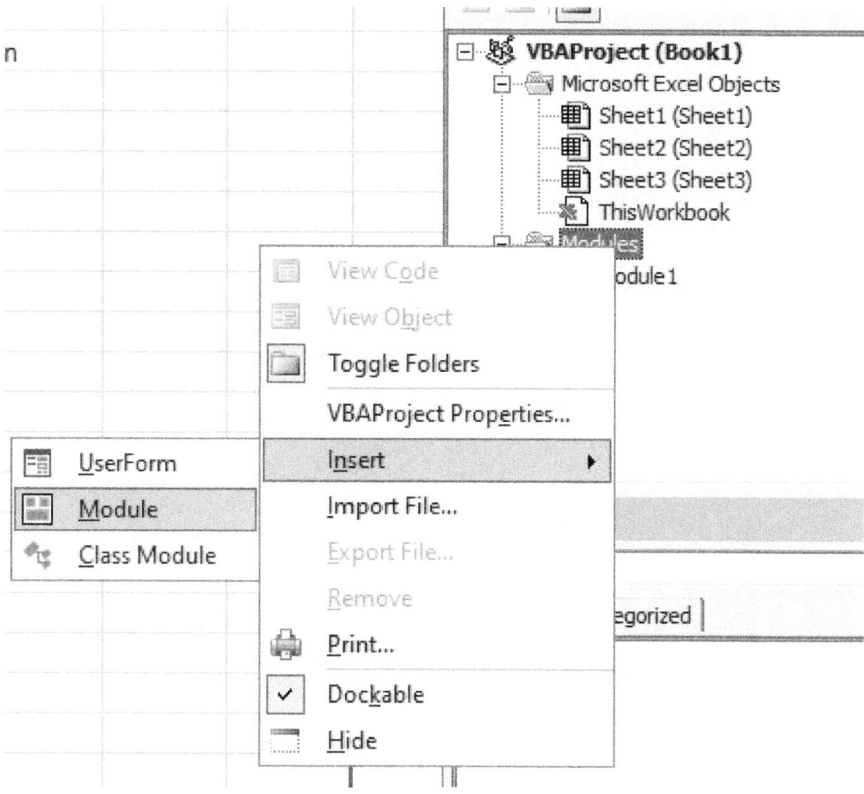

You can put different macros in different modules, based on how you need to organize them.

Don't do this just yet though. There are several considerations you need to consider for this. When macros are in different modules, they can't call each other easily. You need to understand macro scope and variable lifetimes.

When would you use a different module?

Suppose you built, tested and have a rock-solid macro that generates a monthly sales report. The entire process, with all the various macros, is self-contained and does not need any modifications (or just minor modifications) to work in another workbook. Then you can put all that code in one module.

When you need to use the code again, you can right click on the module and select 'Export File..". In the new workbook, you would import the file and use the macro there.

Of course, this is all up to you. You can easily say, "I want all the Sales department related macros in one module and all the Operations department macros in another module". If that works for you, go for it.

Variables

I gotta do it. Might as well get it over with. It's dry and boring but you need to learn about variables. If the term brings back nightmares of high school algebra, I empathize with your pain. Unlike high school though, I'll make this section short and relatively painless. Also, there will not be an exam at the end.

Just like in Algebra, variables are buckets that store something else. You can swap out the contents of the variable without changing the variable itself.

In a macro, the easiest way to define and assign a value to a macro is like this:

```
Sub variables()

    x = 42

End Sub
```

If you wanted to show the value of x to a user, you can add a message box command.

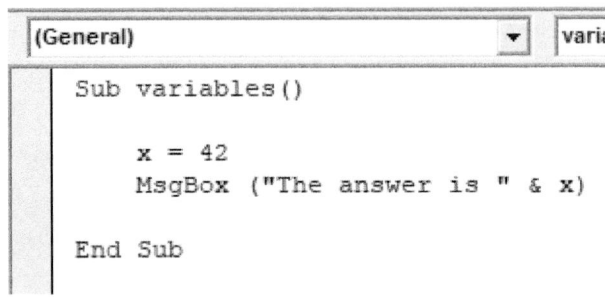

When you run the macro, you will see this popup:

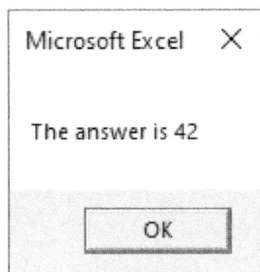

Declaring Variables

Even though the macro above works, it does not follow best practices. You should declare your variables. Declaring variables let's Excel know what to expect in a variable and it will allocate the appropriate memory for storing that variable.

You declare a variable using the Dim keyword.

```
Sub variables()
    Dim x As Integer

    x = 42
    MsgBox ("The answer is " & x)

End Sub
```

In the above example, I have assigned the Integer type to the x variable. That means if I change x to contain the word 'Mark', Excel will generate an error when I run the macro.

```
Sub variables()
    Dim x As Integer
    
    x = "Mark"
    MsgBox ("The answer is " & x)

End Sub
```

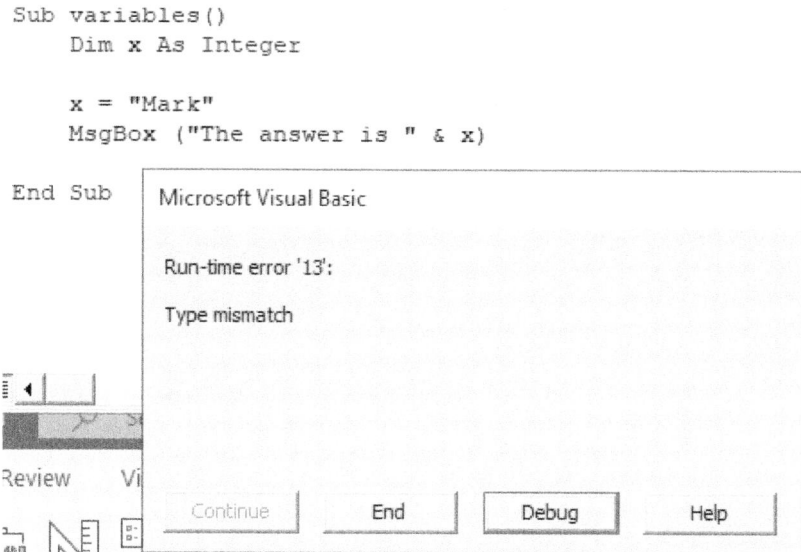

The infamous 'Type mismatch' error. Not very helpful is it?

What it means is that Excel is expecting an integer value (-32,768 to 32,767) but it found a text value ("Mark"), therefore there was a type mismatch; the type expected did not match the type sent.

Why did the first macro work when I didn't declare a type?

When you don't declare a type, like I did in the macro with the message box, Excel will assign a Variant data type. The Variant data type is a jack-of-all-trades type that can handle text and all types of numbers.

There are many types of types that you can use. For pure programming best practices, you should use the data type that is closest to the data you are using. This matters a great deal when you are programming software, you want your program to be as efficient and fast as possible. However, frankly speaking, for small macros, Variant is fine. You won't notice any performance difference when running your macros.

Just in case you want to see the other data types, I'll drop a link to the Microsoft webpage that explains them:

https://docs.microsoft.com/en-us/office/vba/language/reference/user-interface-help/data-type-summary

Passing Variables

Variables have scope and lifetime.

Scope: defines which macro can see and access the variable

Lifetime: defines how long the variable lives before it is destroyed

You are going to need to deal with both of these concepts when building your small, single purpose macros.

Just in case, you're freaking out about now, don't. Everything will come together in a few pages and you'll realize that although it's new material, it isn't hard to master.

All of these last few topics come to bear when you are passing variables between macros. Passing variables is how macros communicate with one another.

Let's do an exercise to get the hang of this.

1. Open a new workbook
2. Insert a new module
    a. Go to the Developer tab
    b. Click on Visual Basic
    c. Right click on Microsoft Excel Objects in the Project pane
    d. Select Insert Module
3. Manually create a main macro (type the following in the blank macro window)
    a. Type sub main
    b. Press Enter

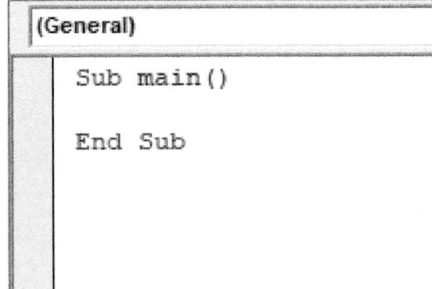

4. Create a second macro under the End sub. Call it Macro2

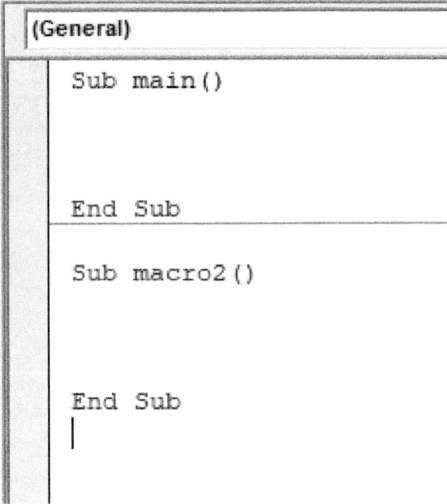

5. Add the next lines of code per the image below:

```
Sub main()
    Dim x As Integer

    x = 42
    Call macro2
End Sub
Sub macro2()
    MsgBox ("variable x is " & x)
End Sub
```

In the code above, main declares the x variable, assigns it the value of 42 then calls macro2. Macro2 displays a message box with text and the value of x.

6. Run the main macro

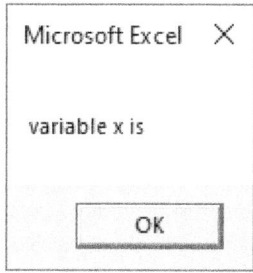

You get the text of the message because that was hard coded into macro2 but you do not see the value of x in the message box. Why is that?

Because x is out of scope of macro2. In other words, macro2 has no clue what main is doing. **I'll prove it.**

7. Add another variable x to macro2
8. Set it equal to the text "hello"

```
Sub main()
    Dim x As Integer

    x = 42
    Call macro2
End Sub
Sub macro2()
    x = "hello"
    MsgBox ("variable x is " & x)
End Sub
```

9. Run main

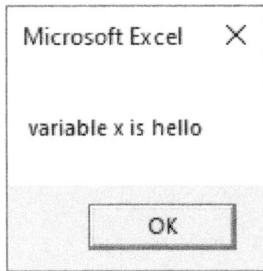

What is going on? How can this be?

What is happening is that each macro has its own version of x. Neither macro knows what the other is doing so they will use their version. The x that is 42 is scoped to main while the x that is "hello" is scoped to macro2.

The main can call macro2 but it isn't talking to it. Main needs to talk to macro2 and let it know that it is sending a piece of information to it. On the other side, macro2 needs to be altered to use a new piece of information.

10. Change macro2 to accept a variable from main and main to pass the x variable. I have highlighted the changes in the image for you.

```
Sub main()
    Dim x As Integer

    x = 42
    Call macro2(x)
End Sub
Sub macro2(y As Integer)
    x = "hello"
    MsgBox ("variable x is " & y)
End Sub
```

Now when you run main, you will see the correct message box.

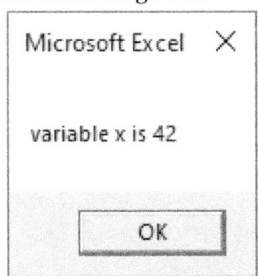

Note that I changed the variable to y in macro2. You can call it x or anything else you want (including words but spaces are not allowed).

That's how you *really* set up main to call the other macros. That first image was just to show you the concept. An updated example is this:

```
Sub main()

    Call FindRegion
    Call FindInvoices(MyRegion)
    Call FindUnitPrice(Invoice)
    Call CalculateSalesTax(MyRegion)

    ThisWorkbook.Save

End Sub
```

A quick note about ThisWorkbook. When you start managing several workbooks from one macro, knowing which one you are manipulating can get tricky. ThisWorkbook always refers to the workbook that has the macro that is currently executing.

Using Excel Formulas in Macros

Eventually, you are going to want to take advantage of regular Excel formulas in your macro. When you get to that point, there are a few things to take into consideration. I'm going to cover them here.

WorksheetFunction

Some functions are available natively in a macro, others need to be called with WorksheetFunction. You'll know which is which if the Intellisense prompt shows up. For example, the images below show that the LEFT function can be used directly in a macro, but VLOOKUP needs to be called with WorksheetFunction.

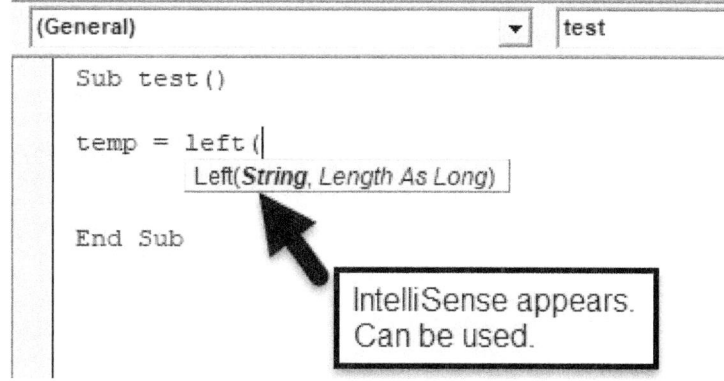

```
Sub test()

temp = worksheetfunction.VLookup(
                        VLookup(Arg1, Arg2, Arg3, [Arg4])

End Sub
```

IntelliSense appears only with WorksheetFunction.

The drawback of WorksheetFunction is that you need to know the parameters of the function. As you can see from the image for VLOOKUP, in a macro, you only get Arg1, Arg2, etc. You need to know what those are. You can always go back to Excel and input the formula there to jog your memory.

In the above example, the answer to the LEFT & VLOOKUP were assigned to a variable. That variable can be used later on in the macro. If you want to put the formula itself in Excel, you need to pretend it is a string and put it in with the = sign.

For example, a cell in a macro is called a range, if you wanted to put the RAND formula in a cell you would do this:

Range("A1").Formula = "=RAND()"

Note that the cell address is a text (enclosed by quotes) and so is the formula. Additionally, you must start the formula with the = sign.

To put the formula in more than one cell, all you need is to make a simple change:

Range("A1:A10").Formula = "=RAND()"

Advanced Formula Use

Putting formulas in cells using macros is where users get confused, frustrated and give up. No one explained how to reference cells in a macro created formula. **The problem is that Excel does exactly what you tell it to do, not what you want it to do.**

Let's work through an example. It will highlight the issue and then I'll explain how to solve it.

1. Open a new workbook
2. Type in these sample numbers in A1:B3

	A	B	C
1	1	1	
2	2	2	
3	3	3	
4			

3. Open the macro environment and create this macro:

MASTERING EXCEL MACROS

```
(General)                                    test
    Sub test()

        Range("C1").Formula = "=SUM(A1:B1)"

    End Sub
```

This macro will put the SUM function in cell C1.

4. Run the macro

You should see the SUM function and the corresponding answer in C1. Cool.

5. Change the macro so that the SUM function will be put in cell C2.

```
(General)                                    test
    Sub test()

        Range("C2").Formula = "=SUM(A1:B1)"

    End Sub
```

6. Run the macro

What happened?

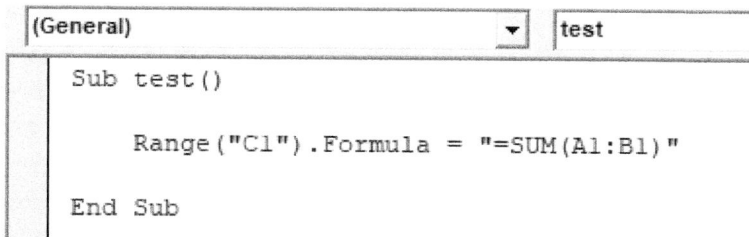

You did not get the right answer. Why? The macro told Excel put =SUM(A1:B1) in C2, and that's exactly what it did...but that's not what you wanted. You wanted the sum of the numbers in row 2.

The manual way to update the macro is to change the formula from =SUM(A1:B1) to =SUM(A2:B2). What if you have thousands of rows? In that case, it's easier to forget about the macro put in the formula by hand and drag it down in Excel.

This is the reason the R1C1 cell notation was developed. It makes referencing cells easier. Not only rows but columns. Can you imagine having to add 1 to column B for a sum going across columns? 1+B does not equal C.

Be forewarned, R1C1 notation will look very strange until you get used to it, but it is very powerful.

- R1C1 uses numbers for both rows and columns.

- [ ] indicate the distance from the active cell
- No brackets indicate an absolute reference
- + means down/right
- - Means up, left

Whenever you use the R1C1 notation, you need to remember two things:

- [ ] are the equivalent of $ in a cell reference
- If you don't put [ ] then everything is based on the cell the formula is in

7. Change the macro so it looks like this:

```
Sub test()
    Range("C1").Formula2R1C1 = "=SUM(RC[-2]:RC[-1])"
End Sub
```

Let's break it down.
This macro will put the formula in C1.
What formula? A SUM function.
What row? Since there is no bracket, just a plain R, that means the same row the formula is in. In this case row 1, because the macro said Range("C1")
What columns?   First cell reference: Two columns to the left of C1
                Second cell reference: One column to the left of C1

From C1, RC[-2] is A1
From C1, RC[-1] is B1

8. Run the macro
9. Change the Range("C1") to Range("C2")
10. Run the macro again
11. Change the Range("C2") to Range("C3")
12. Run the macro again

Now the math works, and the formula is correct because the R1C1 notation uses the relative position based on the cell of interest.

Did you realize the power of this? Look at steps 8 through 12. The only thing you changed what the cell reference on the left of the equal sign, **you never had to change the formula**. With R1C1 notation, **it is always the same formula**. Excel changes it to A1 notation automatically, you don't have to worry about it.

In later lessons, when I get into looping (how to do the same thing several times over) the R1C1 notation becomes very useful because all you need to do is add 1 or subtract 1 to move the formula references over a column or row.

Using R1C1 notation is not mandatory in any way. If you don't like it, you don't have to use it. There are other ways to create formulas in the regular A1 notation.

Excel Trick

Did you know that you can force Excel to use R1C1 notation all the time?

1. Go to File, Options
2. Click on Formulas
3. Check R1C1 reference style
4. Click OK

Now all your formulas were converted to R1C1 notation and your column letters were replaced with numbers.

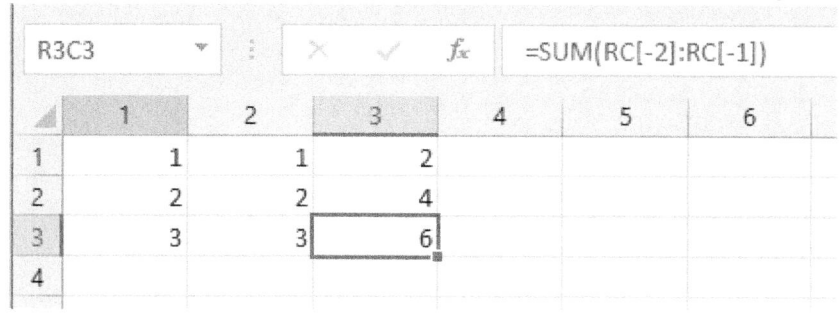

5. You can change it back by unchecking the option.

It is a harmless prank to pull on someone though... ☺

End of Excel Trick

Conclusion

That's it for this introductory lesson. You should have enough tools under your belt to start building macros to automate many routine tasks in Excel.

The best way to learn is to experiment. Keep recording new macros, change them, break them fix them.

Online Excel School

If you would rather watch and hear the Excel lessons, you can take a peek at my online Excel school. The first class lecture is free so you can see if you like the format and my teaching style.

The online school goes beyond the text lessons. There are over 9 hours of material you can watch based on your schedule. As with the text lessons, there are follow along workbooks you can download to practice on.

https://mastering-excel.teachable.com/p/mastering-excel-macros

Lesson:2
Debugging

This lesson will cover the developer ribbon and the VBA editor we reviewed in the introductory lesson. Knowing how to navigate around will make your life much easier. Furthermore, you will spend most of your time in the VBA editor. There are many, time saving features in there that will make debugging (finding errors) in your macro code less painful.

Developer Ribbon

Let's go through each button and what it does.

Code Group

Visual Basic: This button opens up the VBA editor. The components of this window will be covered later in this lesson.

Macros: This button opens up this window.

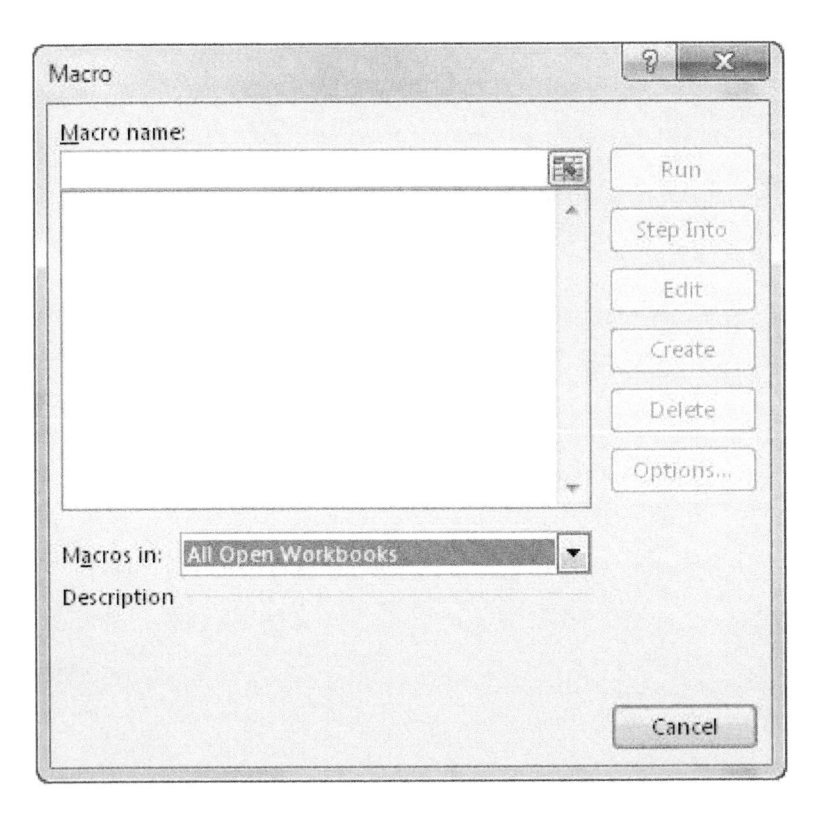

Here you will see all the macros available in all open workbooks. Notice the blue shaded drop box that says 'All Open Workbooks'. You can change that to a specific workbook if you only want to see the macros in that workbook.

The button on the right of the window are:

Run: Lets you run the selected macro

Step Into: Opens the VBA editor and lets you run the macro line by line

Edit: Opens the VBA editor where you can edit the macro

Create: Type in a new macro name and click Create to start coding a new macro

Delete: Let's you delete a macro

Options: Opens this window:

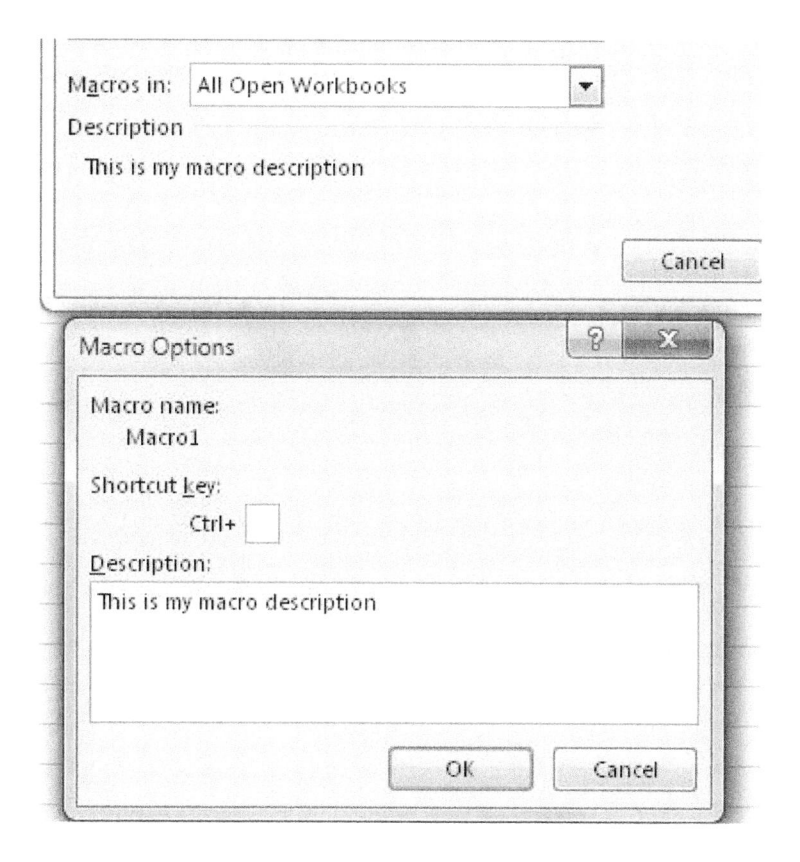

The macro options window is at the bottom of the image. Here you can select a key that you can assign to run a macro. For example, if you choose q, then when this workbook is open, you can press Ctrl+q to run the macro. However, this will override any existing Excel shortcuts. For example, if you choose Ctrl+c in this window, then Ctrl+c will run the macro **not** perform the copy command.

The bottom box is where you can input a description for the macro. The description will appear in the macro window. Notice how the text input appears in the top portion of the image, in the Description section.

Record Macro: This button begins the macro recording process. After entering some basic information, you can have excel record all your actions.

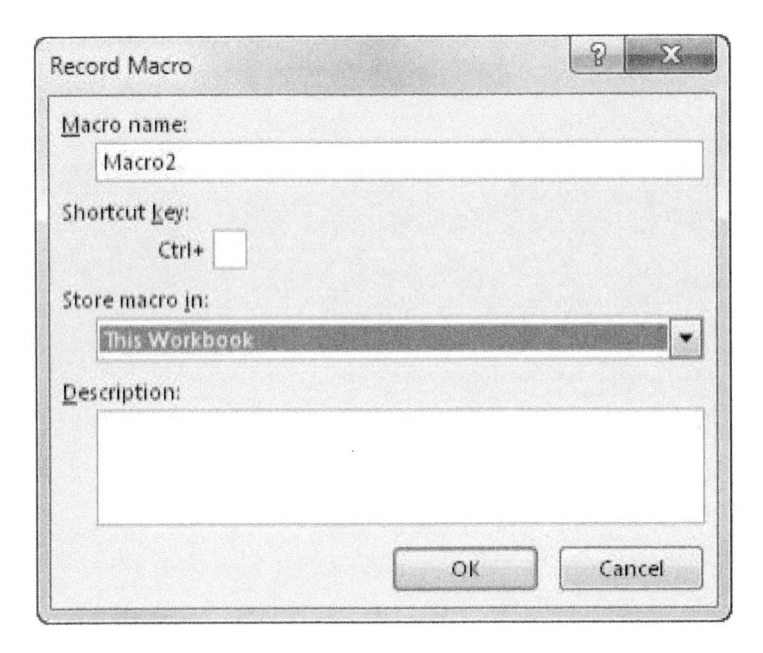

The basic information you enter is:

Macro name: The name of the macro. No spaces nor special characters are allowed. You can use underscores _

Shortcut key: Another place to assign a shortcut key to the macro

Store macro in: The options here are shown below.

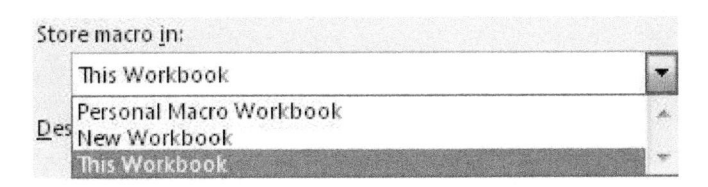

You can store the macro in the currently open workbook (i.e. This Workbook) or a new workbook. The Personal Macro Workbook is a special workbook where you can store macros. This workbook will open every time you open Excel. This means that the macros stored in it will always be available to you to use.

Use Relative References

This function forces the macro use relative references. This means that every location the macro records will based off the original cell selected.

In the following example, I recorded a macro where I selected cell A1 and typed in the text a1 then selected cell B2 and typed in b2.

Here is the macro result without relative references:

```
Sub NoRelativeRef()

    Range("A1").Select

    ActiveCell.FormulaR1C1 = "a1"

    Range("B2").Select

    ActiveCell.FormulaR1C1 = "b2"

End Sub
```

Here is the macro with relative references:

```
Sub WithRelativeRef()

    ActiveCell.Select

    ActiveCell.FormulaR1C1 = "a1"

    ActiveCell.Offset(1, 1).Range("A1").Select

    ActiveCell.FormulaR1C1 = "b2"

End Sub
```

Notice how in the second example Excel does not select cell B2? Instead it selects a cell 1 row to the right and 1 row to the bottom of A1 using the command ActiveCell.Offset(1, 1).Range("A1").Select. Every location is based off the active cell (which is A1).

Why would this ever be useful when recording a macro? Consider a situation where you receive a report that always starts at a different place but other than that, the report structure is always the same. In this case, normal macro recording will not work since every cell will shift rows and columns. However, since the structure is the same but only the starting point is off, recording a macro with relative recording will still allow you to use macros to process the report.

Macro Security

This button opens the Excel Trust Center. This governs how Excel will handle workbooks with macros.

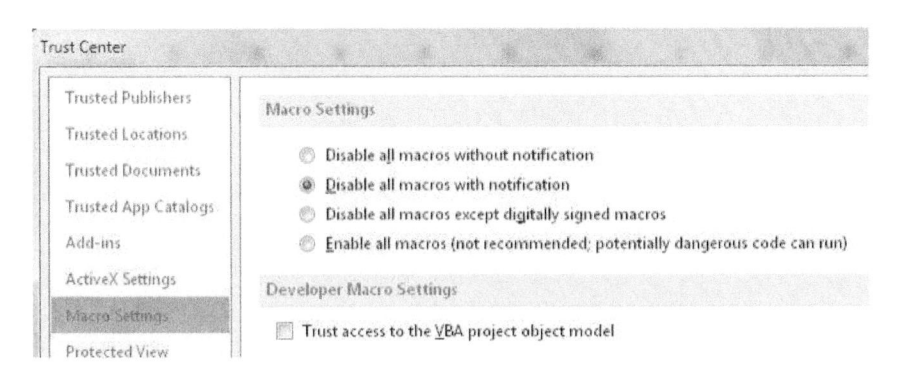

To be safe, choose 'Disable all macros with notification' this means that you will need to select 'Enable macros' whenever you open a workbook with macros.

That last option 'Trust access to the VBA project object model' is for macro developers. Yes, you are one now! Leave it off for now. But here is what this does: You can write macros that write other macros or macros that change themselves. This allows you to write self-replicating and mutating macros. This feature is how computer viruses are created. As an extra security layer, Excel disables this functionality be default.

Add-Ins

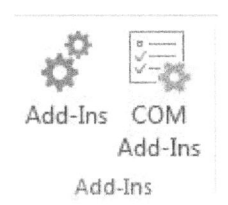

Add-ins are macros that have been saved by other programmers and then imported into Excel. These macros extend Excel's functionality. The macros that I have available on my computer are shown here:

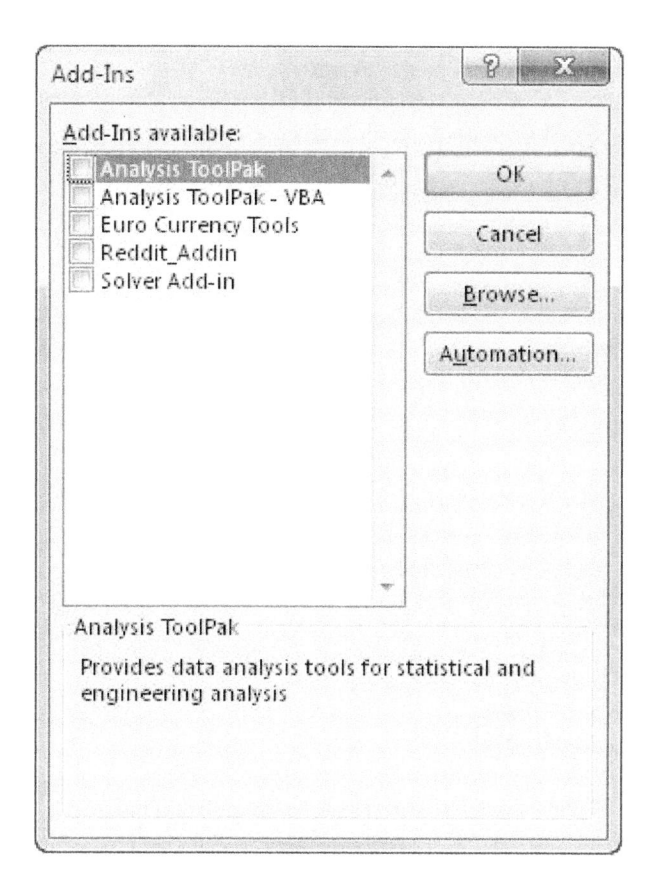

To enable these macros, check the box next to each macro and click ok.

COM Add-ins

COM add-ins are a different type of add-in that are created in Visual Basic (not Visual Basic for Applications). Creating these gets into some complex programming. We will not be covering these types of macros in this series.

Controls

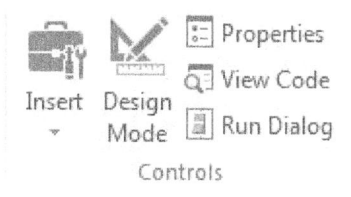

Controls add a definite wow factor to any macro. Controls are drop down boxes, scrollbars, checkboxes and any other graphical input elements that you can add to your spreadsheet or to a custom built dialog box that you build in the macro editor.

Insert

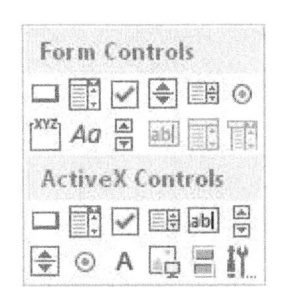

Clicking on insert displays this box. The top controls under the 'Form Control' heading you can use directly in an Excel spreadsheet with no macros. The second set of controls under the 'ActiveX Controls' heading are controls that have the ability to store macro code inside of them. These you cannot use without writing macros.

Properties: Selecting a control and clicking on properties lets you change the properties of the control. Properties are things like the color, text, size, etc.

View Code: Clicking this button opens the VBA editor

Run Dialog: When you have created a custom dialog box, this button will launch it.

XML: XML is a way to store data where each data point is labeled. Excel can use an XML map to interpret the labels and automatically import data. We will not be covering XML data in this series.

Modify

Document Panel

This button is used to display Excel information to other Office compatible programs. We will not be covering this topic in this course.

The VBA Editor

The VBA editor has many options and features. We are just going to cover the most frequently used ones now. As we get into programming, we will cover other less popular, but useful options.

The Window Panes

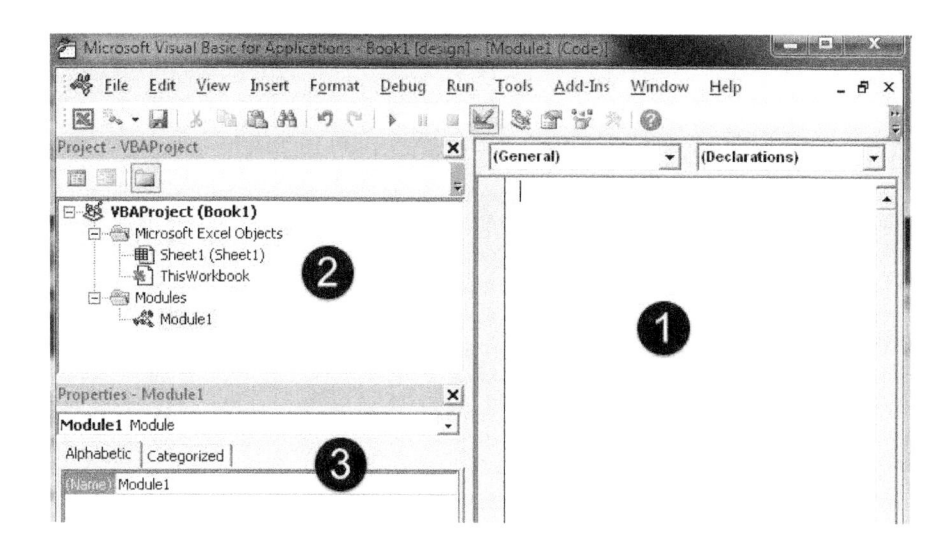

1 - This is where the macro code is stored. You will do most of macro editing here.

2 - VBAProject pane: This shows the structure of the Excel workbook. Every spreadsheet is shown here.

Modules: Macros live in modules. A module can have several macros. You can put all your macros in one module or you can separate them in different modules. Modules are used for organizational purposes. Modules can be exported from one Excel workbook and imported into another.

3 - Properties Pane: This pane displays the properties of the object selected above. In this case Module1.

If I change the selection in the VBAProject pane to Sheet1, my properties window changes to this:

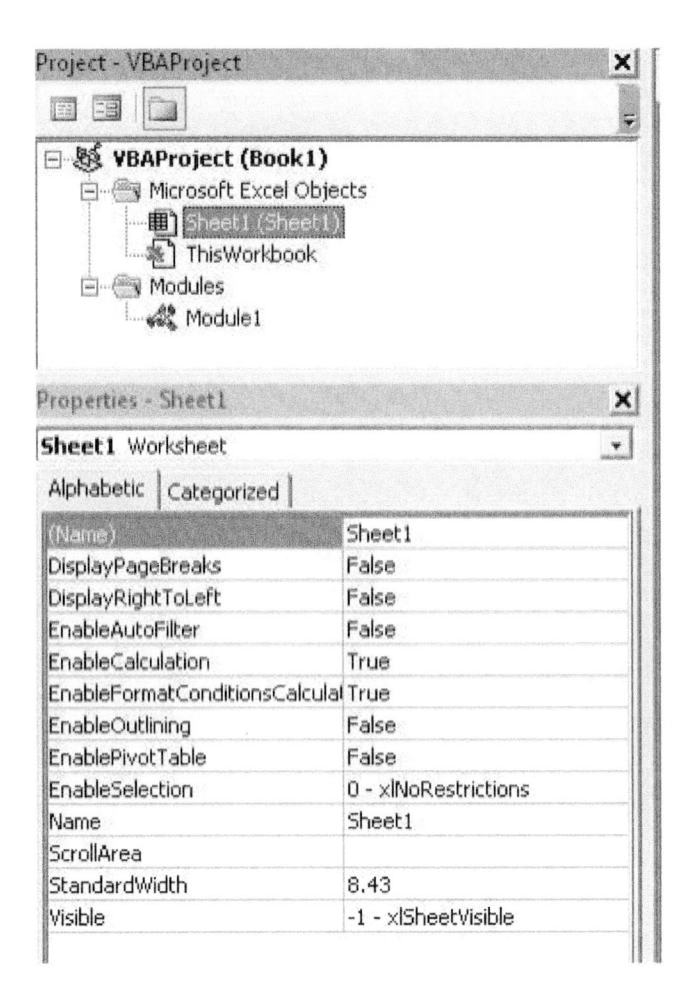

Here I can see all the properties of Sheet1, and I can also change them here. Clicking on the right hand column will let me change the properties for Sheet1.

Debug Menu

This menu is going to make your life so much easier. This is where you can move through a macro, line by line and see what is going on. Let me explain what the options are, then we can debug a simple macro to get some hands on experience.

```
Debug  Run   Tools   Add-Ins   Window
       Compile VBAProject
       Step Into                F8
       Step Over                Shift+F8
       Step Out                 Ctrl+Shift+F8
       Run To Cursor            Ctrl+F8
       Add Watch...
       Edit Watch...            Ctrl+W
       Quick Watch...           Shift+F9
       Toggle Breakpoint        F9
       Clear All Breakpoints    Ctrl+Shift+F9
       Set Next Statement       Ctrl+F9
       Show Next Statement
```

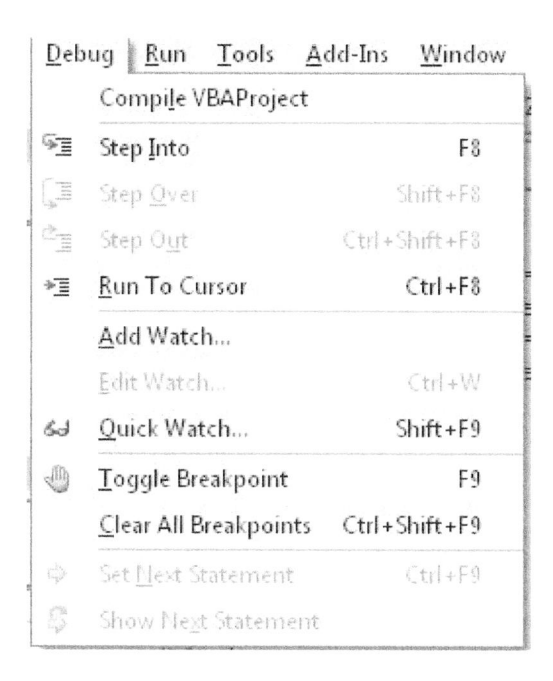

Compile VBA Project: This option compiles the code and checks for errors. You really don't ever need to do this. When you execute a macro it gets compiled automatically.

Step Into: This is what you will use most of the time. Clicking this (press F8 instead on clicking, it's easier) will move the current program execution by one line (This will make sense in a few pages)

Step Over: If one macro calls another, Step Over skips the line-b-line of the second macro. Instead it executes it as a single unit and continues on to the next line

Step Out: Executes the rest of the remaining lines of the macro

Run to Cursor: If you have a long macro and stepping through each line will take too long. Place your cursor where you want to start debugging and click this option. The macro will continue up to the cursor.

Add Watch/Edit Watch/Quick Watch: Watches are small windows that we can use to track variables and values in our code. These options let us set and change them.

Toggle Breakpoint/Clear All Breakpoints: A breakpoint is a pause. You can set a breakpoint at a specific point in the macro and when Excel reaches that point, the macro will pause and you can begin to debug.

Set Next Statement/Show Next Statement: This is used to specify which line should be executed next. For example, if the macro is on line 5 but you want line 25 to be executed next, you would set the Next Statement at line 25. The macro would jump from line 5 to 25.

Debugging a Macro

When working with macros, you are going to spend most of your time debugging. Very, very, very rarely will you program a non-trivial macro and have it work perfectly the first time. Because of this, you will be moving through your code, one line at time, looking for where things went awry.

Although we just reviewed all the options for debugging macros, I am sure your eyes glazed over a bit. You read it but not much of it 'stuck'. Let's go ahead and get our hands dirty with a macro.

I wrote a simple macro that builds this spreadsheet:

	A	B	C	D
1	Salesperson	Qty	Price	Total
2	Lisa	10	50	500
3	Stacy	5	25	125
4	Larry	8	100	800
5	Steve	12	80	960
6				

I'm not going to force you write the lines of the macro. We are interested, right now, in debugging. Instead, take the follow along text file and paste it in a new module.

1 - Open the text file that you received when subscribing to the follow along files for this lesson.

2 - Launch Excel

3 - Click the Developer tab

4 - Click on the Visual Basic button (the first one)

Visual Basic

5 - Insert a module (all macros are stored in modules) by right clicking on Microsoft Excel Objects, Insert, Module

(If you do not see the Project - VBAProject window, display it by clicking the View menu, then selecting Project Explorer)

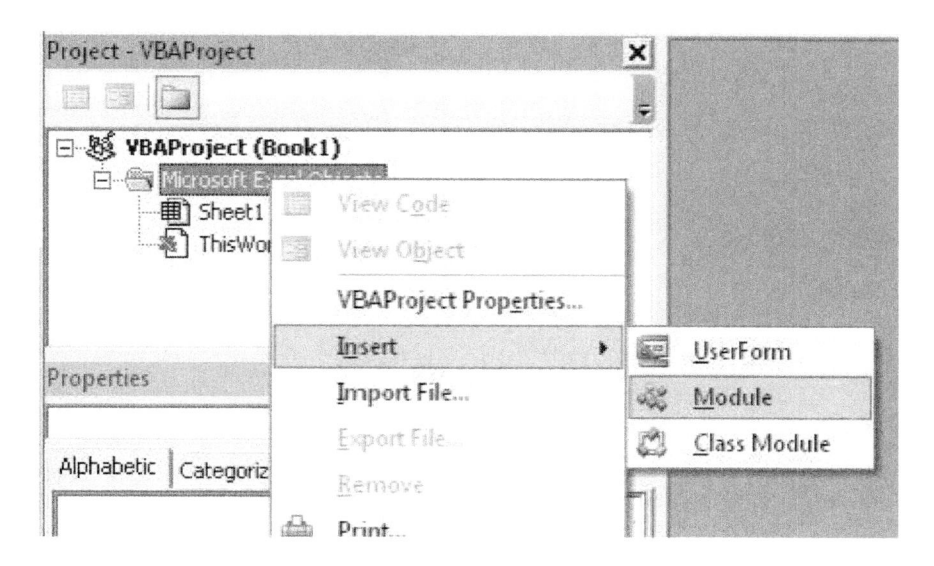

6 - Copy all the text in the SampleMacro.txt file

7 - Click anywhere in the blank macro window

8 - Right click and select Paste

That's it, you have copied the macro from the text file into the Excel workbook.

9 - Save the as Debug.xlsm. Remember to choose file type xlsm. If you choose xlsx, you will lose the macro.

Your VBA editor should look something like this:

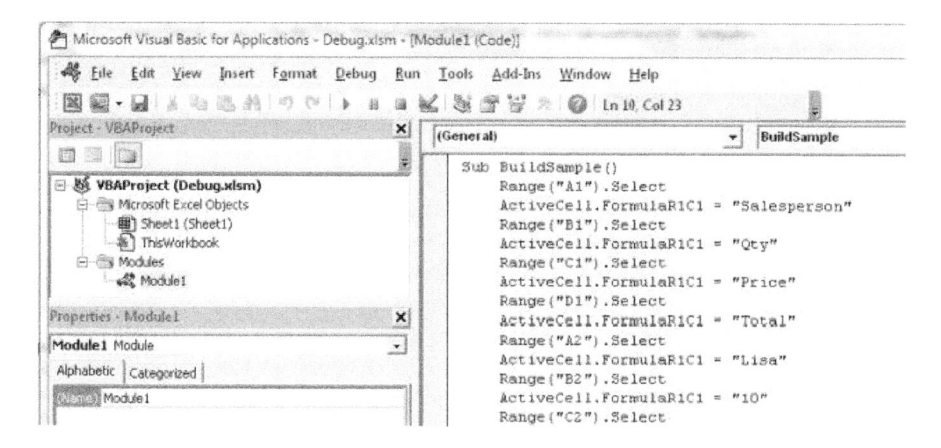

Let's run the macro, right from this window. Click the small arrow under the Debug menu. This is the Run command. You can also press F5 to run the macro.

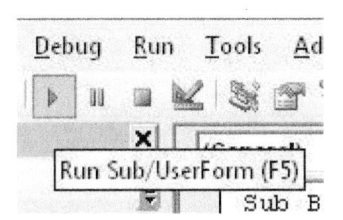

Go back to the Excel worksheet and check it out. The data looks mostly ok but there is a formula missing in cell D5. Let's debug and fix that.

One of the benefits of having the VBA editor in a different window is that you can position the VBA window and Excel side by side. This way you can see the code and what is going on in the Excel spreadsheet.

First, erase everything in the Debug.xlsm workbook. This isn't absolutely required but it will be easier to see what the macro is doing if it's putting data on a blank spreadsheet.

1 – Go back to the VBA editor

2 – Reposition Excel and the VBA editor so you can see them both. This is how I positioned my windows.

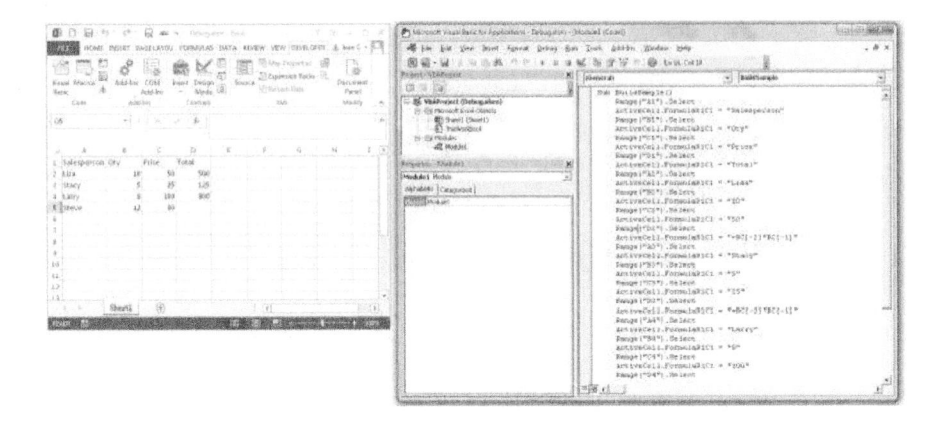

3 – Click anywhere inside the code to make the VBA window active

Let's start debugging!

We are going to run the macro line by line.

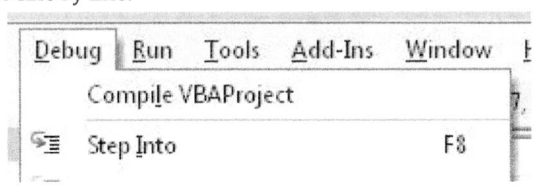

You can use the menu but it's much easier to use the keyboard.

4 – Press F8 once

You should see this:

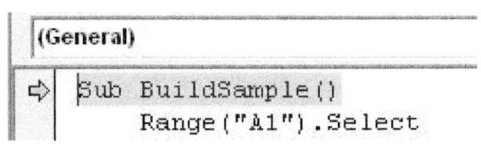

The yellow means that this is the next line that is going to be executed. Right now, the macro is on pause. We can do whatever we want. The macro will only move to the next line when we press F8

5 – Press F8 again
6 – Press F8. The lien highlighted should be this one:

```
Sub BuildSample()
    Range("A1").Select
    ActiveCell.FormulaR1C1 = "Salesperson"
```

If it isn't don't worry about it. Press the Stop button, and start pressing F8 until you get to this line.

7 – Keep an eye on the Excel spreadsheet and press F8 to execute the line with salesperson in it. You should see the word salesperson appear in cell A1.

8 – Keep pressing F8 until you get to the line that says A2

```
Range("A2").Select
ActiveCell.FormulaR1C1 = "Lisa"
Range("B2").Select
```

Skipping Lines

Let's skip a few lines, shall we? Suppose our macro is very long and complicated. We don't have to go through **every single line** until we get to the area of interest.

Let's skip putting the first salesperson's name and go straight to cell B2

9 – Click on the small yellow arrow and keep the left mouse button pressed. The icon should change to this:

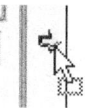

```
ActiveCell.FormulaR1C1 = "Total"
Range("A2").Select
ActiveCell.FormulaR1C1 = "Lisa"
Range("B2").Select
```

10 – Drag the arrow down to this line

```
Range("A2").Select
ActiveCell.FormulaR1C1 = "Lisa"
Range("B2").Select
```

The next thing the macro will do is select cell B2. The macro will not select cell A2 nor put in the name Lisa in that cell since we skipped it.

Run to Cursor

What about if you really do need to have every line executed but you don't want to press F8 thousands of times? You can keep F8 pressed and the lines will execute blazingly fast. The problem then becomes how to get the code to stop at the right place.

We can select the line we want to stop at and then use the Run to Cursor feature.

11 – Click anywhere on this line:

```
Range("B2").Select
ActiveCell.FormulaR1C1 = "10"
Range("C2").Select
ActiveCell.FormulaR1C1 = "50"
```

12 – Right click and choose Run to Cursor

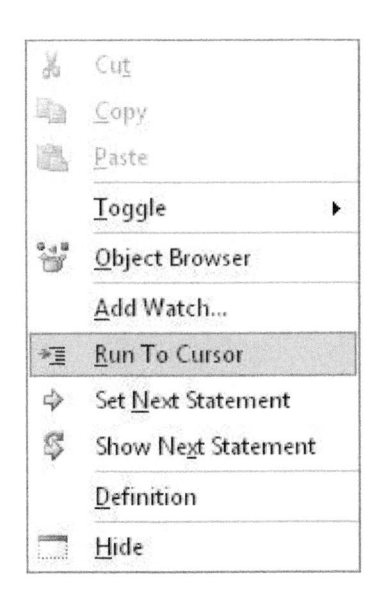

Adding Breakpoints: Breakpoints are like STOP signs in a macro. When you execute a macro using the Run button the macro will stop at each breakpoint (you can put in as many breakpoints as you like). Note that breakpoints have no effect when we are stepping through the code using F8.

You are going to set a breakpoint at line 17:

```
Range("D2").Select
ActiveCell.FormulaR1C1 = "=RC[-2]*RC[-1]"
Range("I3").Select
```

Line Numbers

Knowing the line number of a macro makes it much easier to refer to it. The line numbers are shown at the top menu bar under the Help menu

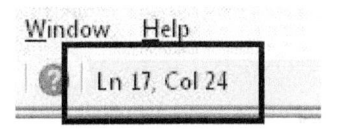

13 – To add a breakpoint on line 17, click on line 17, then click on the area where the yellow arrow **would be** if that were the active line. A brown dot will appear there.

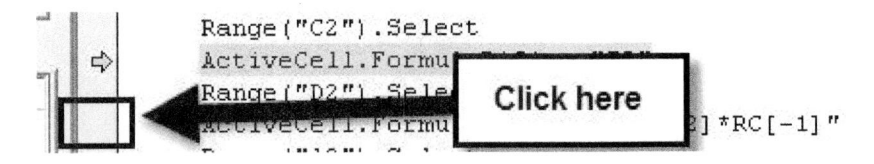

This is how it will look when the breakpoint has been set:

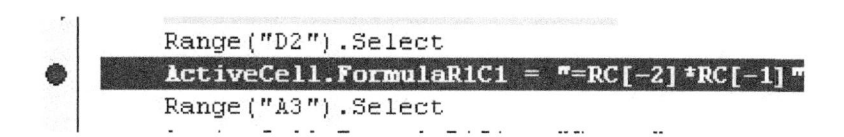

```
Range("D2").Select
ActiveCell.FormulaR1C1 = "=RC[-2]*RC[-1]"
Range("A3").Select
```

14 – Click Stop to stop the macro

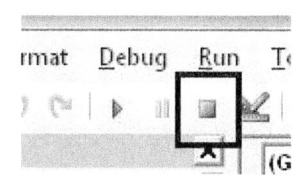

15 – Click Run (or press F5) to run the macro

The macro will run and stop at line 17. Excel will return back to the step mode. Line 17 will be both yellow and brown.

```
Range("D2").Select
ActiveCell.FormulaR1C1 = "=RC[-2]*RC[-1]"
Range("A3").Select
```

Note: Breakpoints will remain in the macro until you remove them. You can remove them by clicking on the brown dot or by going to Debug > Clear All Breakpoints or by pressing Ctrl+Shift+F9

Cell References in VBA

You are probably confused by line 17

ActiveCell.FormulaR1C1 = "=RC[-2]*RC[-1]"

When you record a macro in VBA it uses R1C1 notation. This means that instead of using the column letters and row numbers, Excel uses the **distance from the active cell** to figure out the other cells.

Yes, it is pretty strange but very, very clever.

The first part of the line is the active cell. This is the object that we are manipulating. The active cell is whichever cell we clicked on. We are on line 17. Line 16 selected cell D2 using the Range("D2").Select command. Therefore, for line 17, the active cell is D2.

Note: In VBA cells are called ranges. A range of cells can span one solitary cell to the entire worksheet. To indicate a range of cells, the command would be Range("A1:B2"). If you wanted to select the range A1:B2 the command would be Range("A1:B2").Select.

FormulaR1C1 is the property we are changing.

The macro is at this point:

	A	B	C	D
1	Salesperson	Qty	Price	Total
2	Lisa		10	50

Excel needs to calculate the total price as B2 * C2. Why not just put that in there? **You** can but the Excel macro recorder will not.

First let me explain what the RC notation is and how it works. RC notation refers to other cells based on their position relative to the active cell.

Distances are in whole numbers. Each number represents a column or a row. Positive numbers mean a column to the right or a row downwards. Negative numbers represent a column to the left or a row above the active cell. **Remember, everything is based off the active cell.**

For example, if the active cell is D2 (as in the previous image) you can refer to cell C1 by R[-1]C[-1] because C1 is one cell up and one cell to the left of D2

To refer to cell D1, the notation is R[-1]C. D1 is one row above D2 but in the same column. If we do not specify a row or column number, it means the other cell is in the same row or column.

To refer to cell A2, the notation is RC[-3] because A2 is on the same row as D2 but 3 columns to the left.

So what's the big deal? You probably think that B2 * C2 is much clearer and easier to understand. Well, it is much easier to *understand* but not easier to *program*.

Let's pretend that we are using the normal row and column notation. You use
ActiveCell.Formula = "=B2*C2" and then when you get to the next row you need to use ActiveCell.Formula = "=B3*C3". Ok, that sort of works but now you have to change every single cell and add one to the row number. OK, I will admit, there are ways around this, you can use a variable and other stuff we will cover alter on.

What about if the data is laid out horizontally? The first formula would be ActiveCell.Formula = "=B2*C2" and the second formula would be ActiveCell.Formula = "=C2*D2". There's no easy way to increment the columns. You can't add 1 to B and get C.

That's why relative references are so crafty. Every formula in column D of our spreadsheet is basically the same formula. It is always looking at the cells to the left of it.

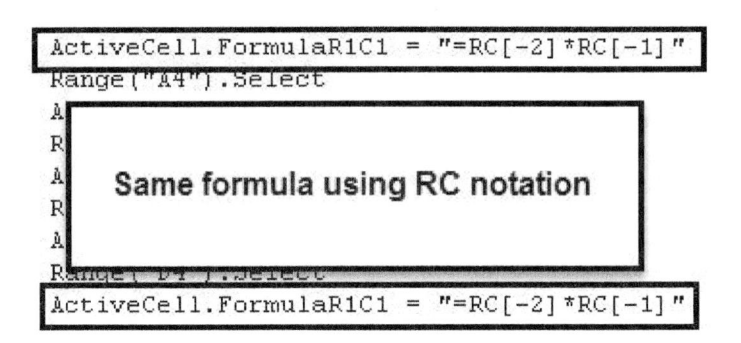

```
ActiveCell.FormulaR1C1 = "=RC[-2]*RC[-1]"
Range("A4").Select
```

Same formula using RC notation

```
ActiveCell.FormulaR1C1 = "=RC[-2]*RC[-1]"
```

16 - The macro should still be paused at row 17. If it is, click on Run. If it is not, run the macro again, when it gets to the breakpoint click Run again to make it continue.

Can you see the error in the macro?

The last cell, D8 is missing the formula. Let's fix that.

17 – Click at the end of line 40 (the last line before Range("D5").Select)

18 – Press Enter

This is where the R1C1 notation becomes useful. You don't have to write B5 * C5 or figure out what the right columns are. Since each formula is the same, copy another formula and put in the new line.

19 – Copy another line with the formula
20 – Paste it into the new empty line
The last part of the macro should look like this:

```
        Range("C5").Select
        ActiveCell.FormulaR1C1 = "80"
        Range("D5").Select
        ActiveCell.FormulaR1C1 = "=RC[-2]*RC[-1]"
  End Sub
```

21 – Test the macro by running the macro again. You can delete the data in the worksheet or leave it in there. It is up to you.

After running the macro, the worksheet will populate everything and cell D5 will have the formula entered.

	A	B	C	D
1	Salesperson	Qty	Price	Total
2	Lisa	10	50	500
3	Stacy	5	25	125
4	Larry	8	100	800
5	Steve	12	80	960

What's Next?

The next lesson, Mastering Excel Macros: Beginning to Code starts a project where you will code a macro that will build a database of invoices. You start be recording a simple macro, then you add macro commands that cannot be recorded.

Lesson: 3
Beginning to Code

Introduction

OK, by now you've been introduced to the Excel macro editor in lesson one and learned how to use all of the debugging tools in lesson two, you're ready to begin coding a macro. If you haven't been following along lesson one in lesson two I encourage you to do so but it's not really necessary, if you already know the basics about macros and the VBA editor and how to debug you can start with this lesson.

Figuring Out Macros

When starting to learn about macros the hardest part is not figuring out what you want to do but how to do what you want to do. In other words, you know you want to insert a row at a certain place in the Excel worksheet but how do you know what the commands are or how to do it? Let's review a couple of ways that you can *learn to learn* macros.

Recording Your Actions

This is by far the fastest and easiest way to learn the various commands available in the Excel programming language. The only thing you have to do is perform the actions that you want to macro to do while recording a macro. When you're done, open up the macro editor and see what Excel recorded for your actions.

Let's try an example now. Later in this lesson, were going to write a macro and part of that macro is going to copy a worksheet in the same workbook but let's figure how to do that right now by using the macro editor to figure out how to do it.

Okay just to be clear, we are going to record a macro that will copy a worksheet and then just see how it's done. Then we can use that knowledge to build a new macro without having to record anything.

1 – Open up the follow along workbook, Invoice.xlsm

2 – Save the workbook with the name Invoice Macro.xlsm.

Make sure you say that as file type xlsm and not file type xlsx. Xlsx files **will not** save macros. Also, saving the workbook under a different name gives us what we called a rollback point. That basically means if you mess up and go back to the original workbook and start again.

3 - Click on the report macro button at the bottom left of the Excel window

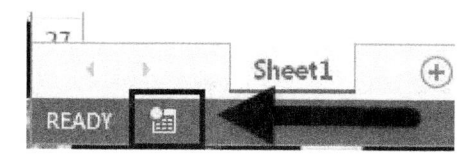

4 - In the new window that pops up, name the macro CopyWorksheet (no spaces in names are allowed).

It is a best practice to name the macros relevantly so that you remember exactly what it does. Note how to write the macro names, it's not necessary to have capital letters between but it does make it more legible. Every new word should have a capital letter. This type of writing name is called "camel case".

5 - Click OK

The report macro button should now be a small white square. This means every action we perform will be recorded.

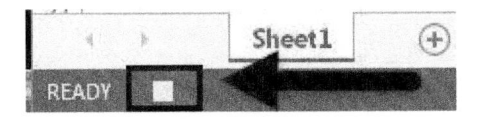

6 - Right-click on the worksheet tab named Sheet1
7 - In the pop-up menu select "Move or Copy..."

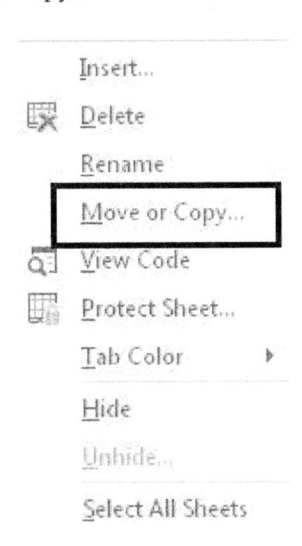

8 – Select (move to end)
9 – Check the box next to 'Create a copy'

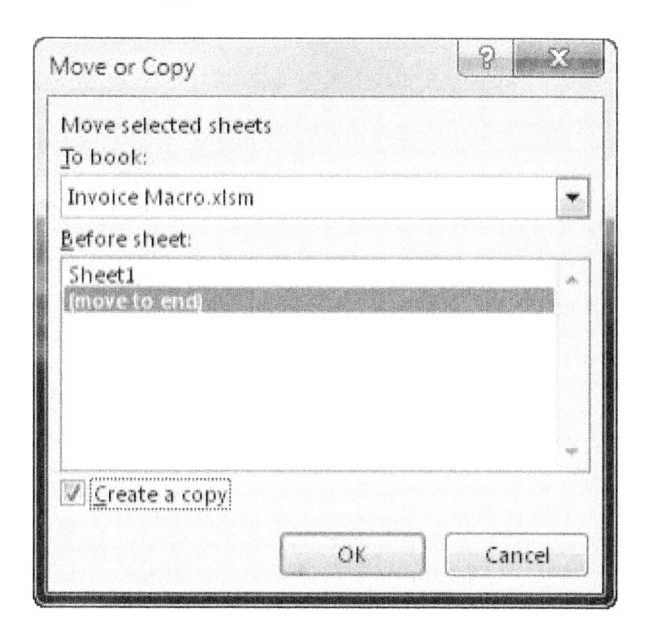

10 – Click OK
11 – Double-click on the new worksheet tab that should read Sheet1(2)
12 – Type in a new worksheet name. Name the worksheet Data
13 – Press Enter

14 - Click the stop recording macro button

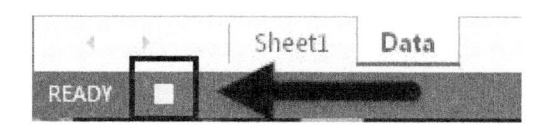

We have just recoded a macro that copies a worksheet and then renames the copied worksheet to Data. Let's look at the generated code.
15 – Click on the Developer tab
If you don't see the develop tab, enable it by going to File > Options > Customize Ribbon and then selecting the box that says Developer tab. Steps will be a slightly different in Excel 2007 & 2010)
16 – Click on the Visual Basic button
17 – If you do not see the macro displayed, double click on Module1
This is the code generated. If yours is a bit different, it just means you did a few additional things in Excel.

```
Sub CopyWorksheet()
'
' CopyWorksheet Macro
'

'
    Sheets("Sheet1").Select
    Sheets("Sheet1").Copy After:=Sheets(1)
    Sheets("Sheet1 (2)").Name = "Data"
End Sub
```

Line by line, here is what the macro does.

Sheets("Sheet1").Select	This line selects the worksheet Sheet1
Sheets("Sheet1").Copy After:=Sheets(1)	This line copies it after Sheets (1)
Sheets("Sheet1 (2)").Name = "Data"	This line renames Sheet 1 (2) to Data

OK, I understand that the := and the Sheets words are pretty confusing but we will cover that later on in other lessons.

Right now, just remember that if you don't know how to program something in Excel, record it, then look at it.

How can we use this? If we need to add a worksheet renaming command to another macro, we can just copy this renaming line and change it suit our needs. We can do something like:

Sheets("Sheet10").Name = "Shopping List"

This will rename sheet 10 (in another hypothetical workbook) to Shopping List.

OK, let's get back to learning how to figure out macros. We just covered recording macros to see the generated code. How else can we learn to do something specific in a macro (excluding these lessons)?

Use Google

Of course, you're going to use Google. It knows just about everything. If you have run into a problem with macros, I can guarantee that someone else has run into the same problem. Launch your browser and do a google search for your problem. To limit results, include the term vba in your search (this will limit results to Excel results). So to learn how to move a worksheet you would input "move an excel worksheet vba"

Use VBA Help

The VBA editor has its own help files that are completely different from the regular Excel help files. When you are in the VBA editor, click the F1 key to launch help. Note that F1 is smart, it will try to find the help topic for the word where the cursor is. For example, if you click in between the word Select in the macro we just recorded and press F1, you will see this window:

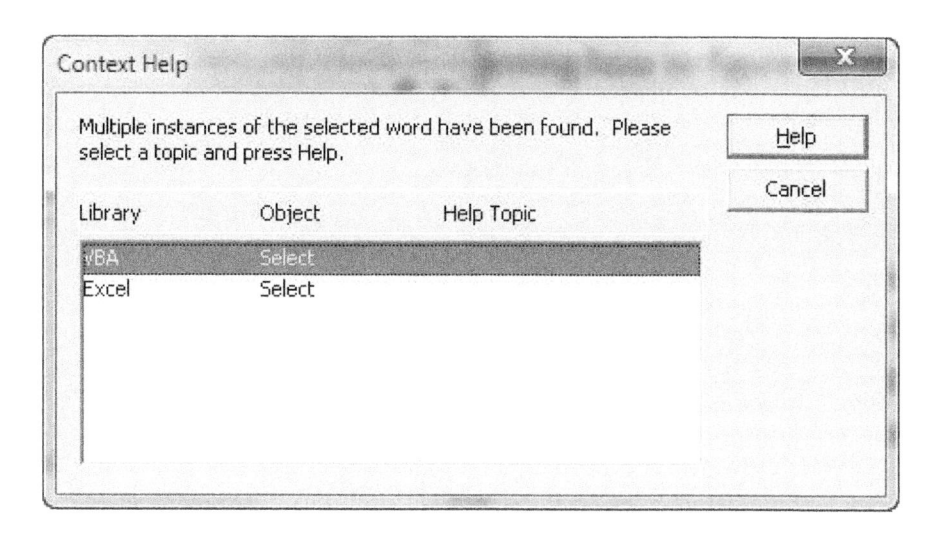

In this case, Excel needs more clarification. Do you want to see the help files for the regular Select in Excel or the VBA Select? In this case, select VBA Select (the first one).

Unfortunately, VBA Excel help is not automatically installed. If you get an error in Excel saying that Help has not been installed, you need to re run the Excel installation and select Custom Installation. Then select 'Run from my computer' in the VBA box.

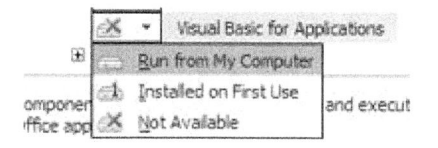

Use Intellisense

When you are writing a macro, Excel has a built in function that tries to help you out by telling you everything that you can do with a particular object.

Let's see how this works.

I am in the process of writing this macro:

```
Sub Intellisense()

    Range("A1").

End Sub
```

I want to do something with cell A1. All the objects have methods and properties that can be changed (We covered this in Mastering Excel Macros: Introduction the first book of the series). I don't know what the properties/methods are. No problem, as soon as I enter a period after range ("A1") a feature called Intellisense will launch and list out all the properties/methods that are applicable to the object (in this case the object is a range). I can then scroll down the list and find the one I want.

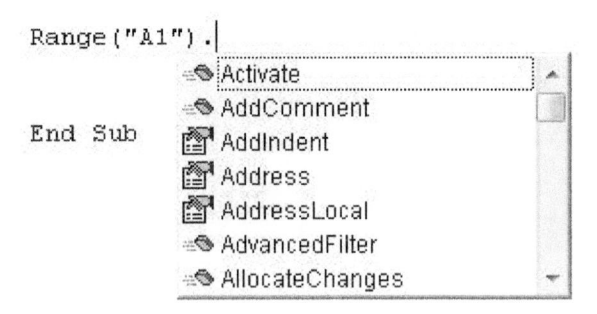

```
Range("A1").
               Activate
               AddComment
End Sub        AddIndent
               Address
               AddressLocal
               AdvancedFilter
               AllocateChanges
```

Notice how each item has a different icon? The green block with the action lines denote a method. This is the action that you can take on the range object; the verb. You can activate the range, add a comment to it, etc. The boxes with the small hand at the corner denote properties; the nouns of the object. A cell has an Address, an Indentation level, etc.

Structure of a Macro

Let's look at a simple macro and review the structure and parts of it.

```
Sub RenameSheet()
    Dim NewName As String
    NewName = "MySheet"
    Sheets("Sheet3").Name = NewName
End Sub
```

Sub [Macro Name] ( )

Every macro starts with the word Sub (this is shorthand for subroutine) and followed by the name of the macro. When naming the macro, use relevant names and use camel case to make it easier to read (ThisIsCamelCase). No spaces or special characters are allowed in macro names. However, you can use the underscore _

The parentheses after the macro name are also required. This is how macros talk to each other. If a macro has variables in between the parenthesis, that means when another macro calls it (yes, one macro can execute another macro) the calling macro needs to 'tell' the second macro the variables. If this doesn't make sense, don't worry about it. This is something we will get into much later in another lesson. For the most part, run of the mill macros will always have nothing in between the parenthesis.

Declare Variables

Dim NewName as String

This line is not at all required. I put it in there because you might need it in the future or you might see it in a website. This line is where you declare all your variables. Usually this is at the top of the macro before anything is really 'done' by the macro.

Why is this needed?

It's not.

What is its purpose then?

For large, complex macros, declaring your variables can make code easier to read and improve performance.

Variables are just like the variable we learned to hate in Algebra class. Something that stands for another thing. In this case, the variable NewName will stand for whatever word we choose to name the sheet. String means text in programming speak.

Why will declaring variables improve performance?

I'm going to try and keep this short and to the point and not get too complicated.

When you need to store a variable, Excel separates a tiny bit of space in memory to store that information. There are different types of information. There are words (i.e. string data), numbers (there are other data types but we are going to skip those for now). Each type of information takes a different amount of memory to store. A very, very large number like 654,321,9876,087,456 takes more memory to store than 42. Declaring variables let's Excel prepare itself to store the variables in the most efficient way possible, because you told it what to do.

If you don't declare your variables (tell Excel what to do) Excel will assign a default variable type called Variant. Variant can handle text and any number.

Does it matter?

For the macros that we will be using, not really. Technically, yes the macro will run faster but if it's not noticeable, don't worry about it. However, if your goal is to start with VBA then move into learning other programming languages, **do** declare your variables. Other languages require all variables to be declared and it is a good habit to acquire.

The Macro Code

Let's deconstruct the sample macro. Here we set a value for the NewName variable

NewName = "MySheet"

Here we rename the sheet

Sheets("Sheet3").Name = NewName

End Sub

Every macro must end with the End Sub command.

In summary, this image shows the structure of a simple macro:

```
Sub ()

Declare variables

Macro code

End Sub ()
```

Comments

Comments are explanations that you put in your code to explain or help you remember things that are happening. They can be anything you like. Excel will ignore all comments when executing macros.

Comments are indicated by starting a line with a single quote '. Everything after that will be highlighted in green to indicate it is a comment.

Beginning to Code

Now that you know the basic parts of a macro, let's use the follow along workbook to add some functionality to our invoice file.

If you followed along with the previous exercise, close that workbook (you don't have to save it) and reopen the original follow along workbook, Invoice.xlsm.

The Scenario

The follow along workbook is an invoice from Klaus Industries. The CEO, S. Klaus in addition to having a thriving toy business also sells goods to other holiday characters. Each invoice is submitted individually. You have a project to build an Excel based database where you can analyze all the invoice data.

To solve this, you are going to have to consolidate all the individual invoices from different worksheets into one worksheet. Then you can build pivot tables and dashboards to see how the business is doing over time.

Since there are so many invoices sent out, you need to use VBA to automate this task.

The Goal

This lesson will start with one invoice. We will copy it to another worksheet and remove extra rows so that we have a simple Excel database (just data with row headers). In later lessons you will continually improve this macro to work with multiple invoices. At each step you will learn one new macro concept.

1 – Open the follow along workbook, Invoice.xlsm

2 – Save it as Invoice Database.xlsm

To create the database, you will need to copy the existing invoice into a new worksheet, then remove all the header information. We will start by creating a new macro, recording our actions, then copy/pasting commands from the recorded macro into the new macro. This really is the best way to learn how to code. In a little while, you'll start to remember the commands and will be able to skip the recording part of the process.

3 – Create a new, empty macro

4 – Click on the Developer tab

5 – Click on the Visual Basic button

6 – In the VBAProject window, right click on Microsoft Excel Objects

7 – Select Insert Module

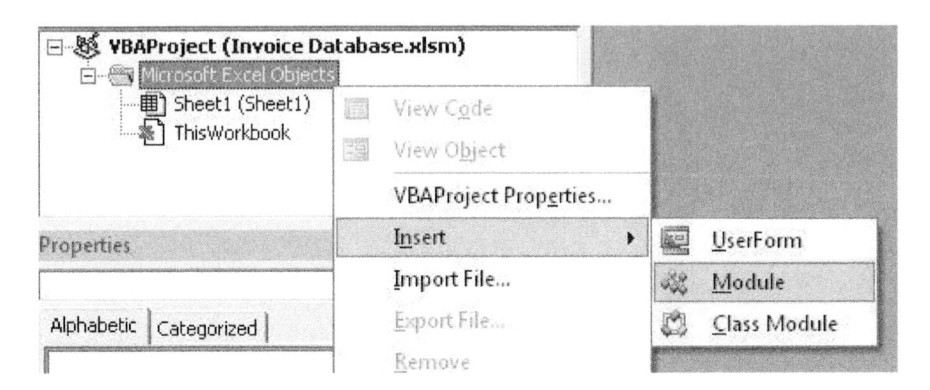

8 – Create a new macro called CreateDatabase (Just type in the following text in the blank module that opened up)

```
Sub CreateDatabase()

End Sub
```

Now let's record a macro that will make a copy of Sheet1 and see how that's done.
9 – Go back to Excel
10 – Click the Record Macro button
11 – Leave the defaults in the Record macro window
12 – Click OK
13 – Right click on Sheet1
14 – Select 'Move or Copy...'
15 – Select (move to end) and check 'Create a copy'

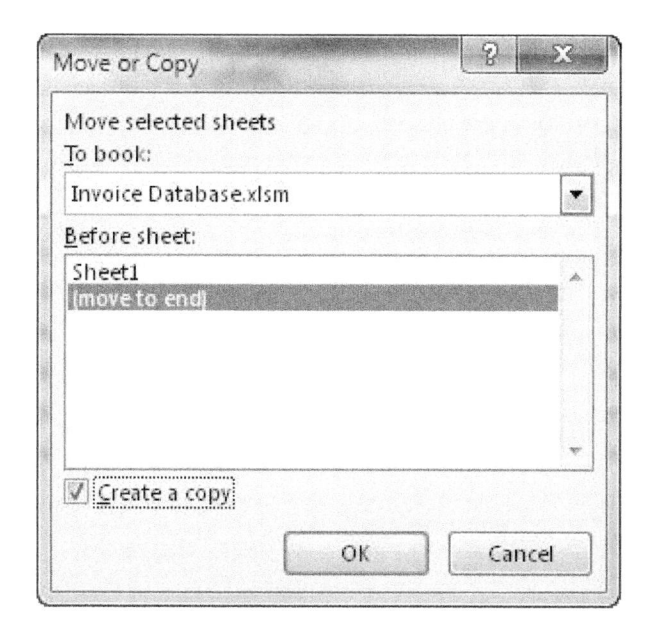

16 – Click OK
17 – Click on the stop recording macro button

18 – Let's go back to the VBA editor window to see the macro
You should now see a Module2 in the VBAProject window. That is where the just recorded macro is stored.
19 – Double click Module2 to open it
20 – The code to add a copy of a worksheet is:

```
Sub Macro2()
'
' Macro2 Macro
'
    Sheets("Sheet1").Select
    Sheets("Sheet1").Copy After:=Sheets(1)
End Sub
```

21 – Copy the commands from Macro2 to the CreateDatabase macro

The CreateDatabase macro should look like this now:

```
Sub CreateDatabase()

    Sheets("Sheet1").Select
    Sheets("Sheet1").Copy After:=Sheets(1)

End Sub
```

22 – We already saw how to rename a worksheet in VBA. Let's add that code to our CreateDatabase macro and have the new sheet be named Database.

After adding the new code, the macro should look like this:

```
Sub CreateDatabase()

    Sheets("Sheet1").Select
    Sheets("Sheet1").Copy After:=Sheets(1)
    Sheets("Sheet1 (2)").Name = "Database"

End Sub
```

Let's test the macro.

23 – Delete Sheet1 (2). (Right click on Sheet1 (2) and select Delete. Click Delete at the warning window). You should only have Sheet1 in the workbook.

24 – In Excel, click on the Developer tab

25 – Click on Macros

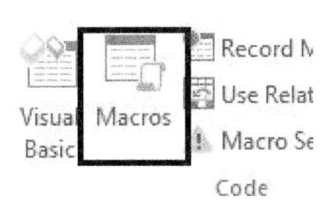

26 – Click on CreateDatabase

27 – Click Run

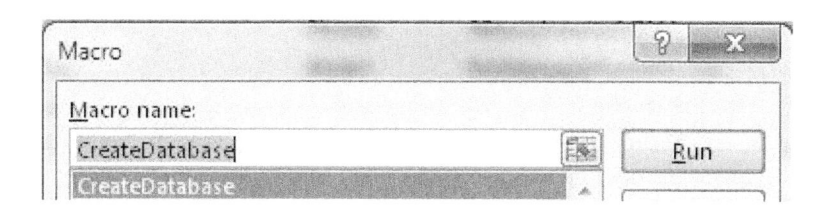

You should now have a new worksheet that is a copy of the invoice on a worksheet named Database.

The last step is to clean up the database. An invoice has a lot of data that is necessary, the header, the selling company address, the phone number, etc. However, in a database a lot of that data is not needed. For example, for our invoice database, we really don't need the phone numbers or the addresses. We do need the Bill To (the customer) and the Invoice #.

You are going to define two variables to store that data and then put it for each line in the invoice

28 – Define the variables. They will both store text (i.e. string data). Call one Customer and the other Invoice.

Once again, do we **need** to do this? No. However, doing so will introduce the concept of variables, variable types and how to use them. Later on, you can choose to skip declaring variables in your macros. You can always go back and declare them.

```
Sub CreateDatabase()
    Dim Customer As String
    Dim Invoice As String

    Sheets("Sheet1").Select
    Sheets("Sheet1").Copy After:=Sheets(1)
    Sheets("Sheet1 (2)").Name = "Database"

End Sub
```

Now the variables will be created but they will be empty. We need to tell Excel what to put inside the variable. This is the stuff you can't record in Excel, you have to start programming.

You want the text inside cell C7 in the Customer variable and the text inside cell H7 in the Invoice variable.

The line to populate the Customer variable is:

Customer = Range("C7").Value

Now all the stuff we reviewed in an earlier lesson about dot notation comes to bear. In VBA, cells are referred to ranges. A range can be as small as 1 cell or as large as all cells in a worksheet. The address of the cell is put within quotations "

What's the deal with the .Value part? Remember I told you in a previous lesson that everything is an object? A range (i.e. a cell) is an object. It has properties and methods. Typing in Range("C7") leaves Excel wondering, "What about C7?" Is it bolded? Centered? Deleted? Shaded pink? You have to be specific and say "I want the value of cell C7." That's what the .Value means.

Similarly, to set the value for the Invoice variable, the line would be:

Invoice = Range("H7").Value

29 – Type in the lines to set the variable values

Customer = Range("C7").Value

Invoice = Range("H7").Value

Your macros should look like this now:

```
Sub CreateDatabase()
    Dim Customer As String
    Dim Invoice As String

    Sheets("Sheet1").Select
    Sheets("Sheet1").Copy After:=Sheets(1)
    Sheets("Sheet1 (2)").Name = "Database"
    Customer = Range("C7").Value
    Invoice = Range("H7").Value

End Sub
```

Now we need to put the values of those variables next to the extended price for each row. The lines are very similar to setting the values for the variable, they are just backwards.

Ok, when we set the variables we used:

Customer = Range("C7").Value

Generally speaking, the format is

[Object that is empty] = [Object that has value to put into empty object]

(i.e. make Customer equal to the value in range C7)

So now that we have data in our variables, what would be the syntax to put Customer data in cell G13 (an empty cell)?

[Object that is empty] = [Object that has value to put into empty object]

Range("G13") = Customer

(i.e. make range G13 equal to whatever value Customer has)

Then to put Invoice data in cell H13 would be:

[Object that is empty] = [Object that has value to put into empty object]

Range("H13") = Invoice

30 – Type in two commands to fill in the customer and invoice data for cells G13 & H13

Range("G13") = Customer

Range("H13") = Invoice

Your macro should look like this now:

```
Sub CreateDatabase()
    Dim Customer As String
    Dim Invoice As String

    Sheets("Sheet1").Select
    Sheets("Sheet1").Copy After:=Sheets(1)
    Sheets("Sheet1 (2)").Name = "Database"
    Customer = Range("C7").Value
    Invoice = Range("H7").Value

    Range("G13") = Customer
    Range("H13") = Invoice


End Sub
```

Now you have to repeat the last two lines for rows 14 through 16
31 – Copy and change the last two lines so they populate rows 14 through 16
Your macro should look like this now:

```
Sub CreateDatabase()
    Dim Customer As String
    Dim Invoice As String

    Sheets("Sheet1").Select
    Sheets("Sheet1").Copy After:=Sheets(1)
    Sheets("Sheet1 (2)").Name = "Database"
    Customer = Range("C7").Value
    Invoice = Range("H7").Value

    Range("G13") = Customer
    Range("H13") = Invoice
    Range("G14") = Customer
    Range("H14") = Invoice
    Range("G15") = Customer
    Range("H15") = Invoice
    Range("G16") = Customer
    Range("H16") = Invoice

End Sub
```

32 - Save the Excel workbook
Test the macro by deleting the Database worksheet and running the CreateDatabase macro.
Your invoice worksheet should now have data in columns G & H

Item	Description	Quantity	Unit Price	Extended Price		
1	Pink Baskets	100	5.75	575.00	Easter Bu	1000
2	Ribbons	500	2.00	1,000.00	Easter Bu	1000
3	Paint	900	1.25	1,125.00	Easter Bu	1000
4	Paint remover	200	2.50	500.00	Easter Bu	1000
5						

The last part of the macro is to delete any rows other than the individual line items.

There are many ways to delete a row or multiple rows, but let's use this one:

Range("A1").EntireRow.Delete

However, we don't have to do it line by line. We can delete rows block by block. Block 1 through 11 is the first block and block 17 through 25 is the second block.

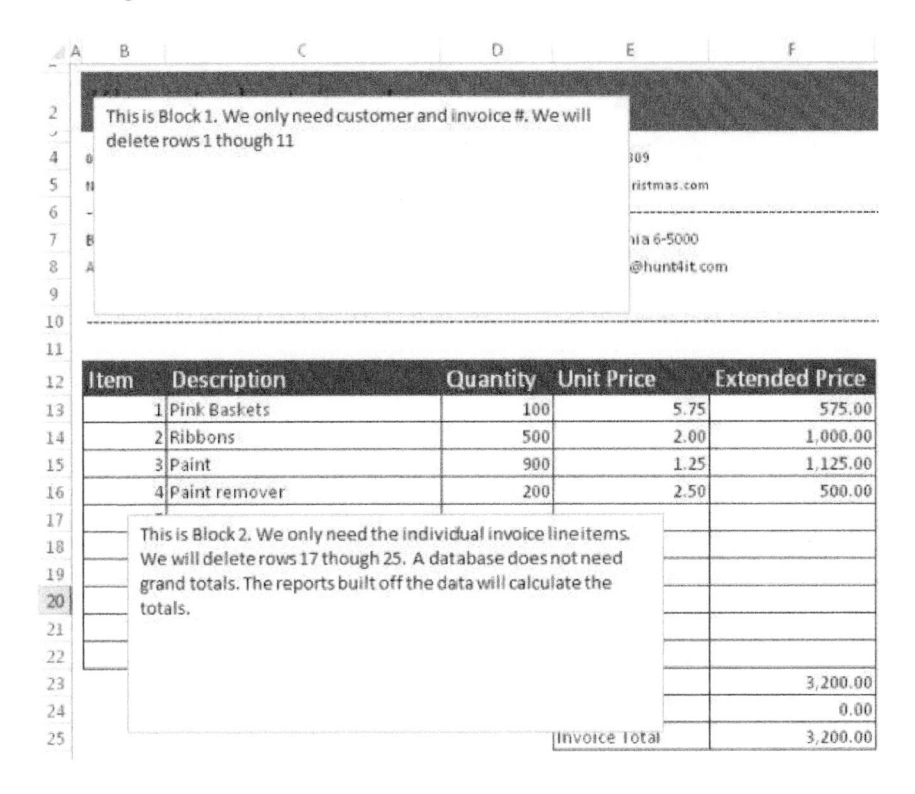

[Spreadsheet image showing Block 1 (rows 1-11) containing customer and invoice # information, and Block 2 (rows 17-25) containing totals information. The line items (Item, Description, Quantity, Unit Price, Extended Price) appear in rows 12-16 with Pink Baskets, Ribbons, Paint, and Paint remover entries. Invoice Total shows 3,200.00.]

To delete rows 1 through 11, use this line:

Range("A1:A11").EntireRow.Delete

33 – Input the delete row line in the macro and use it so that rows 1 through 11 and rows 17 through 25 are deleted

Range("A17:A25").EntireRow.Delete

Range("A1:A11").EntireRow.Delete

(You have to delete the bottom rows first because the row numbers will change if you delete the top rows first)

```
Sub CreateDatabase()
    Dim Customer As String
    Dim Invoice As String

    Sheets("Sheet1").Select
    Sheets("Sheet1").Copy After:=Sheets(1)
    Sheets("Sheet1 (2)").Name = "Database"
    Customer = Range("C7").Value
    Invoice = Range("H7").Value

    Range("G13") = Customer
    Range("H13") = Invoice
    Range("G14") = Customer
    Range("H14") = Invoice
    Range("G15") = Customer
    Range("H15") = Invoice
    Range("G16") = Customer
    Range("H16") = Invoice

    Range("A17:A25").EntireRow.Delete
    Range("A1:A11").EntireRow.Delete

End Sub
```

34 – Include these lines to add column headers for the Invoice & Customer columns

Range("G1").Value = "Customer"

Range("H1").Value = "Invoice"

```
Sub CreateDatabase()
    Dim Customer As String
    Dim Invoice As String
    
    Sheets("Sheet1").Select
    Sheets("Sheet1").Copy After:=Sheets(1)
    Sheets("Sheet1 (2)").Name = "Database"
    Customer = Range("C7").Value
    Invoice = Range("H7").Value
    
    Range("G13") = Customer
    Range("H13") = Invoice
    Range("G14") = Customer
    Range("H14") = Invoice
    Range("G15") = Customer
    Range("H15") = Invoice
    Range("G16") = Customer
    Range("H16") = Invoice
    
    Range("A17:A25").EntireRow.Delete
    Range("A1:A11").EntireRow.Delete
    
    Range("G1").Value = "Customer"
    Range("H1").Value = "Invoice"
    
End Sub
```

Save the workbook, delete the Database worksheet and run the macro to test.
After running the macro, the database worksheet should look like this:

A	B	C	D	E	F	G	H
1	Item	Description	Quantity	Unit Price	Extended Price	Customer	Invoice
2	1	Pink Baskets	100	5.75	575.00	Easter Bur	1000
3	2	Ribbons	500	2.00	1,000.00	Easter Bur	1000
4	3	Paint	900	1.25	1,125.00	Easter Bur	1000
5	4	Paint remover	200	2.50	500.00	Easter Bur	1000

The macro is done. It takes an invoice, copies it over into a new worksheet, renames it and deletes any extra rows. However, it is not complete by a long shot. It will only work for invoices that have four line items. Any extra line items will be removed.

Lesson:4
If Statements

In this lesson we are going to start with the core item used in macro programming: the IF statement. This will be used in just about any but the most basic macros you will write. The IF statement is the way to make macros intelligent and 'think'.

Before we get directly into the IF statements, we will review two concepts: OFFSET and the active cell.

OFFSET

The OFFSET function is one you will use frequently when writing macros. This function lets you refer to other cells without having to move the cursor. You use the OFFSET function to point to a cell x rows and y columns away from a cell. The syntax is

OFFSET([row offset],[column offset])

However, you can't just use that command alone. Excel will think, Offset off of what? Which cell? The full syntax is:

[Range].Offset([row offset],[column offset])

	A	B	C
1	Region	Sales	Commissions
2	North	501	
3	South	525	
4	East	861	
5	West	401	
6	International	276	
7			

Two examples will clear this up. In the above image, the active cell is C2 (that cell has been selected), to work with cell B2 **without** moving to cell B2 (i.e. staying on cell C2 but referring to cell B2) you use

Range("C2").OFFSET(0,-1).Value

What about if the cell that has been selected changes from C2 to C3? We would have to change the macro to Range("C3"). You can use an easier method. Instead of using Range, use active cell.

Activecell.OFFSET(0,-1).Value

Now the line won't be stuck to cell C2, it will look to the left of whichever the active cell is.

Just a last note, positive numbers mean rows below and columns to the right. Negative numbers mean rows above and columns to the left.

Let's review this example:

If ActiveCell.Offset(0, -2).Value = "North" Then

    Sales = ActiveCell.Offset(0, -1).Value

    ActiveCell.Value = Sales * NorthRate

End If

What this code does is the following (based on the above image). If the cell two columns to the left of C2 (the active cell) has North in it, then assign the value of the cell one row to the left (cell B2) to the Sales variable. Then multiply the Sales variable times the North rate and put the value in the active cell (cell C2). Notice how the active cell never moved from C2. The code just calculated the positions of the other cells based on C2. **The macro doesn't have to jump around getting values from different cells. That's too much work. It just needs to plant itself in one spot and refer to the other cells from the active cell's position.**

ActiveCell

Using "ActiveCell" is a very convenient way to learn macros. As you learn to program in Excel, whenever you want to do something, force Excel to move to that cell and then begin your desired actions. When you are debugging your code, since Excel is moving to each cell, you can see exactly what is going on in the worksheet and that makes it much easier to see any errors.

However, using the active cell is inefficient. Excel really doesn't need to move to the cell to affect it. Excel knows where every cell is. It's kind of like having to point at your elbow whenever you talk about it. You know where your elbow is, you can just talk about it without pointing it out.

Does it matter that it's inefficient? It's up to you. If a macro takes 5 seconds to run using the active cell and 2 seconds without, can you live with it? You decide on a case by case basis.

Where possible, I will use the active cell in these lessons. It will let you step through the code and see what is going on and get the hang of Excel programming. There are certain programming topics where you cannot use the active cell but by the time you get to them, you will be pretty comfortable with figuring out what is happening.

Active cell is used like any other range. Consider this line:

Range("A1").Font.Bold = True

This will make the cell A1 bold. This will only work for cell A1. However, if you change it to this:

ActiveCell.Font.Bold = True

the line will then make any cell that is selected bold. To make cell A1 bold, you would do this:

Range("A1").Activate

ActiveCell.Font.Bold = True

Basically, you have split out the one line into two separate lines. When we review the lesson on looping and moving through cells, it is easier to move the active cell than try to figure out that A2 is under A1. You can't add 1 to A1 to make it A2.

IF Statements

If statements are the basic logical function in macros, if you have used IF statements in Excel, you will see how similar they are in VBA Note that there are many variations of the IF statement. We are starting with the most basic one then building on it in later pages. The syntax of the IF statement is shown below.

If [condition] Then

[result]

Else

[other result]

End If

Looking at an example will make understanding this much easier. In the following example, the code adds 25 to the cell if the value is above 100.

Sub FirstIFStatement()

    If Range("A1").Value > 100 Then

        Range("B1").Value = Range("A1").Value + 25

    Else

        Range("B1").Value = "Cell A1 is less than 100"

    End If

End Sub

Just by looking through the macro you can probably tell what it does. The way to identify a cell in VBA is through the range object and the address. Range("A1") means cell A1. If cell A1's value is greater than 100 then take the number in A1 add 25 to it and put it in cell B1. If the value in A1 is less than 100 then put the statement 'Cell A1 is less than 100' in cell B1. Notice that if you want to put any type of text into a cell, you must enclose it in quotations "".

You don't **have** to put the ELSE part of the IF statement. If you just wanted to add the 25 and not put any text if the value in A1 was less than 100, you could have used this code:

Sub FirstIFStatement()

    If Range("A1").Value > 100 Then

        Range("B1").Value = Range("A1").Value + 25

    End If

End Sub

This is great but very rarely do we have such simple conditions in the real world. Let's work with something more realistic. Look at this worksheet in the follow along workbook:

	A	B	C
1	Region	Sales	Commissions
2	North	501	
3	South	525	
4	East	861	
5	West	401	
6	International	276	

The workbook shows regions and their sales. Let's write a macro that calculates the commissions. Each commission will vary based on the region. With what you know now, you could write 5 different IF statements to calculate commissions. It would work, but there are better ways.

Although you could put in as many IF statement in your code as you like, later on, it will be more difficult to edit and improve your code.

ELSEIF

(Note that the IF Statements.xlsm file does not have any macros in it. You will be creating a new one.)

Instead of using 5 IF statements to evaluate 1 condition each, let's use 1 IF statement to evaluate 5 conditions. You will add several ELSEIF conditions to an IF statement.

1 - Open the follow along workbook, IF Statements.xlsm (make sure you enable macros when opening it)

2 - Go to the Developer tab

3 - Click on Visual Basic

You will create a new macro underneath the existing FirstIFStatement macro

4 - Type in Sub FirstElseIf () below the End Sub

5 - Press Enter

```
Sub FirstIFStatement()

    If Range("A1").Value > 100 Then
        Range("B1").Value = Range("A1").Value + 25
    Else
        Range("B1").Value = "Cell A1 is less than 100"
    End If

End Sub
Sub FirstElseIf()

End Sub
```

In this exercise, each region will have a different commission rate. You could go right ahead and start writing the If statement and putting in the rates at the appropriate places. However, next week, next month, or whenever you have to change the macro you will have to pore through the code and find every commission and change it. For this small macro, it isn't that big of a deal but for a large macro going through every line is tedious and error prone. You can 'future proof' your code by putting your variables at the top of the macro. Then, when you have to change them you simply do so in one place.

Since each region has different rates, we will need one variable for each region.

6 - Type these lines in the FirstElseIf macro

NorthRate = .05

SouthRate = .10

EastRate = .07

WestRate = .04

IntRate = .20

Your macro should look like this now:

Sub FirstElseIf()

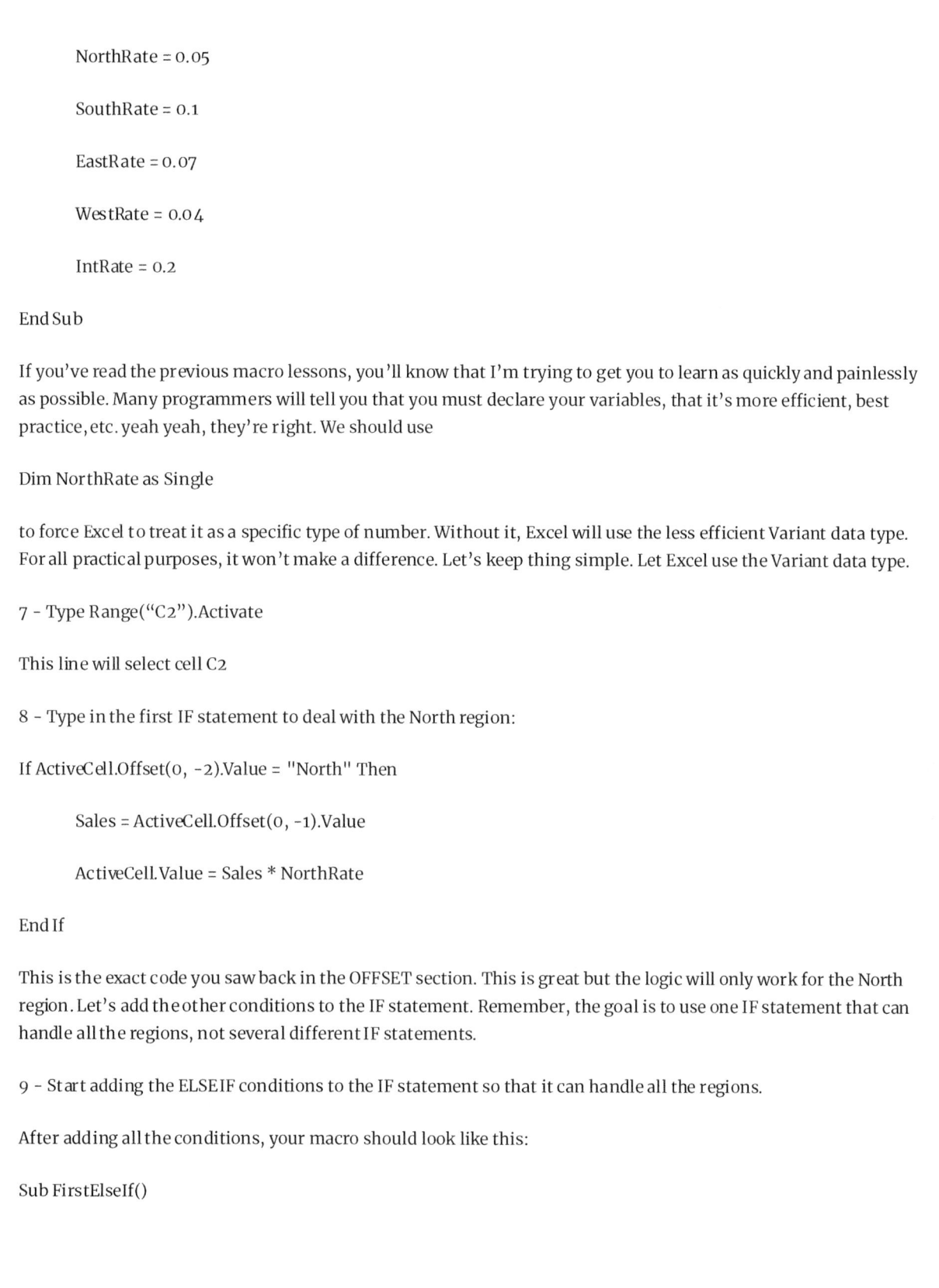

    NorthRate = 0.05

    SouthRate = 0.1

    EastRate = 0.07

    WestRate = 0.04

    IntRate = 0.2

End Sub

If you've read the previous macro lessons, you'll know that I'm trying to get you to learn as quickly and painlessly as possible. Many programmers will tell you that you must declare your variables, that it's more efficient, best practice, etc. yeah yeah, they're right. We should use

Dim NorthRate as Single

to force Excel to treat it as a specific type of number. Without it, Excel will use the less efficient Variant data type. For all practical purposes, it won't make a difference. Let's keep thing simple. Let Excel use the Variant data type.

7 - Type Range("C2").Activate

This line will select cell C2

8 - Type in the first IF statement to deal with the North region:

If ActiveCell.Offset(0, -2).Value = "North" Then

    Sales = ActiveCell.Offset(0, -1).Value

    ActiveCell.Value = Sales * NorthRate

End If

This is the exact code you saw back in the OFFSET section. This is great but the logic will only work for the North region. Let's add the other conditions to the IF statement. Remember, the goal is to use one IF statement that can handle all the regions, not several different IF statements.

9 - Start adding the ELSEIF conditions to the IF statement so that it can handle all the regions.

After adding all the conditions, your macro should look like this:

Sub FirstElseIf()

```
NorthRate = 0.05

SouthRate = 0.1

EastRate = 0.07

WestRate = 0.04

IntRate = 0.2

Range("C2").Activate

If ActiveCell.Offset(0, -2).Value = "North" Then

    Sales = ActiveCell.Offset(0, -1).Value

    ActiveCell.Value = Sales * NorthRate

ElseIf ActiveCell.Offset(0, -2).Value = "South" Then

    Sales = ActiveCell.Offset(0, -1).Value

    ActiveCell.Value = Sales * SouthRate

ElseIf ActiveCell.Offset(0, -2).Value = "East" Then

    Sales = ActiveCell.Offset(0, -1).Value

    ActiveCell.Value = Sales * EastRate

ElseIf ActiveCell.Offset(0, -2).Value = "West" Then

    Sales = ActiveCell.Offset(0, -1).Value

    ActiveCell.Value = Sales * SouthRate

ElseIf ActiveCell.Offset(0, -2).Value = "International" Then

    Sales = ActiveCell.Offset(0, -1).Value

    ActiveCell.Value = Sales * IntRate

Else

    ActiveCell.Value = "Incorrect Region input"
```

        End If

End Sub

That should make sense by now. Each section is very similar, the differences are the region value and the variable it is using.

I did include an ELSE clause there at the end. Why? Because I'm 'future proofing' the macro. Who knows what values users will put into column A? There could be typos or some other incorrect entries. The ELSE catches those errors and put in the phrase "Incorrect Region Input".

10 – Save your workbook with a different name

11 – Click anywhere inside the FirstElseIf macro

12 – Press F8 to start the step by step debugger

13 – Keep pressing F8 to see what the macro is doing, line by line

A few notes about this macro

1 – Did you notice how using OFFSET is much easier than hard coding the cell address? You don't have to input any cell references (i.e. A2, B2, etc.). You just have to say x columns to the left of the active cell.

2 – For many conditions, ELSEIF is better because as soon as Excel finds a valid condition, it skips the rest of them and goes straight to the END IF. If you put 5 individual IF statements, Excel would have to evaluate every one each time.

3 – What about upper and lowercase? Yes, that is a problem.

Test this out:

a) Type in north in cell A2

b) Press F8 and work your way through the macro

What happened? It didn't calculate the North region correctly. Why? Because North **is not equal** to north. Letter case matters! Let's add a bit more intelligence to this macro. Make whatever is in the cell all uppercase and then compare it to the uppercase region value. This way, no matter what case the user inputs, the logic will still work. Here's how you do that, you use the UCASE formula like this:

UCase(ActiveCell.Offset(0, -2).Value) = "NORTH"

Remember to change the last part to NORTH. The new, improved macro using UCASE is below.

```vb
Sub FirstElseIf()

    NorthRate = 0.05

    SouthRate = 0.1

    EastRate = 0.07

    WestRate = 0.04

    IntRate = 0.2

    Range("C2").Activate

    If UCase(ActiveCell.Offset(0, -2).Value) = "NORTH" Then

        Sales = ActiveCell.Offset(0, -1).Value

        ActiveCell.Value = Sales * NorthRate

    ElseIf UCase(ActiveCell.Offset(0, -2).Value) = "SOUTH" Then

        Sales = ActiveCell.Offset(0, -1).Value

        ActiveCell.Value = Sales * SouthRate

    ElseIf UCase(ActiveCell.Offset(0, -2).Value) = "EAST" Then

        Sales = ActiveCell.Offset(0, -1).Value

        ActiveCell.Value = Sales * EastRate

    ElseIf UCase(ActiveCell.Offset(0, -2).Value) = "WEST" Then

        Sales = ActiveCell.Offset(0, -1).Value

        ActiveCell.Value = Sales * SouthRate

    ElseIf UCase(ActiveCell.Offset(0, -2).Value) = "INTERNATIONAL" Then

        Sales = ActiveCell.Offset(0, -1).Value

        ActiveCell.Value = Sales * IntRate

    Else
```

        ActiveCell.Value = "Incorrect Region input"

    End If

End Sub

Testing

- Try typing in a variety of cases, typos etc. and stepping through the macro (using F8) to see how it works.

- Change the active cell from C2, to another cell in column C and the step through the code

ORs and ANDs

This short section will show you that you can also test for several conditions without using ELSEIF.

AND

The AND conditions evaluates two (or more) conditions and if they are **both** true, then the result will be executed. For example, in the code below if the salesperson is Lisa and the region is west then the product is scarf.

	A	B	C	D
1	Salesperson	Region	Product	
2	Lisa	West		
3				

If Range("A1").Value = "Lisa" And Range("B2").Value = "West" Then

    Range("C2").Value = "Scarf"

End If

OR

The OR condition evaluates two (or more) conditions and if any one is true, then the result will be executed. In this example, the product will be scarf if the salesperson is Lisa or Marta.

If Range("A1").Value = "Lisa" Or Range("A1").Value = "Marta" Then

    Range("C2").Value = "Scarf"

End If

What's Next?

Right now, the macro we worked on only works on one cell, the active cell. The next lesson will cover looping. Looping is how you tell Excel to do the actions you specify over and over again.

Lesson:5
Looping

Looping is the way you tell Excel to do an action (or several actions) over and over. Using this feature in conjunction with the previous lesson that covered the IF statement is how most macros operate. You figure out the logic of the macro using one or several IF statements and then you put that logic in the loop and have the logic repeat until the work is done.

There are several types of loops that are covered in this lesson. The main difference between them is the way they stop. In other words, starting a loop is easy, figuring out when/how to stop is the tricky part.

Once all the different types of loops are covered, you will revisit the invoice macro and use IF statements and loops to improve it.

However, before we get into looping, let's talk about collections.

Collections

In the introductory lesson, we reviewed how Excel is made up of objects. These objects have properties and methods. Macros change properties (e.g. set the Bold property to True) or use methods (e.g. use the ClearContents method on a cell) to do work. Objects can contain other objects. For example, the Worksheet object contains range objects (remember ranges are how you refer to cells in macros) and maybe some chart objects or some textbox objects, etc. You get the idea.

Collections are groupings of similar objects. Each item (the object) in the collection will have the same methods and properties. Writing macros using collections is much easier than accessing each object individually. You can write macros that process the collection of objects instead of changing each object individually.

Let's set up an example. Suppose we have a workbook with 50 worksheets, one for each US State. You need to write a value in each worksheet in a certain cell. One way to do this is to do something like this:

```
Sub USStates()
'
' Access each worksheet
'
Worksheet("AL").Activate
Range("B1") = "South Region"

Worksheet("AK").Activate
Range("B1") = "South Region"

Worksheet("AZ").Activate
Range("B1") = "Central Region"

'etc etc for each worksheet

End Sub
```

Of course, now the problem is that you have to do this for every worksheet. Each worksheet is a member of the worksheets collection. If this is confusing, just think of a collection as a group of like objects, in this case worksheets. If you add a new worksheet, it is automatically added to the collection. In simple terms, the sheets collection is the group of all worksheets in a workbook. The next section explains how to process items in a collection.

Stopping a Running Macro

Before we even start talking about looping, let's review how to forcibly stop a macro. Eventually, you will run a macro that will have an infinite loop. It happens to all of us. We will cover infinite loop macros in the next section where you will see how one works. When that does happen, don't worry just press CTRL+BREAK a few times and this will force the macro to stop.

For Each Loop

Collections have their own properties and methods that are specific to the collection and not applicable to the members. For example, the Worksheets collection has the Count property. This code will assign the number of worksheets to the x variable.

```
Sub SheetsCount()

    x = Worksheets.Count

End Sub
```

It doesn't make sense for the worksheet to have the Count property because it is only a single worksheet. However, the Worksheets collection can have several worksheets and having the Count property is useful. How do you tell what other properties and methods the Worksheet collection has? Let Excel tell you.

Type in the code shown above in any workbook. When you get the point where you type in the period after Worksheets, Intellisense will display a pop up window where you can see all the properties/methods.

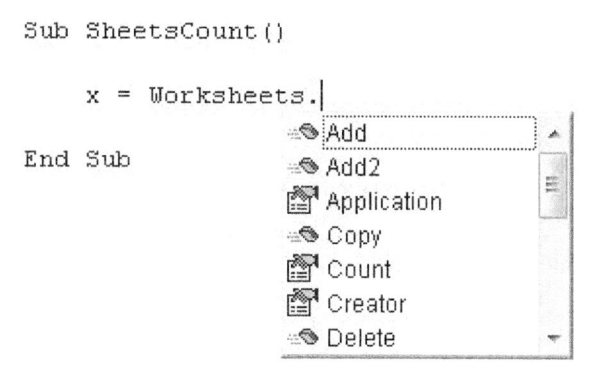

```
Sub SheetsCount()

    x = Worksheets.|
                    Add
    End Sub         Add2
                    Application
                    Copy
                    Count
                    Creator
                    Delete
```

The green flying bricks are methods (i.e. verbs) and the boxes with a hand are properties (i.e. nouns). For collections, the properties are of the collection itself (like Count) but the methods operate on the objects **inside** the collection. The Add method does not add a collection, it adds a worksheet to the collection. Similarly, the Delete method does not delete the collection, it deletes a worksheet from the collection.

You can use the worksheet name to get to the worksheet:

```
Worksheets("FL").Activate
```

Accessing worksheets by name is just as tedious as the previous code. The previous code used the individual worksheet, the code snippet above used the collection to get to the worksheet. the difference is only an 's'. Worksheet vs. worksheets. To be clearer and prevent confusion, from now on I will use the short cut name for the worksheets collection: Sheets.

These macros all do the same thing. Programming is like writing an essay. There are a million ways to say the same thing. There are three ways to reference a worksheet. You can use Worksheet, Worksheets or Sheets.

```
Sub USStates()
'
'  Access each worksheet
'
Worksheet("AL").Activate
Range("B1") = "South Region"

Worksheet("AK").Activate
Range("B1") = "South Region"

Worksheet("AZ").Activate
Range("B1") = "Central Region"

'etc etc for each worksheet

End Sub
```

```
Sub USStates()
'
'  Access each worksheet
'
Worksheets("AL").Activate
Range("B1") = "South Region"

Worksheets("AK").Activate
Range("B1") = "South Region"

Worksheets("AZ").Activate
Range("B1") = "Central Region"

'etc etc for each worksheet

End Sub
```

```
Sub USStates()
'
' Access each worksheet
'
Sheets("AL").Activate
Range("B1") = "South Region"

Sheets("AK").Activate
Range("B1") = "South Region"

Sheets("AZ").Activate
Range("B1") = "Central Region"

'etc etc for each worksheet

End Sub
```

Using any of the above macros saves you no time compared to the original macro. You still have to refer to each worksheet individually. Instead of doing that, you are going to have Excel loop through **each** member of the collection (each worksheet); each is the keyword here.

The Goal: You will write a macro that loops through every worksheet in the US States workbook and writes the worksheet name in cell A1.

1 - Open the follow along workbook 'US States.xlsm'

2 - Open Module 1 in the VBA editor

3 - Type in the following code so your For Each macro looks like this:

```
Sub ForEach()

    For Each s In Sheets


    Next s

End Sub
```

This is the basic For Each loop. It is saying for every item in the Sheets collection do something. In the above example, the something is still blank but we will fill it in shortly. Then at the bottom, the 'Next s' tells the macro to move on to the next item in the sheets collection

I'm going to take a paragraph or two to explain the 's' in the 'For Each s In Sheets' because it really confused me when I started out programming macros. The s is a variable, it is just a place holder for the current sheet. The US

States workbook has 50 different sheets. Each worksheet is in the Sheets collection (remember that the Worksheets collection can also be referred to as the Sheets collection). When using a For Each loop, the s variable will 'be' the current worksheet that is being processed. The variable doesn't have to be s, it can be anything you like; t, i, bob, etc.

It just doesn't look quite right to say 'For Each Bob in Sheets'. To make things clearer, programmers usually assign a variable that makes sense and indicates what is being manipulated. In this case the s represents the first letter of the word sheet.

4 - You want to put the sheet name in cell A1 in each sheet. In between the 'For each' and the 'Next' statement, type in the following code: Range("A1").Value = s.Name. Your macro should now look like this:

```
Sub ForEach()

    For Each s In Sheets

        Range("A1").Value = s.Name

    Next s

End Sub
```

5 - Go to the AL worksheet

6 - Run the macro.

What happened? If it went by too fast, use the step by step debugger to see what is going on (in case you forgot, click inside the macro and press F8 to move line by line)

Computers are dumb, they only do what we **tell** them to do, not what we **want** them to do. The macro tells the computer to put each worksheet name in cell A1. That's exactly what it is doing, **in the same worksheet**. The macro needs to move to each worksheet **then** put the name in cell A1. Luckily, it is a very minor change. Add the line s.Activate to the macro

```
Sub ForEach()

    For Each s In Sheets

        s.Activate
        Range("A1").Value = s.Name

    Next s

End Sub
```

Now you can run the macro or step through it and see it working as expected.

Note that this loop will perform the same action for every worksheet in the workbook. Sometimes you want this, sometimes you don't. What if you wanted to skip a worksheet and not have the worksheet name in Cell A1? How would you do that?

.

Did you get it?

You would put an If statement in the loop. Suppose you wanted to skip a worksheet names "Summary" the loop would look like this:

```
Sub ForEach()

    For Each s In Sheets

        s.Activate
        If s.Name <> "Summary" Then
            Range("A1").Value = s.Name
        End If
    Next s

End Sub
```

Looping through a range of cells

You can use the same method to loop through a range of cells and process them. Note this macro can be written on the US States.xlsm workbook or in a new workbook. It doesn't matter, it's just a simple example to illustrate looping through cells.

1 - Under the ForEach macro (under the End Sub) type in Sub LoopCells () to start a new macro

I could use s as a variable but I want to be clear so I am changing the macro to use c (which represents a cell). Look at the code below and see how similar it is to the loop through sheets macro we worked on.

```
Sub LoopCells()

    For Each c In Range("A1:C10")
        c.Value = c.Address
    Next c

End Sub
```

The macro will loop through all the cells inside the range A1:C10 and insert the cell address. Granted, it's a simple macro but it shows how once you understand how one for each loop works, you can apply it to any other collection.

This was your first venture into loops. Please take some time to re-read and work through the exercises in this section. This looping structure was a bit more complex because you had to learn and deal with the concept of a collection. However, once you 'get' this, you'll see how the other loops in the next sections much easier to work with.

For Loop

The For loop doesn't iterate through a collection. Instead you tell the For loop what to iterate by. You make up a counter and then you increase (or decrease) the counter until the target value is met. The counter can be anything you like but programmers have gotten into the habit of using i as an initial counter. I will also use i but remember it can be any letter or word.

Here is a sample of a For Loop:

```
Sub ForLoop()

For i = 1 To 10
    MsgBox ("The counter is now " & i)
Next i

End Sub
```

This macro will execute 10 times. Each time a pop up window (the message box) will appear with a statement letting you know the current counter value.

How can you use this? If you need to write a macro that only does something for the first 100 rows of a worksheet you can use a For I = 1 to 100 loop.

Do Until Loop

The Do Until loop does almost the same thing as the For Each loop. This loop will continue until a specified condition is met; it will 'do' 'until' a condition is met. The main difference is how you tell the loop to stop. The For Each stops when it encounters the last item in the collection, the Do Until stops when the condition you specify is met.

The syntax for the Do Until Loop is:

Do Until [Criteria]

Loop

For example, if I wanted a macro to move down a column until the active cell had the text 'Stop' in it, I would write this code:

```
Sub DoUntilStop()

    Do Until ActiveCell.Value = "Stop"
        ActiveCell.Offset(1, 0).Activate
    Loop

End Sub
```

Look at the DoUntil workbook and plan out what the macro is going to do.

The worksheet has a list of US States going down column A. You will write a macro that will fill in the correct salesperson in column B. Right now, you only know that Tony is responsible for the States of FL, CA and TX.

	A	B
1	State	Salesperson
2	AL	
3	AK	
4	AZ	
5	AR	
6	CA	
7	CO	
8	CT	
9	DE	
10	FL	
11	GA	
12	HI	

The first thing you have to do is put the active cell in cell B2. Then you need to evaluate the value of the cell to the left of it (using the Offset function). If that value is FL or CA or TX then put the value of Tony in the active cell and move the active cell down one cell (once again using the Offset function).

Go ahead and try to write the macro on your own. You aren't going to break anything. See if using the previous lessons and the previous loop examples, you can figure it out. If you run into trouble or get frustrated, don't worry about it. Just read on to see the solution below.

1 - Open the workbook DoUntil.xlsm

2 - Add a new module

3 - Type in Sub FirstDoUntil() and press Enter to create a new macro

```
Sub FirstDoUntil()



End Sub
```

4 - Set the start point at cell B2. Type in Range("B2").Activate

5 - Type in the loop statement (I like to write the loop structure then fill in the logic later)

```
Sub FirstDoUntil()

    Range("B2").Activate
    Do Until ActiveCell.Offset(0, -1).Value = ""

    Loop
End Sub
```

Whoa, what is all that stuff? Well, you want the macro to run and process all the States, right? You tell the macro to do that by setting the criteria to = "". The two double quotes with nothing in between (nothing, not even a space) means a blank. This macro will stop running when a cell is blank. Which cell? The cell that is one column to the left of the active cell. Active cell is B2, one column to the left is A2.

A quick reminder about the Offset property. The syntax is OFFSET(Cell, Rows away from cell, columns away from cell). positive numbers mean up a row or right a column. Negative numbers mean down a row or left a column.

In essence, when the value of the cell one column to the left of the active cell is blank, the macro will stop. **Do not run this macro now!** Why? Because the value of the cell to the left will **never** be blank. Any why is that? Because we are always stuck in cell B2. We never told the macro to move down one cell. This macro will loop into infinity and never end.

If you chose not to follow my advice and you ran the macro, press CTRL+BREAK a few times to force Excel to stop executing the macro.

6 - Type in ActiveCell.Offset(1,0).Activate right above the Loop statement.

```
Sub FirstDoUntil()

    Range("B2").Activate
    Do Until ActiveCell.Offset(0, -1).Value = ""

        ActiveCell.Offset(1, 0).Activate
    Loop
End Sub
```

The line you just typed in tells the macro to move the active cell one row down. Now this eliminates the infinite loop because eventually a cell in column A will be blank. The loop structure has been built. You just have to add the logic to test for the state and put in Tony in the appropriate place.

7 - Add the logic for the loop statement. Notice how the If statement has an Or in it? That's because you have to evaluate three conditions. You have to see if it is FL or CA or TX. **The macro below is cut off.** Having a long line of code is not that easy to read.

```
Sub FirstDoUntil()

    Range("B2").Activate
    Do Until ActiveCell.Offset(0, -1).Value = ""
        If ActiveCell.Offset(0, -1).Value = "FL" Or ActiveCell.Of:
            ActiveCell.Value = "Tony"
        End If

        ActiveCell.Offset(1, 0).Activate
    Loop
End Sub
```

You can split a line of code into two lines by typing in a space and an underscore. Here is the entire macro with the long If statement broken into several lines to make it easier to read.

```
Sub FirstDoUntil()

    Range("B2").Activate
    Do Until ActiveCell.Offset(0, -1).Value = ""
        If ActiveCell.Offset(0, -1).Value = "FL" _
        Or ActiveCell.Offset(0, -1).Value = "CA" _
        Or ActiveCell.Offset(0, -1).Value = "TX" Then
            ActiveCell.Value = "Tony"
        End If

        ActiveCell.Offset(1, 0).Activate
    Loop
End Sub
```

Do While Loop

The While loop is extremely similar to the Do Until loop we just covered. Instead of stopping when a condition is met, this loop will continue until a condition is met. I will show the previous Do Until loop changed into a Do While loop below.

In the macro below, the opposite of = is <>.

```
Sub FirstDoWhile()

    Range("B2").Activate
    Do While ActiveCell.Offset(0, -1).Value <> ""
        If ActiveCell.Offset(0, -1).Value = "FL" _
        Or ActiveCell.Offset(0, -1).Value = "CA" _
        Or ActiveCell.Offset(0, -1).Value = "TX" Then
            ActiveCell.Value = "Tony"
        End If

        ActiveCell.Offset(1, 0).Activate
    Loop
End Sub
```

Almost the same thing right? Here you tell the macro, while the cell to the left is not blank, go do stuff.

This begs the question, when do you use one loop vs. another? The For Each loop is used to loop through items in a collection. Using Do Until and Do While is really a matter of preference. One can be easily changed into another...with one exception: putting the Do condition at the end of the Do Until loop (the Do Until - Variation sections explains this). This forces the loop to execute once whereas the same While loop might never execute if the condition is met before the loop ever starts (like if a cell was changed by another macro).

More Practice

Below is a screenshot of a workbook that tracks the overtime payments for 100 fictional employees. This is the follow along workbook named Overtime Calculations.xlsm

	A	B	C	D	E	F	G	H	I	J	K
1	First Name	Last Name	Mon	Tue	Wed	Thu	Fri	Total Hours	Overtime? (Only if hours > 40) (Input Y or N)	Hourly Wage	Weekly Gross Salary
2	Naqi	Miscevic	10	9	9	10	7	45		$ 12.00	
3	Keeva	Trystram	7	8	8	7	6	36		$ 14.00	
4	Markos	Calverley	9	9	6	9	10	43		$ 13.00	
5	Youan	Thalassinos	10	10	9	7	7	43		$ 11.00	
6	Debjani	Theory	6	7	6	7	10	36		$ 15.00	
7	Dannert	Rocca	7	7	7	10	8	39		$ 9.00	
8	Nakoda	Lanto	6	9	8	9	6	38		$ 8.00	

All the hours have been input and column K has a formula that calculates total gross pay. If the employee has worked more than 40 hours, then you need to input a Y in column I for the employee. If the employee has not worked 40 hours, input an N in column I. The formula in column K will adjust accordingly. Write a macro that automates the input of a Y or N in column I.

Go ahead and try to figure it out. Use whichever loop structure you want (as long as it stops at the last employee). You will need to use an If statement in the macro. That's it, I'm not giving you any more hints.

Of course, I'm not going to leave you stranded, one way to write the loop is in the answer file OvertimeCalculations_Complete.xlsm.

Acknowledgements

I want to thank Jim from Vegas and Jim Holland for their great feedback. You guys are great!

Lesson: 6
Object Variables

Object variables are tricky to learn. In all the previous lessons, you have learned programming topics using the active cell. This is a great way to learn because when you step through code you can see exactly what is going on. If there is anything wrong, you can fix it and then step through again to ensure everything is working as expected.

However, using the active cell can cause many headaches (which I will explain in a few paragraphs) and in many cases object variables will eliminate these issues.

Keep in mind, like I have said before, programming is like writing a paragraph. There are millions of ways to say the same thing. If you have a macro and you got it working by only using the active cell method, you don't have to change it. You can use object variables, you just don't have to.

Declaring Variables

In all the lessons so far, I have mentioned but not enforced the programming concept of declaring variables. In case you forgot, declaring variables means that you are explicitly telling Excel what to expect when using a variable. For example, the code shown below tells Excel exactly what Variable1 is.

```
Sub SampleMacro()

Dim variable1 As Integer

    variable1 = 100

End Sub
```

The Dim statement stands for Dimension. It is how you tell Excel that the next word is going to be a variable. Then you use the As keyword and finally the type of variable (an integer in this case). Most programming languages insist on variable declaration because it makes the language much more efficient. The language knows exactly what actions are, and are not possible with a variable. The language knows exactly how much memory space to allocate to a variable; it's super-efficient.

I know what you are thinking, 'If it is so great, why did we skip over it?' Because it is not practical for non-programmers, and it opens a whole complicated can of worms. For example, an integer data type can only hold numbers between -32,768 to 32,767. Any number outside that range must use another data type. You can use Long Integer or Single or Double. The issue is that each data type has its ranges. Any numbers falling outside the data type range will cause an error. That means that now on top of learning how to program, you also have to keep in mind the possible ranges of the data the macro will use.

I'm not short changing you by skipping topics; it's just that learning all of this is not time well spent for learning basic macro programming. Instead, we skip the variable declaration part and let Excel assign the Variant data type to all our variables.

However, when working with object variables, you **must** declare them. Excel needs to know that it is an object so that you can use all their features.

What is an Object Variable Anyway?

Variables, as we have used them so far in the lessons, have consisted of numbers or text. An object variable, on the other hand, is an entire object that we can use as needed. Remember that everything in Excel is an object. Objects have properties (height, width, etc.) and methods (delete, insert, etc.). Similar objects are grouped into collections (for example, the sheets collection is the grouping of all the worksheets in a workbook). You assign a variable to an object, thus creating an object variable. Once the object variable has been set, you can use all of the object's methods and properties in the macro.

Code Without Object Variables

Consider the situation shown below. You receive data from distributors, but the data is not clean. You don't know what system the distributor uses or how they get their data. All you know is you get it in the format shown in column A:D, and you need to make it look like columns F:K so you can build reports off the cleaned up data.

The major issue you have is that the item#, salesperson, and region are all together in column A. Because you will receive this data regularly, you are going to write a macro to automate this as much as possible. You also need to skip any sales made by Tom.

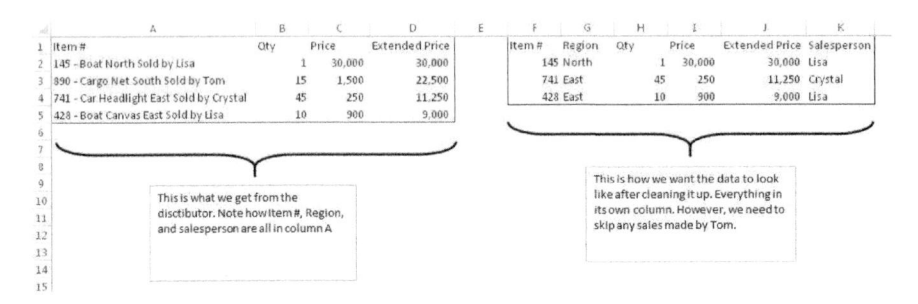

Item #	Qty	Price	Extended Price		Item #	Region	Qty	Price	Extended Price	Salesperson
145 - Boat North Sold by Lisa	1	30,000	30,000		145	North	1	30,000	30,000	Lisa
890 - Cargo Net South Sold by Tom	15	1,500	22,500		741	East	45	250	11,250	Crystal
741 - Car Headlight East Sold by Crystal	45	250	11,250		428	East	10	900	9,000	Lisa
428 - Boat Canvas East Sold by Lisa	10	900	9,000							

This is what we get from the disctibutor. Note how Item #, Region, and salesperson are all in column A

This is how we want the data to look like after cleaning it up. Everything in its own column. However, we need to skip any sales made by Tom.

How would you do this? Let's start by writing some pseudo code. Pseudo code is just an outline of what we want the code to do. This is a good practice to get into for complex macros. It helps you think through the steps needed without having to worry about getting everything perfect. It is an exercise to order the steps and get the logic right.

1 - Select cell A1

2 - Loop until the cell in column A is blank

3 - In the active cell, extract the Item #, Region, and Salesperson

4 - If salesperson is Tom, skip the row

5 - Get Qty, Price, and Extended Price from the cells next to the active cell

6 - Store the address of the active cell in column A

7 - Go to the first blank line in column F

8 - Input the Item # in column F

9 - Input the Region in column G

10 - Input the Qty in column H

11 - Input the Price in column I

12 - Input the Extended Price in column J

13 - Input the Salesperson in column K

14 - Go back to the last cell processed in column A (this was the cell address from step 6)

15 - Move the active cell one row down

16 - Repeat the loop that started in step 2

That's the big picture. The code gets data from columns A:D, then processes it and puts it in in columns F:K. The problem is that this involves a lot of "bouncing back and forth". The code needs to remember where the last processed row in column A was, then find the first blank row in column F, put in the processed data, then go back to the last row in column A and repeat the process.

Instead of bouncing back and forth between columns and finding the last cell the code left off at, you are going to set up a few object variables to keep track of this for you.

Code With Object Variables

Let's start working with object variables.

The object you will use in this exercise is the range object. The range object can represent either a single cell or multiple cells. You will use two object variables to keep track of two cells: the cell where the data is coming from (i.e., the source in columns A:D) and the cell where the data is going to (i.e., the destination in columns F:K). By doing this, you will not have to worry about remembering where the program left off in both columns; the object variables will store this for you.

1 - Open the follow along workbook named Range Object Variable.xlsm

(Remember, you can sign up to get the workbook at my website: http://markmoorebooks.com/macros-object-variables/)

You will see this spreadsheet:

	A	B	C	D	E	F	G	H	I	J	K
1	Item #	Qty	Price	Extended Price		Item #	Region	Qty	Price	Extended Price	Salesperson
2	145 - Boat North Sold by Lisa	1	30000	30000							
3	890 - Cargo Net South Sold by Tom	15	1500	22500							
4	741 - Car Headlight East Sold by Crystal	45	250	11250							
5	428 - Boat Canvas East Sold by Lisa	10	900	9000							
6											
7											

This is the same spreadsheet you saw before. Your goal remains the same: take the records from columns A:D, process them, and then put them in columns F:K. You need to skip records that have Tom as a salesperson.

2 - Open the VBA editor and add a module

3 - Create a new ProcessRows macro

Your macro should look like this now:

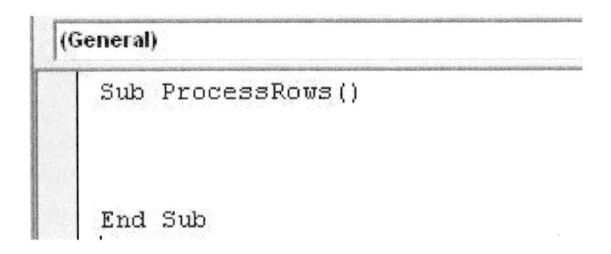

```
(General)

Sub ProcessRows()



End Sub
```

The logic of what the program should do has already been set. Remember the pseudo code you looked at earlier? That's what the program should do. You have the logic; now you just have to implement it and use object variables where appropriate.

Before we get into the logic, we need to declare our object variables. Add these lines to the macro:

```
Sub ProcessRows()

Dim source As Range
Dim destination As Range


End Sub
```

4 - Set the new variable to the appropriate ranges

You created the variable, but it is empty. What range should it be? You need to tell it what range it should represent. You need to use the *Set* command to set the object variables to something, in this case a range. Add these new lines to your code:

```
Sub ProcessRows()

    Dim source As Range
    Dim destination As Range

    Set source = Range("A2")
    Set destination = Range("F2")

End Sub
```

Now you have told Excel that the object variable is going to be initially set to range A2. In effect, you have made a reference to range A2 through the object source. The very cool part of this is that your source variable is an object. It has everything that a range object has (column number, row number, bold status, etc.).

Try this: in the line right above the End Sub type in source. (Include the period). Did you see this pop up?

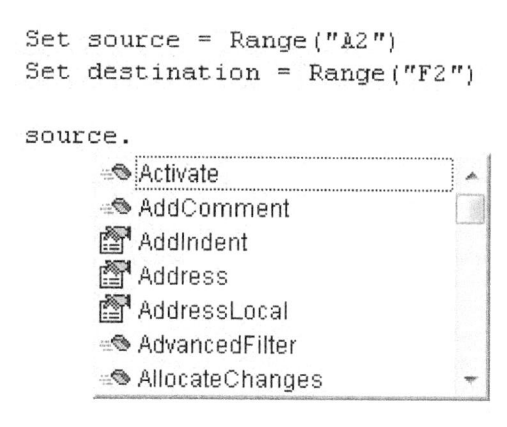

```
    Set source = Range("A2")
    Set destination = Range("F2")

    source.
```
- Activate
- AddComment
- AddIndent
- Address
- AddressLocal
- AdvancedFilter
- AllocateChanges

Excel's Intellisense window appeared with all of the range object's methods and properties. Why? Because we declared *source* to be a range, and now we can do anything to it that we could do to a normal range. Then in turn, whatever we do to *source* will be done to A2 because we set *source* to A2.

OK, delete the source. reference, and get your code back to this, and let's continue with the pseudo code:

```
Sub ProcessRows()

    Dim source As Range
    Dim destination As Range

    Set source = Range("A2")
    Set destination = Range("F2")

End Sub
```

PseudoCode Step 1 - Select cell A2

After the set destination line, set the active cell to select cell A2

```
Sub ProcessRows()

    Dim source As Range
    Dim destination As Range

    Set source = Range("A2")
    Set destination = Range("F2")

    source.Select

End Sub
```

Note that I could have used Range("A2").Select but why? I already have a variable set to it. I'm using that instead.

PseudoCode Step 2 - Loop until the cell in column A is blank

There are many types of loops (we covered them in a previous lesson); looking at the data, you can see that all columns are filled out. Let's use a Do Until loop that will process rows until a blank cell is found in column A.

This is where things are going to get a bit different. Look at the loop code below:

```
Sub ProcessRows()

    Dim source As Range
    Dim destination As Range

    Set source = Range("A2")
    Set destination = Range("F2")

    source.Select

    Do Until source.Value = ""

        Set source = source.Offset(1, 0)
    Loop

End Sub
```

The Do Until uses source.value instead of activecell.value. That's because we aren't using active cell anymore. We are using *source* (which might or might not be active). The last line in the loop is where you move the *source* to the next cell underneath the current *source*. As a quick reminder, the OFFSET function is a way to refer to one cell based on its distance from the source cell. source.Offset(1,0) means one row underneath *source*. *Source* is set as A2; therefore, source.Offset(1,0) means A3.

Yes, it's a bit confusing. In reality, you can't add something to itself. You can, however, do so in programming. You are using the current *source* (on the right side of the = sign) to set itself (on the left side of the = sign) one cell under it. Think of it as Excel making a temporary copy of *source* (the one on the left side of the = sign is the temporary one). Once Excel figures out what source.offset(1,0) is, it then gets rid of the original *source* and converts the temporary one into the new *source*.

The very cool thing about this is that *source* is kind of a marker. You can now have the code go do some other stuff and not worry about *source* at all. When the code is done doing whatever it was doing, it can go back to *source* by using source.activate. As a theoretical example, suppose you have code that is doing something over in column XFD and then you need to get the value that was in *source*. All you need to do is use source.value. There is no need to go all the way back to source and see its value (you would have had to do that if you only used active cell to do stuff).

I hope this is starting to make more sense and showcase how powerful object variables are. From wherever the code is, it can easily access any property (i.e., source.value, source.address) or method (i.e., source.activate) of the object variable.

Pseudocode Step 3 - In the active cell, extract the Item #, Region, Salesperson

Here I'm going to show you some text parsing tricks that you can only use in VBA. Look at the text in the first cell that we need to parse:

	A
1	Item #
2	145 - Boat North Sold by Lisa
3	890 - Cargo Net South Sold by Tom
4	741 - Car Headlight East Sold by Crystal
5	428 - Boat Canvas East Sold by Lisa

Item #: In this example, all the item numbers are three characters long. You will use the LEFT function to extract the first three characters from the cell and that will give you the item number.

Region: This is a tricky one. There are only four possible regions in this example: North, South, East, or West. The problem is that they can be anywhere in the text. You can't use LEFT, RIGHT, or MID. What to do? You can use the VBA function INSTR. INSTR is short for 'In String'; this function finds one instance of a text string inside another instance. If it finds the string, the function returns the starting position. If the string is not found, the function returns 0.

You can use this to find any region name inside the text of column A.

INSTR

First let's understand the INSTR function. The syntax is:

INSTR([Start],[String1],[String2],[Compare])

Start: The position to start the search. Use 1 to start at the beginning.

String1: The text you are searching through.

String2: The text you are looking for.

Compare: The type of comparison. 0 for Binary (i.e. case sensitive) or 1 for text (i.e. case insensitive).

Start and Compare are both optional arguments. If you omit Start, the functions automatically starts at position1 and if you omit Compare it will usually default to text.

To find the occurrence of the region 'North' in the *source* object, you would use this:

INSTR(1, source.value, "North")

If INSTR returns anything other than 0, North has been found in the *source* object variable.

Salesperson: In this example (and keeping it simple) there are only three salespeople. You can use INSTR to figure out which salesperson is in source.value.

Let's work through it step by step. Your macro should look like this:

```
Sub ProcessRows()

    Dim source As Range
    Dim destination As Range
    
    Set source = Range("A2")
    Set destination = Range("F2")
    
    source.Select
    
    Do Until source.Value = ""
    
        Set source = source.Offset(1, 0)
    Loop
    
End Sub
```

Inside the Do Until Loop, input an INSTR function that will search for the word "North" inside source.value. If it is found, assign the word "North" to the Region variable. The IF statement I used looks like this:

```
If InStr(1, source.Value, "North") <> 0 Then Region = "North"
```

Repeat the same IF statement for each region. After doing that, your code should look something like this:

```
Sub ProcessRows()

    Dim source As Range
    Dim destination As Range

    Set source = Range("A2")
    Set destination = Range("F2")

    source.Select

    Do Until source.Value = ""

        'Get Region
        If InStr(1, source.Value, "North") <> 0 Then Region = "North"
        If InStr(1, source.Value, "South") <> 0 Then Region = "South"
        If InStr(1, source.Value, "East") <> 0 Then Region = "East"
        If InStr(1, source.Value, "West") <> 0 Then Region = "West"

        Set source = source.Offset(1, 0)
    Loop

End Sub
```

Try stepping through the code to see if it is working. Based on the first value in cell A1, the first IF statement should populate the Region variable with the value "North".

Debugging

Unfortunately, using a range object variable, you can't 'see' the macro operate and select a different cell. Granted, you could use source.activate to force Excel to always select the source but the point is to not have to do that. How can you tell if the *source* object is in the right cell? There must be a way to check. There most certainly is.

While you are stepping through this code, after the source has been set, go to View > Immediate Window. In the window that appears, type in ?source.address. The window displays the address of the *source* object.

```
Immediate
?Source.Address
$A$2
```

Now you need to get the Item # and Salesperson. For the Item # you use the LEFT function and to derive the salesperson you use the same logic with INSTR but look for the salesperson's name instead. There are only three salespeople, Lisa, Tom and Crystal.

```
Sub ProcessRows()

    Dim source As Range
    Dim destination As Range

    Set source = Range("A2")
    Set destination = Range("F2")

    source.Select

    Do Until source.Value = ""

        'Get Region
        If InStr(1, source.Value, "North") <> 0 Then Region = "North"
        If InStr(1, source.Value, "South") <> 0 Then Region = "South"
        If InStr(1, source.Value, "East") <> 0 Then Region = "East"
        If InStr(1, source.Value, "West") <> 0 Then Region = "West"

        'Get Item #
        ItemNumber = Left(source.Value, 3)

        'Get Salesperson
        If InStr(1, source.Value, "Lisa") <> 0 Then Salesperson = "Lisa"
        If InStr(1, source.Value, "Tom") <> 0 Then Salesperson = "Tom"
        If InStr(1, source.Value, "Crystal") <> 0 Then Salesperson = "Crystal"

        Set source = source.Offset(1, 0)
    Loop

End Sub
```

Pseudocode Step 4 – If salesperson is Tom, skip the row

Here we are going to get crafty. Instead of skipping a row when it is Tom, we are going to process the row when it is NOT Tom. Add the IF statement to your code (I'm only going to put the new code from now on, at the end I will put the complete code):

```
'Get Salesperson
If InStr(1, source.Value, "Lisa") <> 0 Then SalesPerson = "Lisa"
If InStr(1, source.Value, "Tom") <> 0 Then SalesPerson = "Tom"
If InStr(1, source.Value, "Crystal") <> 0 Then SalesPerson = "Crystal"

'Do stuff when SalesPerson is not Tom
If SalesPerson <> "Tom" Then


End If
```

Pseudocode Step 5 – Get Qty, Price, Extended Price from the cells next to the Source cell

Take a look at the data source again:

	A	B	C	D
1	Item #	Qty	Price	Extended Price
2	145 - Boat North Sold by Lisa	1	30000	30000
3	890 - Cargo Net South Sold by Tom	15	1500	22500
4	741 - Car Headlight East Sold by Crystal	45	250	11250
5	428 - Boat Canvas East Sold by Lisa	10	900	9000

Your *source* object is in cell A2. You do not need to hop over to B2 to get Qty; you can use the OFFSET function to get that value and store it in a variable. Do the same for Price and Extended Price.

Pseudocode Step 6 - Store the address of the active cell in column A

Pseudocode Step 7 - Go to the first blank line in column F

You do not have to code step 6 or step 7 since we are not using the active cell. The address of where we left off is already stored in source.address (this deals with step 6) and you already set the destination object variable (this deals with step 7).

Pseudocode Steps 8 through 13

- Input the Item # in column F

- Input the Region in column G

- Input the Qty in column H

- Input the Price in column I

- Input the Extended Price in column J

- Input the Salesperson in column K

Now you need to use the OFFET function on the **destination** object variable and populate the cells. Note that you do not have to activate nor move to the destination. Excel knows where it is since we used the SET command to set it to Range("F2")

```
'Do stuff when SalesPerson is not Tom
If SalesPerson <> "Tom" Then
    'Get values from cell to the right of source
    Qty = source.Offset(0, 1).Value
    Price = source.Offset(0, 2).Value
    ExtPrice = source.Offset(0, 3).Value

    'populate destination and cells to right of it
    destination.Value = ItemNumber
    destination.Offset(0, 1).Value = Region
    destination.Offset(0, 2).Value = Qty
    destination.Offset(0, 3).Value = Price
    destination.Offset(0, 4).Value = ExtPrice
    destination.Offset(0, 5).Value = SalesPerson

End If
```

At this point, you have completed the original pseudo code steps. However, there are two extra steps you need to take.

The loop you wrote moves the *source* down one cell but you also need to move the destination down one cell. If you don't, the destination will always stay in F2. You need the destination to move down one row.

Finally (this is important for object variables), you need to some garbage cleanup. Object variables take up memory. If you run this macro over and over again, there will be several copies of *source* and *destination* created and recreated every time. You need to destroy the object variables you use when you are finished with them. You destroy an object variable by setting it to Nothing. Like this:

Set source = Nothing

Here is the complete code:

```vba
Sub ProcessRows()

    Dim source As Range
    Dim destination As Range
    
    Set source = Range("A2")
    Set destination = Range("F2")
    
    source.Select
    
    Do Until source.Value = ""
    
        'Get Region
        If InStr(1, source.Value, "North") <> 0 Then Region = "North"
        If InStr(1, source.Value, "South") <> 0 Then Region = "South"
        If InStr(1, source.Value, "East") <> 0 Then Region = "East"
        If InStr(1, source.Value, "West") <> 0 Then Region = "West"
        
        'Get Item #
        ItemNumber = Left(source.Value, 3)
        
        'Get Salesperson
        If InStr(1, source.Value, "Lisa") <> 0 Then SalesPerson = "Lisa"
        If InStr(1, source.Value, "Tom") <> 0 Then SalesPerson = "Tom"
        If InStr(1, source.Value, "Crystal") <> 0 Then SalesPerson = "Crystal"
        
        'Do stuff when SalesPerson is not Tom
        If SalesPerson <> "Tom" Then
            'Get values from cell to the right of source
            Qty = source.Offset(0, 1).Value
            Price = source.Offset(0, 2).Value
            ExtPrice = source.Offset(0, 3).Value
            
            'populate destination and cells to right of it
            destination.Value = ItemNumber
            destination.Offset(0, 1).Value = Region
            destination.Offset(0, 2).Value = Qty
            destination.Offset(0, 3).Value = Price
            destination.Offset(0, 4).Value = ExtPrice
            destination.Offset(0, 5).Value = SalesPerson
            
            Set destination = destination.Offset(1, 0)
        End If
        
        Set source = source.Offset(1, 0)
        
    Loop
    
    Set source = Nothing
    Set destination = Nothing

End Sub
```

OK, here's one last tip. Remember that writing code is like writing a paragraph. There are many ways to say the same thing. Now that I look at this code, I see I can make some improvements. This is like editing a paragraph.

Notice these lines:

Qty = source.Offset(0, 1).Value

destination.Offset(0, 2).Value = Qty

If they are both equal to the same thing, I should be able to make them equal to each other. *Source* is indeed equal to destination. This line should work:

$$source.Offset(0, 1).Value = destination.Offset(0, 2).Value$$

This says the cell immediately to the right of *source* is equal to the cell two columns to the right of *destination*. If you look at the data it works out; qty (cell B2) needs to be equal to qty (cell H2).

	A	B	C	D	E	F	G	H	I	J	K
1	Item #	Qty	Price	Extended Price		Item #	Region	Qty	Price	Extended Price	Salesperson
2	145 - Boat North Sold by Lisa	1	30000	30000		145	North	1	30000	30000	Lisa
3	890 - Cargo Net South Sold by Tom	15	1500	22500		741	East	45	250	11250	Crystal
4	741 - Car Headlight East Sold by Crystal	45	250	11250		428	East	10	900	9000	Lisa
5	428 - Boat Canvas East Sold by Lisa	10	900	9000							
6											

You can apply the same logic to all other variables. Now, should you change it? That boils down to a judgment call. It is slightly more efficient but less understandable. It's your macro, if you think you will remember how this works or can put in enough comments to help you remember, go ahead and change it. If you like things simpler and more readable, leave it as is.

Invoice Creator

Let's do one more exercise with object variables. This time, instead of using an object variable on a range object, we are going to use an object variable on a workbook object.

The Situation: You frequently get a list of customers and you need to create a blank invoice for each customer. Then you take the blank invoice and email it out to the sales staff and they fill it out. Right now, you are entering the customer names by hand and doing a Save As for each customer. You want to automate this task.

High Level Solution: Create one workbook with the list of customers that need invoices and a blank invoice on another worksheet. This is the master template. For each customer, the macro will create one invoice, fill in the name, and do a "save as." Then the macro will move on to the next customer in the list.

Pseudo code:

1 - Set variables

2 - Loop through each customer

3 - In the loop, copy the master invoice worksheet to the object variable

4 - Rename the worksheet

5 - Save the workbook

Let's write the macro.

1 - Open the workbook named Invoice Master.xlsm. This is the master workbook that will spawn all the other

invoices.

2 - Insert a new module

3 - Create a new macro named CreateInvoice

You might think that we will need two object variables, like we did before, one for the source workbook and another for the newly created invoice. Yes, that will work. However, I'm going to show you a trick. Instead of creating a source workbook object you can use the ThisWorkbook object. ThisWorkbook is very convenient because it refers to the workbook that contains the macro that is running. The master workbook contains the macro so we can use this built-in object.

4 - Add one workbook object variable called Invoice. (Use the Dim statement)

```
Sub CreateInvoice()

Dim Invoice As Workbook



End Sub
```

5 - Create another object variable. This one is a range object and you will use it to move down the customer list. Call it Customer. (No, I'm not that creative. Keep it simple!)

```
Sub CreateInvoice()

Dim Invoice As Workbook
Dim Customer As Range


End Sub
```

6 - Set the Customer variable to Range("A2") in the Customers worksheet

```
Sub CreateInvoice()

    Dim Invoice As Workbook
    Dim Customer As Range

    Set Customer = Sheets("Customers").Range("A2")

End Sub
```

Why did I change the range syntax and add the Sheets("Customers") to it? Because as you work through this exercise, I won't know which worksheet you have active. It could be Customers or it could be Master. If I only used Range("A2") the object would be set on the Range("A2") of the worksheet that is active. Adding the complete address prevents this error.

7 - Add a Do Until loop based on the value in Customer. The loop needs to stop when the value of Customer is empty. Remember to move customer down one cell before the end of the loop. If you don't do that, you will be in an infinite loop.

```
Sub CreateInvoice()

    Dim Invoice As Workbook
    Dim Customer As Range

    Set Customer = Sheets("Customers").Range("A2")

    Do Until Customer.Value = ""

        Set Customer = Customer.Offset(1, 0)
    Loop

End Sub
```

Note that you set the customer object variable to the cell. That means you can access the value of the cell by using customer.value. You do not need to create another variable to store the customer name. The object variable already has it.

8 - Use the Workbooks.Add method to create a new workbook and assign it to Invoice

```vb
Sub CreateInvoice()

    Dim Invoice As Workbook
    Dim Customer As Range

    Set Customer = Sheets("Customers").Range("A2")

    Do Until Customer.Value = ""
        Set Invoice = Workbooks.Add

        Set Customer = Customer.Offset(1, 0)
    Loop

End Sub
```

9 - Copy the Master worksheet to Invoice

```vb
Sub CreateInvoice()

    Dim Invoice As Workbook
    Dim Customer As Range

    Set Customer = Sheets("Customers").Range("A2")

    Do Until Customer.Value = ""
        Set Invoice = Workbooks.Add
        ThisWorkbook.Sheets("Master").Copy Before:=Invoice.Sheets(1)

        Set Customer = Customer.Offset(1, 0)
    Loop

End Sub
```

Now that the Master worksheet is in its own workbook, you can start changing it.

10 - Rename the worksheet to the customer name.

```
Sub CreateInvoice()

    Dim Invoice As Workbook
    Dim Customer As Range

    Set Customer = Sheets("Customers").Range("A2")

    Do Until Customer.Value = ""
        Set Invoice = Workbooks.Add
        ThisWorkbook.Sheets("Master").Copy Before:=Invoice.Sheets(1)
        Invoice.Sheets("Master").Name = Customer.Value

        Set Customer = Customer.Offset(1, 0)
    Loop

End Sub
```

I want to cover what the new line did because it ties together many topics and if you 'get' this you will truly understand how Excel macros work.

Remember that Excel is made up of objects. These objects have properties (color, bold, italic, etc.) and methods (delete, add, insert, etc.). Objects have other objects inside of them (a workbook has a worksheet object inside it). Furthermore, similar objects are grouped into collections. These collections have different properties and methods than the individual objects (a worksheet doesn't have a count because it is only one, but the Sheets collection has a count of how many individual worksheets it contains).

You just used all of these concepts in this line:

Invoice.Sheets("Master").Name = Customer.Value

Invoice is an object variable that is a workbook. You accessed the Sheets collection inside Invoice workbook. Wait, there are many sheets. Which one did you access? The one named "Master". You can think of it as 'drilling down' the object hierarchy. You started at the biggest object, the workbook, then you accessed the Sheets collection and specified one individual worksheet. When you got to where you wanted to be, you then accessed the Value property of the Customer range object. This is another drill down but a much simpler one (from range to value). I hope that makes sense.

11 - Now put the customer name in the right cell in the invoice. It should go in cell C7

```
Sub CreateInvoice()

    Dim Invoice As Workbook
    Dim Customer As Range
    
    Set Customer = Sheets("Customers").Range("A2")
    
    Do Until Customer.Value = ""
        Set Invoice = Workbooks.Add
        ThisWorkbook.Sheets("Master").Copy Before:=Invoice.Sheets(1)
        Invoice.Sheets("Master").Name = Customer.Value
        Invoice.Sheets(Customer.Value).Range("C7").Value = Customer.Value
        
        Set Customer = Customer.Offset(1, 0)
    Loop

End Sub
```

The new line:

Invoice.Sheets(Customer.Value).Range("C7").Value = Customer.Value

did a similar thing to the previous line. This time, it just went a bit deeper into the object hierarchy. Instead of renaming the worksheet, it went to a range on the worksheet and changed the value property of it.

Note that we can no longer use Invoice.Sheets("Master"). Why? Because we renamed it to the customer name. You don't know the **specific** customer because it is going to change as the loop moves on to the next customer (remember you are in a loop that will process all customers). You don't need to know the specific customer. All you need to know is that the customer name, whatever it is, is stored in the value property of the customer variable (i.e., customer value).

12 – Save the workbook. Where are you going to save it? My path is different than yours. No problem, create a variable to store the path. Then when/if you want to change it, you simply change the variable. I am using C:\Common but you can use any path you like. You will need to create this directory before running the macro.

Note that you need to complete the SavePath, C:\Common is not going to work. You need the filename, you can't just add it right after C:\Common, you need to add the \ so it conforms to the standard Windows path syntax. That is why the line has SavePath & "\" & Customer.Value.

```
Sub CreateInvoice()

    Dim Invoice As Workbook
    Dim Customer As Range

    SavePath = "C:\Common"

    Set Customer = Sheets("Customers").Range("A2")

    Do Until Customer.Value = ""
        Set Invoice = Workbooks.Add
        ThisWorkbook.Sheets("Master").Copy Before:=Invoice.Sheets(1)
        Invoice.Sheets("Master").Name = Customer.Value
        Invoice.Sheets(Customer.Value).Range("C7").Value = Customer.Value
        Invoice.SaveAs Filename:=SavePath & "\" & Customer.Value

        Set Customer = Customer.Offset(1, 0)
    Loop

End Sub
```

13 - After the SaveAs method has been called, you need to close the invoice.

```
Sub CreateInvoice()

    Dim Invoice As Workbook
    Dim Customer As Range

    SavePath = "C:\Common"

    Set Customer = Sheets("Customers").Range("A2")

    Do Until Customer.Value = ""
        Set Invoice = Workbooks.Add
        ThisWorkbook.Sheets("Master").Copy Before:=Invoice.Sheets(1)
        Invoice.Sheets("Master").Name = Customer.Value
        Invoice.Sheets(Customer.Value).Range("C7").Value = Customer.Value
        Invoice.SaveAs Filename:=SavePath & "\" & Customer.Value
        Invoice.Close

        Set Customer = Customer.Offset(1, 0)
    Loop

End Sub
```

14 - The last thing we have to do is destroy the object variable once all the customers have been processed.

```vba
Sub CreateInvoice()

    Dim Invoice As Workbook
    Dim Customer As Range
    
    SavePath = "C:\Common"
    
    Set Customer = Sheets("Customers").Range("A2")
    
    Do Until Customer.Value = ""
        Set Invoice = Workbooks.Add
        ThisWorkbook.Sheets("Master").Copy Before:=Invoice.Sheets(1)
        Invoice.Sheets("Master").Name = Customer.Value
        Invoice.Sheets(Customer.Value).Range("C7").Value = Customer.Value
        Invoice.SaveAs Filename:=SavePath & "\" & Customer.Value
        Invoice.Close
        
        Set Customer = Customer.Offset(1, 0)
    Loop
    Set Invoice = Nothing
    
End Sub
```

Run the macro and test it out. It should loop through all the customers, create a new workbook and save it in the specified path.

Look over the macro above. It is taking data from one object and putting it into another object. Did you notice that you did not move the active cell at all?

Note: This macro is not robust. This means you have not added any error trapping. For example, there are certain characters that are not allowed in a worksheet name. To make the macro robust, you will need to look for these characters and remove them or replace them with something else before renaming the worksheet. If you want to see what happens when an invalid character is input, try adding a new customer and include a question mark in the name. The macro will generate an error.

Optional Enhancement

Once you test the macro and are happy with how it is working, you can make this minor enhancement. When you add a new workbook and save it, you will see those actions. You can actually hide screen updates when running a macro. You use the Application.ScreenUpdating property and set it to False in the beginning of the macro. Then you **must** set it back to True when the macro is finished. If you don't, your screen will not update! This is how the macro will look with this enhancement.

```
Sub CreateInvoice()

    Dim Invoice As Workbook
    Dim Customer As Range

    Application.ScreenUpdating = False

    SavePath = "C:\Common"

    Set Customer = Sheets("Customers").Range("A2")

    Do Until Customer.Value = ""
        Set Invoice = Workbooks.Add
        ThisWorkbook.Sheets("Master").Copy Before:=Invoice.Sheets(1)
        Invoice.Sheets("Master").Name = Customer.Value
        Invoice.Sheets(Customer.Value).Range("C7").Value = Customer.Value
        Invoice.SaveAs Filename:=SavePath & "\" & Customer.Value
        Invoice.Close

        Set Customer = Customer.Offset(1, 0)
    Loop
    Set Invoice = Nothing

    Application.ScreenUpdating = True

End Sub
```

Last Word

The topics in this lesson are advanced. I hope the detailed explanations and numerous screenshots helped you understand the topic. You wrote some very useful and complex code. Granted, there are a lot of steps involved but taken in isolation, none of them are terribly complex. Macros aren't magic; they are just small actions that a computer follows under your direction. A good way to tackle any future projects is to just work on one tiny piece at a time. The accumulation of all those tiny pieces is where you get an amazingly useful macro. Then for your next project after that, don't reinvent the wheel! Take the pieces from the previous project and reuse them.

See you in the next lesson!

Acknowledgements

I would like to thank Sharon Deitch for her valuable help in getting this lesson published.

Lesson:7
PowerPoint Automation

Intended Audience and Prerequisites

This lesson continues with the concept of object variables. You will be manipulating PowerPoint from within Excel. This is not a complete course into how to program PowerPoint. To do that, I would have to make this a very long lesson, and go into programming concepts and methodologies that the average/intermediate Excel user does not need to know.

If you want to learn to complete intricacies of Automation with PowerPoint, this lesson is not for you. This lesson is merely a starting point to show you what is possible.

I am going to show you how to get data from Excel into PowerPoint. That's it. Nothing else. Of course, I will explain the how and why behind the concepts covered.

This lesson has prerequisites; you must have worked through the previous lesson, Mastering Excel Macros: Object Variables because this lesson builds on the concepts introduced in that lesson. I am not going to leave you stranded though; here is a brief review of Object Variables.

A Quick Note about Spacing

Some macro lines in this lesson are longer than the page width and they will wrap around when you read this lesson. All the lines should be typed in a single line in your macro even if they appear as two lines.

The **only** time a macro line can cross rows is when it ends with a space and an underscore. You can use this to make your macro easier to read. Here's an example.

This should all go in one line in the macro:

pptFileName = Application.GetOpenFilename("All PowerPoint Presentations (*.pptx), *.pptx", , "Select PowerPoint file to open")

If you want, you can break it up into two lines by doing this:

pptFileName = Application.GetOpenFilename _
("All PowerPoint Presentations (*.pptx), *.pptx", , "Select PowerPoint file to open")

Yeah, you can split the macro line right down the middle if you want. Just remember, it has to be a **space followed by an underscore**.

Background

Object variables are very powerful because when you create an object variable, you have access to that object's properties and methods. The object variable can do many things that a simple numerical or string variable cannot do.

For example, you need to declare an object variable by using the Dim keyword like this. Declaring the variable lets Excel set aside memory to handle the new object.

```
Sub test()

    Dim myCell As Range




End Sub
```

Then you need to use the Set keyword to set it to something. In this example, I am setting the myCell variable to cell A1:

```
Sub test()

    Dim myCell As Range

    Set myCell = Range("A1")


End Sub
```

Now you have all the object properties and methods available to use. If you type in the variable name followed by a period, Excel's Intellisense will display a list of everything that is available for the range variable. (Intellisense offers you assistance with VBA syntax, either on the fly or on demand.)

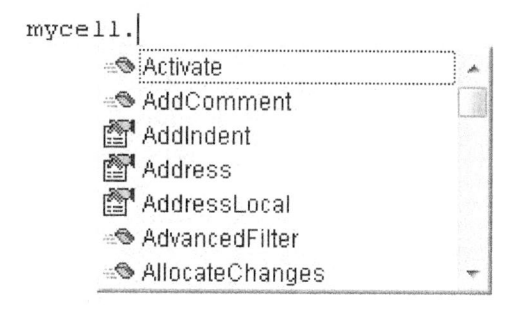

```
mycell.
    Activate
    AddComment
    AddIndent
    Address
    AddressLocal
    AdvancedFilter
    AllocateChanges
```

Everything in Excel is an *object*. Pivot tables, cells, worksheets, charts, and so on. As a matter of fact, Excel *itself* is an object. Excel is the biggest object and all the other objects live inside it. This largest object, Excel, is called the **Application object**. Just like a cell is inside a worksheet, the worksheet is inside Excel. Therefore, by extension, the cell is also inside Excel.

Here's where we are getting pretty creative. You 'get' that Excel is an object. You can create object variables and play with them. What about PowerPoint or Word? They are part of the Office Suite too. Are they objects? They most certainly are. What you are going to learn in this lesson is how to create a PowerPoint object and then **control it from Excel**.

Think of it. You have your list of customers, part numbers, etc. in Excel and you can put it into a PowerPoint presentation. The process of creating an object of another program and controlling it is called *Automation*. You will learn how to automate PowerPoint.

NOTE: In order to follow-along with this lesson you must have PowerPoint installed on your PC. If you only have one application, you can only do the exercises for that application. Automation will not install PowerPoint; it will only let you control it after you buy it and install it.

You can use automation to control many, many other programs. The specifics of how to manage each program is different and you will need to read that program's documentation. In this lesson, we are sticking to PowerPoint.

References

Excel lives in a bubble. It only knows the objects that it was programmed to deal with: worksheets, cells, columns, charts, etc. Excel has no knowledge of Slides, Titles, and Pages. In order to get Excel to automate (programmatically control) another program, you first need to let Excel know what objects that program has. Only then can Excel start to do its magic.

The collection of all of a program's objects, its properties and methods is called a library. You need to add a reference in Excel to the other program's library.

Follow these steps to add a reference to the PowerPoint library:

1 In Excel, open the macro editor. (Press ALT+F11).

2 Click on Tools ->References.

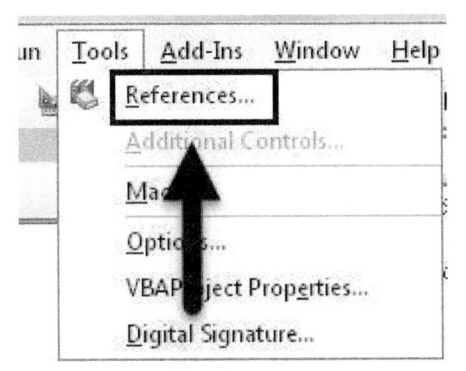

The References window will appear:

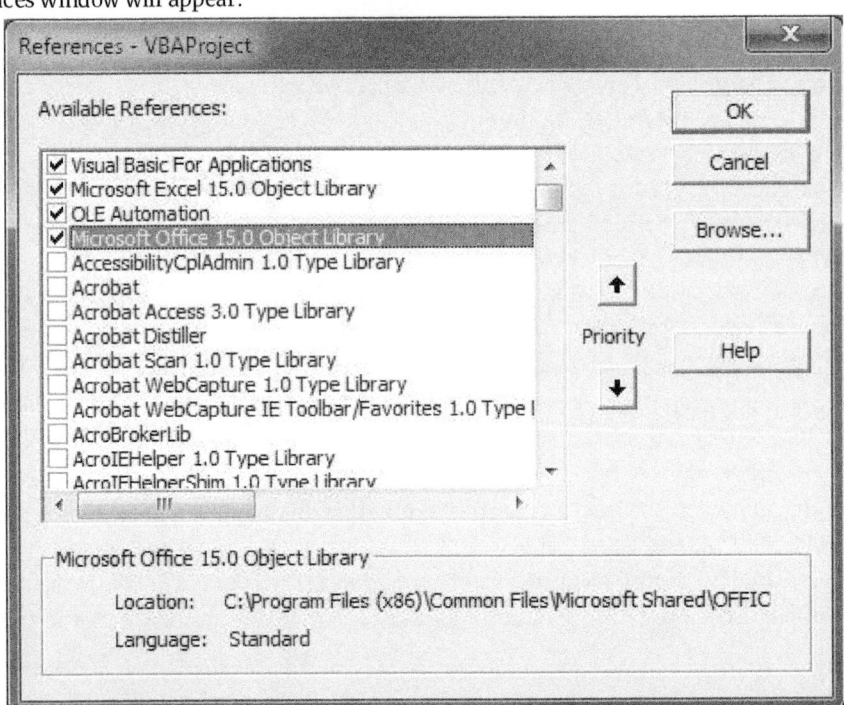

This window displays all the other programs that Excel can manipulate via VBA. There are TONS of them. For this lesson, you are only interested in PowerPoint. Scroll down until you see the Microsoft PowerPoint 15.0 Object Library.

1. Click on the Microsoft PowerPoint 15.0 Object Library checkbox to select it.

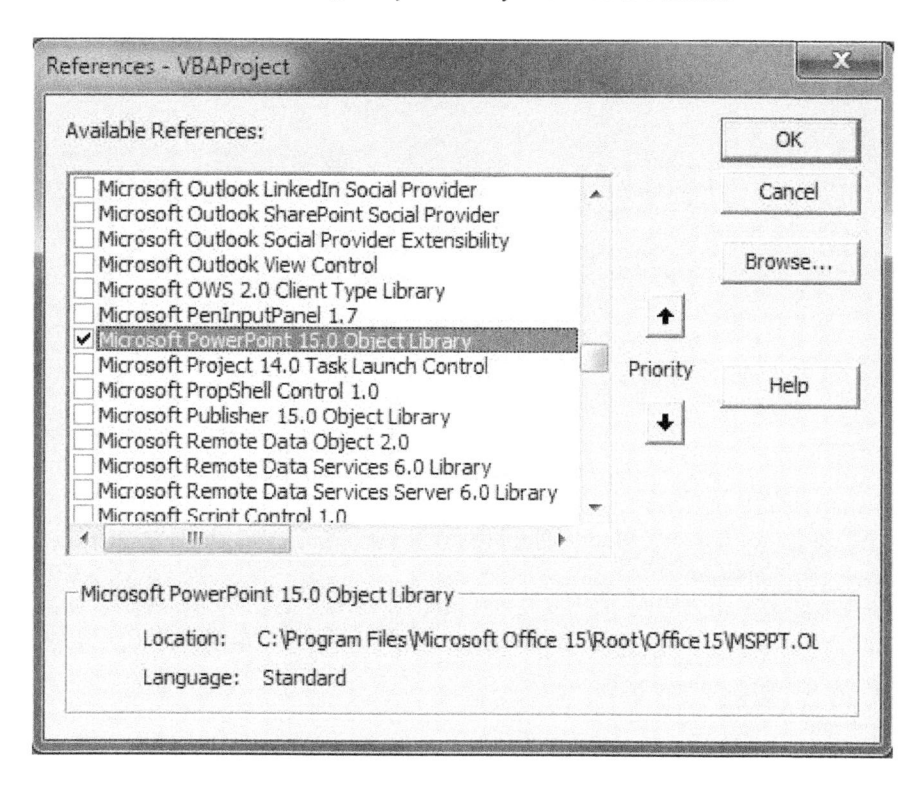

1. Click OK.

Although it looked like nothing happened when you clicked OK, Excel added a reference to the object library of PowerPoint.

Next you are going to learn how to use those references to control PowerPoint from Excel.

PowerPoint

The macro you are going to build in this lesson will create a set of personalized certificates that were prepared in PowerPoint.

This is what the certificate looks like in PowerPoint:

CERTIFICATE OF EXCELLENCE

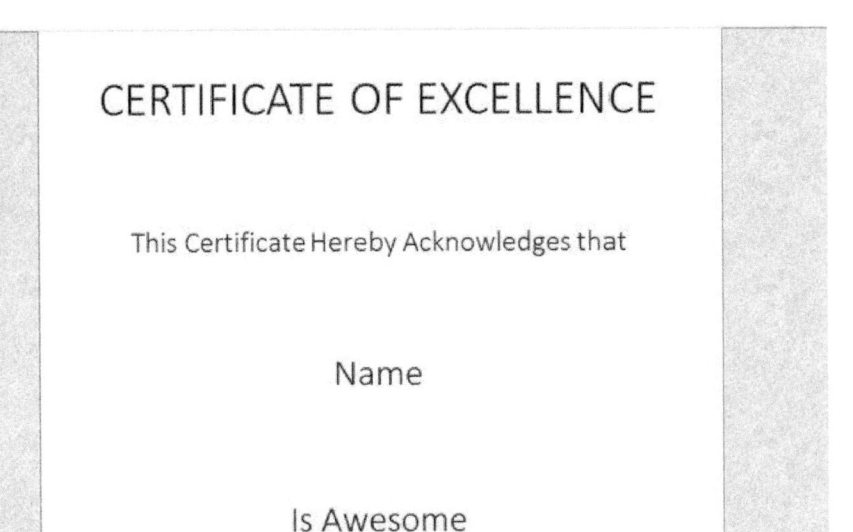

This Certificate Hereby Acknowledges that

Name

Is Awesome

Yes, it's pretty basic. It's just a sample slide I built to cover this topic.

What this macro is going to do:
The follow-along workbook has a list of names. You are going to write a macro that "loops" through the names, creates a new slide for each name and replaces the word 'Name' in the slide with the correct name.

These are the names in the follow-along workbook:

	A
1	Name
2	Santa Claus
3	Easter Bunny
4	Tooth Fairy
5	Rudolph
6	

PowerPoint Background
Unlike Excel, PowerPoint does not have a macro recorder. This means you can't record a macro then pick it apart and figure out how it works. The only way to write VBA code in PowerPoint is to do it from scratch.

The macro I will cover in this lesson can be modified to work with other presentations. If you want to write more complex macros for PowerPoint, then you will need to learn the PowerPoint object model.

This website lists all the PowerPoint objects, their properties and methods. If Microsoft changes the URL of the webpage, you can find the new one by doing an internet search for the terms 'PowerPoint object model'.
https://msdn.microsoft.com/en-us/library/office/ff743835.aspx

The PowerPoint presentation has nothing extraordinary about it. However, there is one thing that I did that will make your programming easier. Let's explore that now.

2. Open the PowerPoint file, Certificate.pptx. Click on the word 'Name'.

You will see that Name is inside a rectangle object in PowerPoint.

Name

When you create a PowerPoint object, PowerPoint assigns a sequential name to it. Names like Rectangle1, Rectangle2, etc.

Your goal is to replace the text inside this rectangle. To make things a bit easier, you are going to assign a specific name to this rectangle. That way, you can refer to it easily in your code.

The cursor should be blinking (waiting for text input) in the rectangle.

3   Click on the Format tab.

4   In the Arrange group, click on Selection Pane.

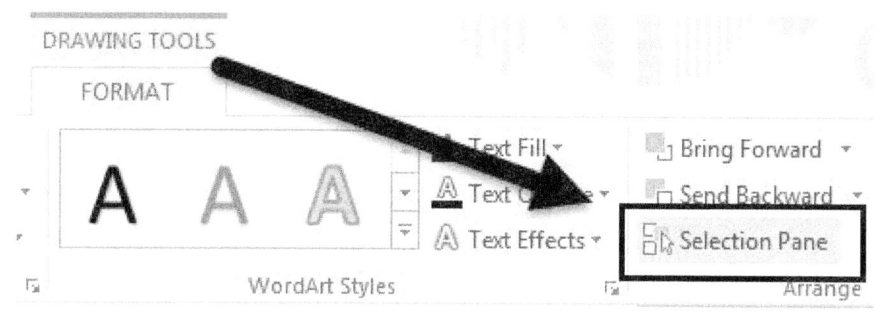

In the Selection Pane, the highlighted rectangle is the one you selected.

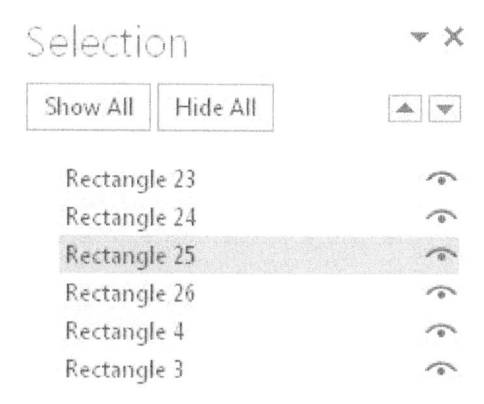

5   Click on the highlighted 'Rectangle 25'.

6   Rename it to 'NameBox'.

You have renamed the rectangle from "Rectangle 25" to "NameBox". This means that when you are working from Excel you can locate this rectangle by its specific name.

7   Save the file and close PowerPoint.

Some Perspective

Before we get into the good stuff, let me give you some more perspective on what you are going to do. This is actually some advanced, deep stuff you are going to do here.

By adding a reference in Excel, you have exposed PowerPoint's objects. Now Excel can access all the definitions of PowerPoint 'stuff', like slides, animations, titles, etc. You can do the same thing with Microsoft Word, Internet Explorer or any of the other references that you saw in the Reference dialog box.

What you are going to do in this lesson is get data from a cell in Excel and put it in a named box in PowerPoint. If you find that you need to control PowerPoint in a more complex way, you will need to go the Microsoft website and start learning the PowerPoint object model. That is beyond the scope of this introductory lesson.

OK let's continue.

1   Open the follow-along workbook, PersonList.xlsm. (The .xlsm file extension means that this is an Excel spreadsheet with macros enabled.)

NOTE: If you do not see the Developer menu at the top of Excel, you need to enable it.

2   Add a new VBA module. (Press ALT+F11).

3   Create a new program called CreateSlides.

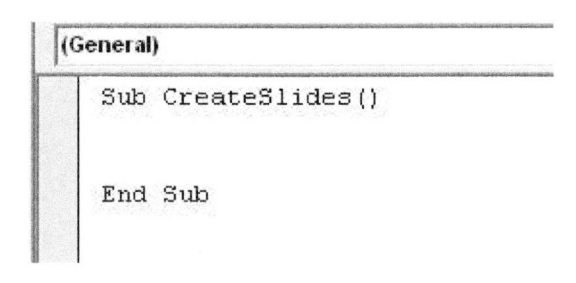

4   Type in the first line of the macro:

Dim ppt As PowerPoint.Application

```
Sub CreateSlides()

Dim ppt As PowerPoint.Application


End Sub
```

Remember the Dim statement? This is how to explicitly tell Excel what type of variable it is going to be. For normal macros, you don't really have to use the Dim statement. If you don't, Excel will assign a general purpose variable type called a Variant.

NOTE: Variants are not going to work for you when you use automation. You need to let Excel know that you need an object variable of type PowerPoint.Application.

Yes, the ppt is an object variable, of type PowerPoint. In other words, all of PowerPoint will be 'inside' the ppt variable. Of course, you don't have to call it ppt. You can call it whatever you want but I find it easier to work with variables that are named by what they represent.

Telling Excel what you want at the beginning of the macro is called **early binding**. There is also late binding, where you tell Excel about PowerPoint later in the macro. They both have their uses but I prefer early binding. Why? Because with early binding, Excel will use PowerPoint's Intellisense. You might not remember about Intellisense right now but when you see it in a few pages, you will be thankful you have it at your disposal!

Ok, now you have the PowerPoint object. The first thing you have to do is open the file. Which file? Where is it? What drive? You have no clue where the file is. Even if you did, and hard-coded the exact file path into the macro, if you ever change the path, you have to change the macro.

You are going to use a built-in Excel method to let the user tell you where the file is. Make the user do some work!

5   Type in this next line in your macro:

pptfilename = Application.GetOpenFilename("All PowerPoint Presentations (*.pptx), *.pptx", , "Select PowerPoint file to open")

The GetOpenFilename method opens up the dialog box that Excel itself uses to open files.

The syntax is:

```
application.GetOpenFilename(
    GetOpenFilename([FileFilter], [FilterIndex], [Title], [ButtonText], [MultiSelect])
```

FileFilter: This is how the box prevents other files from appearing. In your case, you will prevent the dialog from showing anything other than pptx files.

FilterIndex: You can have more than one filter. If you want to initially apply the second one, you would put a 2 here. Since we only have one filter, we will leave this blank.

Title: The title of the dialog box.

ButtonText: This only applied to Macs.

MultiSelect: You can allow users to select more than one file. However, if this is set to true the results are returned in something called an array. Arrays have special rules that have to be followed to use them. I will cover that in a future lesson.

Your macro should look like this now:

Sub CreateSlides()
    Dim ppt As PowerPoint.Application
    pptfilename = Application.GetOpenFilename("All PowerPoint Presentations (*.pptx), *.pptx", , "Select PowerPoint file to open")
End Sub

6. Set a breakpoint at the End Sub line. You want the macro to stop right before finishing. If you forgot how to set a breakpoint, look at this image for a quick refresher. The breakpoint line will turn to a dark color.

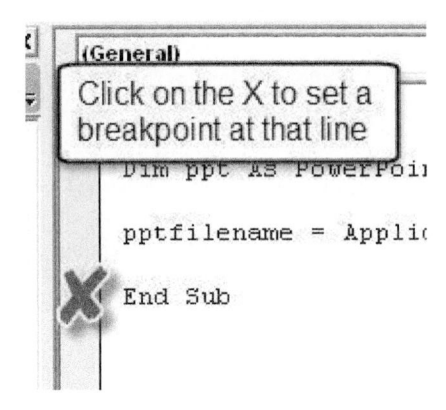

7. Run the macro to see what it does. It will stop at the breakpoint.

This box will appear:

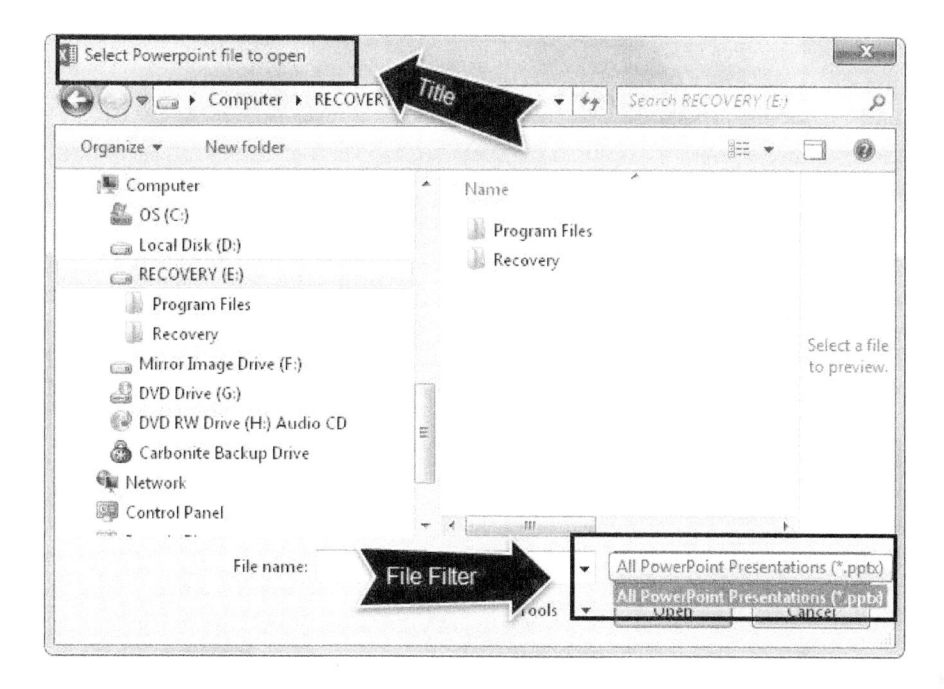

8   Select the Certificate.pptx file.

9   Click Open.

The file won't open, you haven't gotten to that part yet but the file name and path are now stored in the pptFileName variable.

I checked the value of the pptFileName variable in the Immediate tab. This is what it gave me:

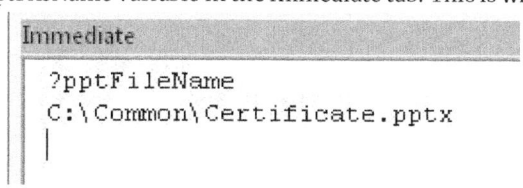

```
?pptFileName
C:\Common\Certificate.pptx
```

You now have the full path and filename that the user gave you by using the dialog box.

10 Stop the macro (click the small box in the VBA toolbar labeled "Reset").

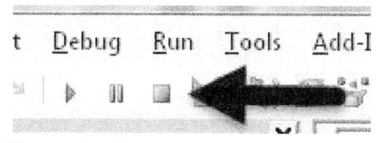

Okay, the next step will cover several lines of code.

11 Type in the following next lines:

Set ppt = New PowerPoint.Application

ppt.Visible = True
ppt.Presentations.Open (pptFileName)
ppt.ActivePresentation.Slides(1).Name = "Template"

Intellisense

What happened when you typed in ppt.? You got a nice drop down with all the ppt properties and methods. That's Intellisense.

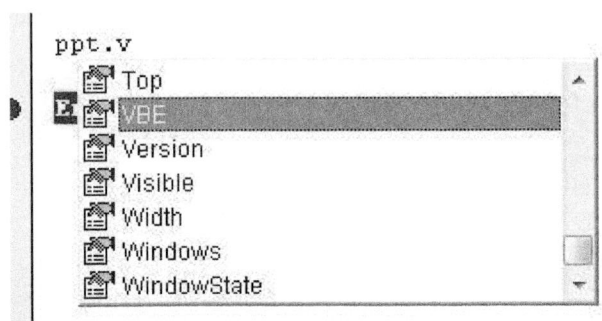

You can scroll up and down to find what you are looking for but you can also scope out other things that are available. It is very convenient to have this **but this is only available if you use early binding**. That is why I recommend you use the Dim statement when working with Automation.

Below is the code with some comments to help you understand what is going on.

```
Set ppt = New PowerPoint.Application 'Open PowerPoint
ppt.Visible = True 'Need to make PowerPoint visible
ppt.Presentations.Open (pptFileName) 'Open the file the user chose

'Name the first slide Template so I can refer to it by name in later steps
ppt.ActivePresentation.Slides(1).Name = "Template"
```

Most of the code above you should be able to understand by now. I want to review the last line in more detail. The following concepts were covered in a previous lesson but they are important enough to have a quick refresher.

Remember when we talked about collections? A collection is a group of like objects. A worksheet is an object; all the worksheets in a workbook are in the Worksheets collection. You refer to an individual item in a collection by its number. If there are three worksheets in a workbook Worksheets(1) would be the first worksheet. Note that Worksheet(1) is the entire object. If you want to find something out about worksheet, you need to use the dot notation. To return the worksheet name you would use Worksheets(1).Name.

Object, properties & methods. All of MS Office (and really everything in Windows) uses them, including PowerPoint. You can see that the PowerPoint object model is a bit different than Excel's but it still follows a logical structure.

ppt.ActivePresentation refers to the presentation you opened (i.e. the ActivePresentation).

ppt.ActivePresentation.Slides(1) tells you that the ActivePresentation has many slides inside it in the Slides collection. Furthermore, you are going to do something with the first slide, Slide(1).

ppt.ActivePresentation.Slides(1).Name = "Template" tells you that this line is going to rename the first slide to "Template".

Consider this code in Excel:

ActiveWorkbook.Worksheets(1).Name = "My Worksheet"

That looks kind of similar to the PowerPoint code doesn't it? They are doing the same thing, just in a different program. See how you can leverage these lessons? Yes, I'm teaching you Excel programming but you can extend your macros to other programs. That's the power of macros. Once you get the mechanics and a bit of what's going on behind the scenes, you can apply that knowledge to all other MS Office applications.

The data source in Excel has all these names:

	A
1	Name
2	Santa Claus
3	Easter Bunny
4	Tooth Fairy
5	Rudolph
6	

Creating the Macro

You are going to write a loop that gets each name and puts it in Slide(1). However, you need to make copies of the first slide. At the end of the macro, you want a presentation with 5 slides, one for each name.

12. Type in the following lines:

```
'Start at the first name
Range("A2").Activate
'Loop down until the cell is empty
Do Until ActiveCell.Value = ""
    'Copy the template slide
    Set NewSlide = _ ppt.ActivePresentation.Slides("Template").Duplicate
    'name it with the new name from Excel
    NewSlide.Name = ActiveCell.Value
    'Change the text of the NameBox rectangle in PowerPoint
    ppt.ActivePresentation.Slides("Template").Shapes("NameBox").TextFrame.TextRange = ActiveCell.Value
    'Move to the next cell down
    ActiveCell.Offset(1, 0).Activate
Loop
```

Note that a few of these lines wrapped into two separate lines in the text but should not be input as two lines in the code. You can only wrap a line in a macro by using a space and an underscore.

This code sets the active cell to A2 then starts a loop that will finish when the active cell is blank. Inside the loop, for each cell, Excel will tell PowerPoint to:

- Make a copy of the Template slide

- Name it according to the value in the active cell

- Change the text inside the NameBox to the value of the cell

- Move to the cell underneath the active cell

- Type in this line after the Loop

Set ppt = Nothing

This last line is your cleanup. You must destroy the object you created! If you do not, then every time you run the macro, you will have an instance of PowerPoint running. Do this enough times and you will need to restart your PC.

Here is the complete macro:

```
Sub CreateSlides()
    Dim ppt As PowerPoint.Application
    pptFileName = Application.GetOpenFilename("All PowerPoint Presentations (*.pptx), *.pptx", , "Select PowerPoint file to open")
    'Open PowerPoint
    Set ppt = New PowerPoint.Application
    'Need to make PowerPoint visible
    ppt.Visible = True
    'Open the file the user chose
    ppt.Presentations.Open (pptFileName)
    'Name the first slide Template so I can refer to it by name in later steps
    ppt.ActivePresentation.Slides(1).Name = "Template"
    'Start at the first name
    Range("A2").Activate
    'Loop down until the cell is empty
    Do Until ActiveCell.Value = ""
        'Copy the template slide
        Set NewSlide = ppt.ActivePresentation.Slides("Template").Duplicate
        'Name it with the new name from Excel
        NewSlide.Name = ActiveCell.Value
        'Change the text of the NameBox rectangle in PowerPoint
        ppt.ActivePresentation.Slides("Template").Shapes("NameBox").TextFrame.TextRange = ActiveCell.Value
        'Move to the next cell down
        ActiveCell.Offset(1, 0).Activate
    Loop
    Set ppt = Nothing
End Sub
```

Miscellaneous Topics

The following text I originally put directly in in the lesson but I thought it interrupted the flow too much. Instead, I moved it to its own section.

This is the magic line of the macro:

ppt.ActivePresentation.Slides("Template").Shapes("NameBox").TextFrame.TextRange = ActiveCell.Value

This line is what moves data from Excel to PowerPoint. I bet you thought it was going to be some huge complicated process to do this. Nope, just one line. Basically it does this:

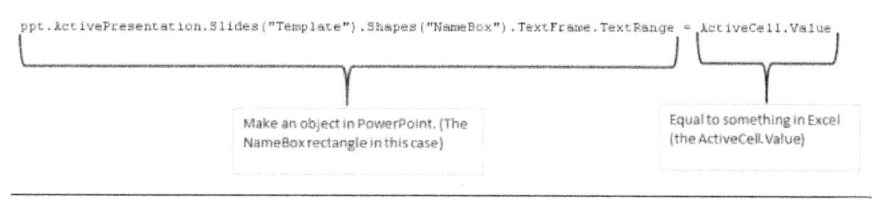

```
ppt.ActivePresentation.Slides("Template").Shapes("NameBox").TextFrame.TextRange = ActiveCell.Value
```

Make an object in PowerPoint. (The NameBox rectangle in this case)

Equal to something in Excel (the ActiveCell.Value)

The trick is to figure out how to refer to the rectangle in PowerPoint. Honestly, I had no idea how you change the text in a textbox until I began this lesson. I know the Excel object model pretty well but I rarely deal with programming PowerPoint.

I'll tell you how I figured it out so you can do the same in the future.

I knew that the rectangle was in Slide(1). Since I used Early Binding, I used Intellisense to help me explore how to access the rectangle. I saw this:

```
ppt.ActivePresentation.Slides("Template").
```
- PublishSlides
- sectionIndex
- Select
- Shapes
- SlideID
- SlideIndex
- SlideNumber

Aha! I see Shapes in there. I bet that's a collection and that the rectangle is in there. How did I know it was a collection? Well, I could have looked at the Help but instead I typed in a "(".

```
ppt.ActivePresentation.Slides("Template").Shapes(
```
Item(*Index*) As Shape

Shapes is plural and I see that Excel expects an index number. That definitely tells me it's a collection. I don't have to use an index number since I renamed the slide. I will use the slide name instead.

Once I was using the collection, I knew that I just had to poke around and find which property stored the text. I saw TextFrame. That seemed like a logical choice.

I chose TextFrame and then typed in another period to see what else was available. I saw TextRange and thought that might be it.

Then I took the entire line and put it in the Immediate Window (preceded with a ?). It returned the text Name. I had found how to access the text in the rectangle!

Note that I like poking around and figuring stuff out. You can just read the VBA help for PowerPoint or more likely, do a web search and find the answer. I just wanted to show you my thought process.

Using the Immediate Window

The Immediate Window is great for seeing what are the current values of variables in your macro. It is a very useful debugging tool but it is kind of dumb.

Here's what I mean by that. To use this line in the Immediate Window, you need to follow certain rules.

?ppt.ActivePresentation.Slides("Template").Shapes("NameBox").TextFrame.TextRange

```
Sub CreateSlides()

Dim ppt As PowerPoint.Application

pptFileName = Application.GetOpenFilename("All PowerPoint Presentations (*.pptx)")

Set ppt = New PowerPoint.Application 'Open PowerPoint
ppt.Visible = True 'Need to make PowerPoint visible
ppt.Presentations.Open (pptFileName) 'Open the file the user chose

'Name the first slide Template so I can refer to it by name in later steps
ppt.ActivePresentation.Slides(1).Name = "Template"

'Start at the first name
Range("A2").Activate
```

Immediate:
```
?ppt.ActivePresentation.Slides("Template").Shapes("NameBox").TextFrame.TextRange.Name
```

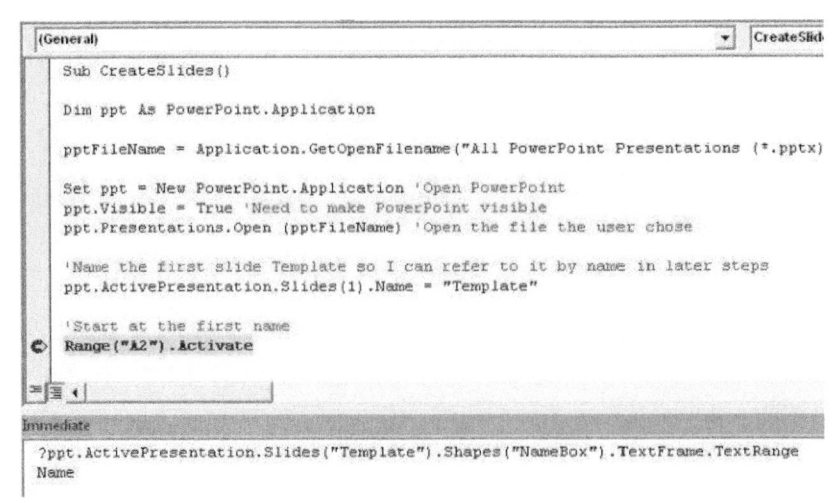

Rule 1: The macro must be running and paused at a breakpoint.
Rule 2: You need to place the breakpoint at the right place. **Everything must be defined**.

If you put the breakpoint at a line before you rename Slide(1) to "Template", the Immediate Window will display an error like this:

> Microsoft Visual Basic for Applications
>
> Run-time error '-2147188160 (80048240)':
>
> Item Template not found in the Slides collection.

You are using ppt as an object variable. The breakpoint must be placed after the Set command. You already saw that you need to put it after the slide has been renamed because we are using the name.

Yes, I know I covered this in lesson #2, Debugging Macros. I wanted to review it here in case you forgot.

Summary

I hope you were able to follow-along with this lesson. This is a very complex programming topic where you dealt with two different programs simultaneously. I just barely scratched the surface of what can be done with Automation. I thought that using PowerPoint was an easily accessible starting point. As I said before, you can also control Microsoft Word, Internet Explorer, Outlook and many, many other programs right from Excel.

You know, let me rephrase that last sentence. I am definitely biased towards Excel (as if you couldn't tell) but truthfully, you can control almost any Office product from any other one. You can have Outlook control Excel, Excel control Internet Explorer, One Note control Excel, etc.

VBA is the common language that ties everything together. Keep working towards an understanding of VBA in one program and you will be able to use it in the other with only a little bit of extra effort. When all is said and done, once you know how to use a loop, how to write an IF statement, how to use object variables, you can carry that over into any other program.

Ok, that's it for this lesson. Hopefully, I'll see you in the next one.

Lesson: 8
File System Object

Intended Audience and Prerequisites

This lesson continues with the concept of object variables. You will be manipulating a new object called the FileSystemObject from within Excel.

The FileSystemObject object is a strange one. It's not like PowerPoint or Word (both objects) that you can see and touch. It's an object that 'lives' in Windows and controls the file structure of Windows. FileSystemObject is the program that creates folders, subfolders, files, deletes files, and moves files around. You are going to work through several exercises where you will learn how to get Excel to manipulate files.

This lesson has prerequisites; you must have worked through the previous lesson, Mastering Excel Macros: Object Variables because this lesson builds on the concepts introduced in that one. I'm not going to leave you stranded though; here is a brief review of Object Variables.

Background

Object variables are very powerful because when you create an object variable, you have access to that object's properties and methods. The object variable can do many things that a simple numerical or string variable cannot do.

For example, you need to declare an object variable by using the Dim keyword like this. Declaring the variable lets Excel set aside memory to handle the new object.

```
Sub test()

    Dim myCell As Range




End Sub
```

Then you need to use the Set keyword to set it to something. In this example, I am setting the myCell variable to cell A1:

```
Sub test()

    Dim myCell As Range

    Set myCell = Range("A1")



End Sub
```

Now you have all the object properties and methods available to use. If you type in the variable name followed by a period, Excel's Intellisense will display a list of everything that is available for the range variable.

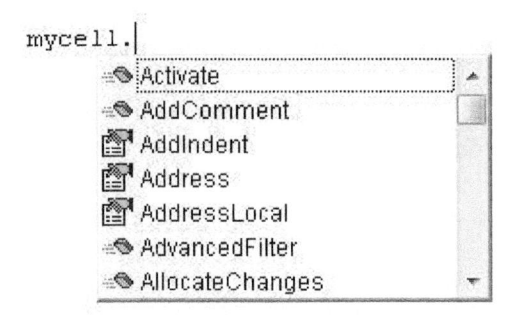

```
mycell.
    Activate
    AddComment
    AddIndent
    Address
    AddressLocal
    AdvancedFilter
    AllocateChanges
```

Everything in Excel is an object. Pivot Tables, cells, worksheets, charts, and so on. As a matter of fact, Excel itself is an object. Excel is the biggest object and all the other objects live inside it. This largest object, Excel, is called the *Application Object*. Just like a cell is inside a worksheet, the worksheet is inside Excel. Therefore, by extension, the cell is also inside Excel.

In this lesson you are going to work with an object that is not visible, the FileSystemObject, but one that you probably use every day. Anytime you create a folder, or move a file, you are using the FileSystemObject.

References

Excel lives in a bubble. It only knows the objects that it was programed to deal with: worksheets, cells, columns, charts, and so on. For example, Excel has no knowledge of Slides, Titles, or Pages. In order to get Excel to automate (programmatically control) another program, you first need to let Excel know what objects that program has. Only then can Excel start to do its magic.

The collection of all programs' objects, their properties and methods is called a *library*. You need to add a reference in Excel to the other program's library.

Follow these steps to add a reference to the FileSystemObject library:

1. In Excel, open the Macro Editor.

2. Click on Tools, References.

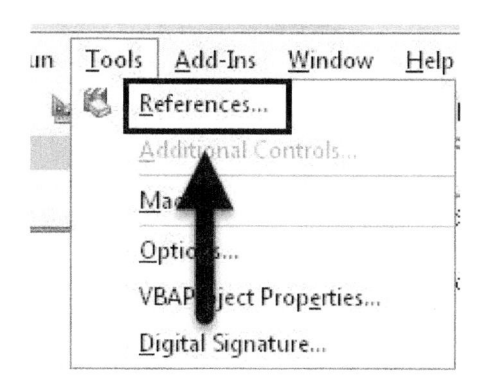

The **References** window will appear. This window displays all the other programs that Excel can manipulate via VBA (Visual Basic for Applications). There are TONS of them. **Note:** For this lesson, you will need to add the Microsoft Scripting Runtime reference.

3   Scroll down to find Microsoft Scripting Runtime.

4   Click the checkbox to select it.

5   Click **OK**.

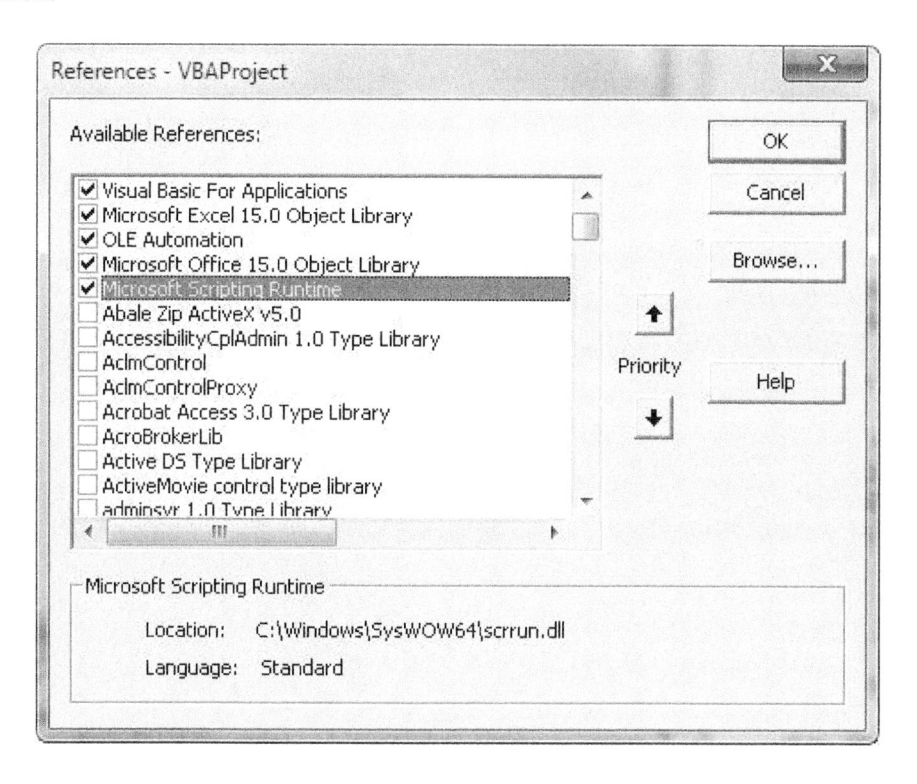

Create Folder

There are many ways to use the FileSystemObject (I'm going to call it FSO from now on). You can delete files, move them, copy them, and read attributes off of them (such as, last time altered, last time saved, and so on.). Anything you can do in Windows to a file or folder, you can do with FSO. The benefit is that you can manage hundreds or thousands of files easily, by using Excel.

I am not going to cover every single possible use case, but by the time the lesson is over you will have a good understanding of how to use this object.

OK, let's get started.

The first macro you are going to build is to use the FSO object to create a new folder.

1. Open Excel.

2. Save a new workbook as FSO.xlsm (remember you must save it as xlsm, which is a *macro-enabled* file).

3. Create a new macro called CreateFolder.

```
Sub CreateFolder()

End Sub
```

4. When working with automation objects, you need to tell Excel that a variable is an object. Create a new FSO variable of type Scripting.FileSystemObject by entering this line:

    Dim FSO As Scripting.FileSystemObject

If you remember this from a previous lesson, this is called *early binding*. You are explicitly telling Excel that you are creating a Scripting.FileSystemObject. This then gives you the benefit of having Intellisense help you later as you type in code.

5. Create an instance of the FSO object.

    Set FSO = New Scripting.FileSystemObject

6. Now you need to delete the object you just created. Use the SET command to do it, like so:

    Set FSO = Nothing

Why are you deleting it right after you created it? It's a best practice. If you don't delete it and you run the macro 25 times, you will have 25 instances of the FSO object running in the background, consuming memory and making your computer run slower. By putting in the Delete statement now, you can run the macro as many times as you like and no orphan objects will be left behind.

The macro should look like this now:

```
Sub CreateFolder()
    Dim FSO As Scripting.FileSystemObject
    Set FSO = New Scripting.FileSystemObject

    Set FSO = Nothing
End Sub
```

Now you need to create the folder. As soon as you type in FSO. Intellisense will appear and give you all the properties and methods you can use. This is why early binding is so useful. Without it, this convenient drop down box would not appear.

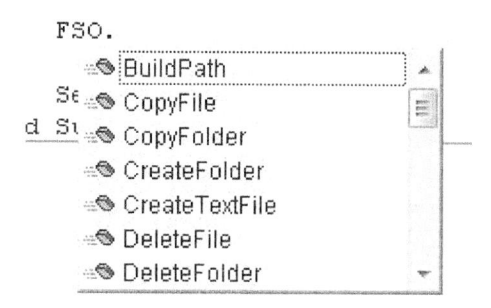

```
FSO.
    BuildPath
  Se   CopyFile
  d Su CopyFolder
       CreateFolder
       CreateTextFile
       DeleteFile
       DeleteFolder
```

7   Above the 'Set FSO = Nothing' line, type in FSO. and enter a space.

Intellisense isn't done; it displays a small box telling you what parameters are available.

```
FSO.CreateFolder |
    CreateFolder(Path As String) As Folder
```

8   Type in ("C:\Common") including the parentheses and quotation marks. The full macro should look like this:

```
Sub CreateFolder()
    Dim FSO As Scripting.FileSystemObject
    Set FSO = New Scripting.FileSystemObject

    FSO.CreateFolder ("C:\Common")

    Set FSO = Nothing
End Sub
```

9   Run the macro.

10 Go to Windows Explorer to see if the folder was created.

11 Run the macro again.

What happened?

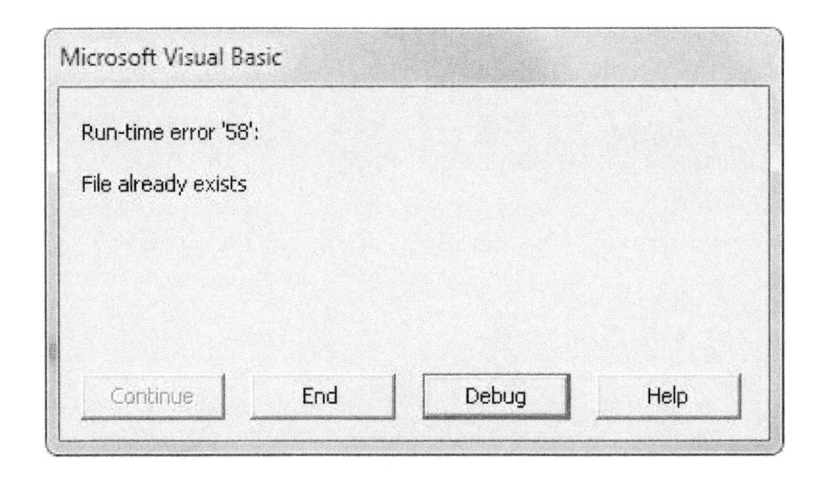

```
Microsoft Visual Basic

Run-time error '58':

File already exists

    Continue      End      Debug      Help
```

From the error you can tell that the file (it's really the folder) is already there. Windows can't create another folder with the same name in the same place. Excel is just handing off commands to Windows. Windows generates an error and hands the error right back to Excel. You need to implement some type of error trapping so this doesn't happen in the future.

12 Click on **End** to close the dialog box.

Exploring Options

Let's explore to see how we can prevent this error. If the folder is already there, we do not want Excel to create the folder. In a blank line above the FSO.CreateFolder line, type in FSO. and scroll down the list to see if you can find anything that might help.

There's one method that is exactly what you need: FolderExists

```
FSO.|
    DeleteFile
    DeleteFolder
    DriveExists
  E1  Drives
    FileExists
    FolderExists
    GetAbsolutePathName
```

The parameter is:

```
FSO.FolderExists
    FolderExists(FolderSpec As String) As Boolean
```

Note: This is how you read the parameters:

- Anything **bold** is required.
- Anything after the 'As' is the return type. Not all methods return data. These will have nothing after the closing parenthesis. FolderExists does return something; it returns a Boolean value.

Boolean values mean TRUE or FALSE. This means that whenever you use FolderExists, the answer will either be TRUE (the folder does exist) or FALSE (the folder does not exist). What you need to do now is write an IF statement that will create the folder if it does not exist.

There are many ways to write this IF statement. Some ways are shorter, some are longer. As long as you get the job done, it's ok. Here are a few ways to write out this IF statement:

```
'Most explicit method
If FSO.FolderExists("C:\Common") = True Then
    'do nothing
Else
    FSO.CreateFolder ("C:\Common")
End If

'Clear method. Don't need = TRUE because
'when something is TRUE the first condition will always execute
If FSO.FolderExists("C:\Common") Then
    'do nothing
Else
    FSO.CreateFolder ("C:\Common")
End If

'Shorter. Only test for the FALSE condition
If Not (FSO.FolderExists("C:\Common")) Then
    FSO.CreateFolder ("C:\Common")
End If

'Shortest method. If you only have one TRUE condition,
'you can collapse everything into one line
If Not (FSO.FolderExists("C:\Common")) Then FSO.CreateFolder ("C:\Common")
```

I will use the first example for the IF statement.

Your macro should look like this:

```vba
Sub CreateFolder()
    Dim FSO As Scripting.FileSystemObject
    Set FSO = New Scripting.FileSystemObject
    
    'Most explicit method
    If FSO.FolderExists("C:\Common") = True Then
        'do nothing
    Else
        FSO.CreateFolder ("C:\Common")
    End If
    
    
    Set FSO = Nothing
End Sub
```

Now that you have added the error trapping, you can run the macro as many times as you want and no errors will be generated on account of the folder already existing.

Create Text Files

Now you have an empty 'C:\Common' folder, I'm going to show you how to create text files.

1. Create a new macro called CreateTextFiles.

2. Create the basic skeleton of the macro. Input the Dim statement, the Set statement and the garbage collection statement (where you set FSO = Nothing). Your macro should look like this:

```vba
Sub CreateTextFiles()

    Dim FSO As Scripting.FileSystemObject
    Set FSO = New Scripting.FileSystemObject
    
    Set FSO = Nothing

End Sub
```

You are going to create 50 different text files. To do this you are going to use a For loop that will increment a variable 50 times.

3. Type in these lines.

Folder = "C:\Common\"

For i = 1 To 50

```
Filename = "File " & i & ".txt"

FSO.CreateTextFile Filename:=Folder & Filename, overwrite:=True
```

Next i

The variable Folder stores the path where all the text files will be stored.

Next the macro sets up the For loop. It uses the variable "i" as a counter. The macro will perform the code inside the loop fifty times since that's the limit specified.

Inside the loop there are two lines. The first line uses the i variable to generate a filename. The ampersand "&" is used to join text together. This line will make files that will be named File 1.txt, File 2.txt, and so on.

The second line is where the magic happens. This line uses the FSO CreateTextFile method to create the text file. The Filename parameter must have the entire path and the file name. Using Folder & Filename will generate something like C:\Common\File 1.txt. You need to set the second parameter, overwrite to True because you might want to run this macro a few times. With overwrite set to true, you are telling Windows to replace any existing files with the new ones.

The CreateTextFiles macro should look like this:

```
Sub CreateTextFiles()

    Dim FSO As Scripting.FileSystemObject

    Set FSO = New Scripting.FileSystemObject

    Folder = "C:\Common\"

    For i = 1 To 50

        Filename = "File " & i & ".txt"

        FSO.CreateTextFile Filename:=Folder & Filename, overwrite:=True

    Next i

    Set FSO = Nothing

End Sub
```

4. 4 Run the macro and look in the C:\Common folder to see your new files.

List Folders

Now you are going to write a macro that loops through all the subfolders in a folder and lists them in column A of the active worksheet.

1. Create a new macro called ListFolders.

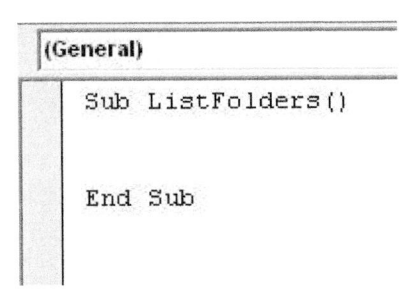

```
(General)

Sub ListFolders()

End Sub
```

2. Add the same three lines you have added in the previous section.

```
Sub ListFolders()

    Dim FSO As Scripting.FileSystemObject
    Set FSO = New Scripting.FileSystemObject

    Set FSO = Nothing

End Sub
```

The goal of this macro is to list all the folders in a drive. You will need a variable to store the path of the folder. In my example, I am going to use the folder C:\Program Files since any Windows users will have this folder.

3. Type in the line below for the new variable. You can type in the comment if you like.

'Specify target folder

targetFolder = "C:\Program Files"

Range("A1").Select

The last line selects cell A1 and sets the starting point for the list.

4. Type in this line (you can type in any comment in addition to the one I wrote to help remind you of what this does).

Note: This line is the one that creates the Folder object that corresponds to the path specified.

'Get folder

Set Folder = FSO.GetFolder(targetFolder)

Now you are going to write a loop that cycles through each folder and lists them in column A. It is much easier than it sounds!

5   Type these lines:

'Loop through folders

For Each Folder In Folder.Subfolders

    ActiveCell.Value = Folder.Name

    ActiveCell.Offset(1, 0).Activate

Next Folder

You've seen the 'For Each' loop before. This time the loop is cycling through each Subfolder in the Folder object. The active cell's value (it is cell A1 because you selected it earlier in the macro) is set to the subfolder name. After that, the active cell moves down one row using the OFFSET function.

Your macro should look like this now:

Sub ListFolders()

    Dim FSO As Scripting.FileSystemObject

    Set FSO = New Scripting.FileSystemObject

    'Specify target folder

    targetfolder = "C:\Program Files"

    Range("A1").Select

    'Get folder

    Set Folder = FSO.GetFolder(targetfolder)

    'Loop through folders

    For Each Folder In Folder.Subfolders

ActiveCell.Value = Folder.Name

ActiveCell.Offset(1, 0).Activate

Next Folder

Set FSO = Nothing

End Sub

6. Go ahead and run it. You should have a list of all the folders in C:\Program Files in column A of the worksheet.

List Files

If you look over the list the last macro created, you'll see that it only listed folders, not files. That's because the Folders.Subfolders object you used in the 'For Each' loop only looks for folders, not files. Now you are going to write a macro that will list the files in a folder. Luckily, you don't have to start from scratch; you can leverage the ListFolders macro you just wrote.

1. Under the End Sub of ListFolders type in Sub ListFiles.

2. Press **Enter** and Excel will create the new macro.

```
        Set FSO = Nothing

    End Sub
    Sub ListFiles()

    End Sub
```

3. Highlight all the lines of the ListFolders macro (except for the first and last lines - Sub and End Sub lines.)

4. Right-click and select **Copy**.

5. Paste the code inside the new ListFiles macro.

```vba
Sub ListFiles()

    Dim FSO As Scripting.FileSystemObject
    Set FSO = New Scripting.FileSystemObject
    
    'Specify target folder
    targetFolder = "C:\Program Files"
    Range("A1").Select
    
    'Get folder
    Set Folder = FSO.GetFolder(targetFolder)
    
    'Loop through folders
    For Each Folder In Folder.Subfolders
        ActiveCell.Value = Folder.Name
        ActiveCell.Offset(1, 0).Activate
    Next Folder
    
    Set FSO = Nothing

End Sub
```

Most of the functionality of ListFolders is applicable to ListFiles; the only thing you have to do is change a few lines to work with files instead of subfolders. Look at the image below to see which lines need to be changed. I have highlighted the added or changed lines for easier reference.

```
Sub ListFiles()

Dim FSO As Scripting.FileSystemObject
Set FSO = New Scripting.FileSystemObject

'Specify target folder
targetFolder = "C:\Common"                    [Change target folder]
Range("A1").Select

'Get folder
Set Folder = FSO.GetFolder(targetFolder)

'Get files
Set AllFiles = FSO.GetFolder(targetFolder).Files

'Loop through files
For Each File In AllFiles                     [Add these lines]
ActiveCell.Value = File.Name
ActiveCell.Offset(1, 0).Activate
Next File                                     [Note where folder
                                               changed to file
Set FSO = Nothing                              and
                                               ActiveCell.value
End Sub          [Note where folder            changed]
                  changed to file]
```

6 Change the targetFolder to "C:\Common".

Why? Because C:\Program Files probably doesn't have any files to list. If you've been doing the exercises in this lesson, then 'C:\Common' will have many text files to list.

7 Add remark and line in your code ("Add these lines") to match the image.

Truthfully, you don't need to change the variable Folder to AllFiles. I just like to be specific in my naming.

I want to talk a bit about the AllFiles variable declared in the code. I covered this before but I think it is worth repeating. The File is a variable I made up. I could have called it f, MyFile, ThisFile, and so on. I could have even left it as Folder; Excel doesn't care. However, for clarity, I suggest you name all your variables clearly and sensibly.

8 Be sure to change 'folder' to 'file' where needed.

9 Once you made those changes, run the macro.

You'll see that column A now has file names.

Now, all you will have to do is change the path specified in targetFolder and you can get a list of any files in Excel.

However, there's one last tweak I think you should make. You need to clear column A before starting the list. Why is that? Think of it. You run the macro for a folder and let's say it listed 42 files. So far, so good. Then you change the path and you run it again. However, this time the targetFolder only has 2 files. What will happen? You will get the 2 files from the current path but Excel will still have the remaining 40 files from the previous folder. You need to erase column A to prevent this from happening.

10. Type in Range("A1").EntireColumn.Clear after the line where you set the targetFolder variable.

With this last tweak, the macro looks like this:

```
Sub ListFiles()

    Dim FSO As Scripting.FileSystemObject
    Set FSO = New Scripting.FileSystemObject

    'Specify target folder
    targetFolder = "C:\Program Files"
    Range("A1").EntireColumn.Clear
    Range("A1").Select

    'Get folder
    Set Folder = FSO.GetFolder(targetFolder)

    'Get files
    Set AllFiles = FSO.GetFolder(targetFolder).Files

    'Loop through files
    For Each File In AllFiles
        ActiveCell.Value = File.Name
        ActiveCell.Offset(1, 0).Activate
    Next File

    Set FSO = Nothing

End Sub
```

Modular Programming

This section is entirely optional. You can write macros without doing anything in this section and you will be okay. However, if you predict that your macros will get more complex in the future, then this section is recommended. It will make your large, complex macros easier to manage.

The best practice to make your macros easier to manage and more robust is to follow the 'Single Responsibility Principle'. This means that the macro should do one thing and one thing only. You will end up having a 'main' macro that has some logic but it principally calls the other task-specific macros when needed. If something ever goes wrong (and it will), you will know which macro has the problem and then be able to find it and fix it quickly.

The additional benefit is that each single-purpose macro can be used for other projects. If you have a long complex macro, you will need to reacquaint yourself with the code, find the lines of interest and then copy them into your new macro. If every macro does a single task, you can copy the entire macro and use it; just plug and play.

For example, you wrote two macros, one that list all files in a folder and another that lists all subfolders in a parent folder. What if you want to list all files and folders in a parent folder? You could take both macros and combine them. The resulting macro would have two loops in it. that would be manageable but think of continually adding more functionality to the macro. You would quickly have many loops and other logic that would make the macro a mess.

Let's work through an exercise where we can use the Single Responsibility Principle.

1. Create a new macro in the existing workbook. Call it 'Main'.

The Main macro is going to do all the prep work and then call the macros to list files and list folders. You will need to make new macros for list files and list folders because you will need to make some changes to them.

The Main macro should clear column A and then select cell A1 as the starting point for the list.

2. Enter these lines for Main:

```
Sub Main()

    Range("A:A").ClearContents
    Range("A1").Select


End Sub
```

OK, now think of Main handing off the work to a new ListFolders macro. (You need to make a new ListFolders macro (with a different name) because there already is a ListFolders macro. You can't have two macros with the same name.) ListFolders will need to know the starting point (so it doesn't overwrite anything) and the target folder.

The variables are declared (that is, created) in Main. No other macro knows about these variables; they are in 'local scope'. What you are going to do is pass the variables from Main to ListFolders. Then ListFolders can use it. It'll make more sense when you actually do it.

3. Type in this line next in Main:

Call ListFoldersHelper("C:\Program Files", Range("A1"))

This line will call the ListFoldersHelper macro (you haven't created it yet), and pass it the targetFolder variable and starting cell address.

This is how Main should look:

```
Sub Main()

    Range("A:A").ClearContents
    Range("A1").Select

    Call ListFoldersHelper("C:\Program Files", Range("A1"))

End Sub
```

4   Create a new macro. Call it ListFoldersHelper.

5   Copy all the interior code from ListFolders to ListFoldersHelper.

```
Sub ListFoldersHelper()

    Dim FSO As Scripting.FileSystemObject
    Set FSO = New Scripting.FileSystemObject

    'Specify target folder
    targetFolder = "C:\Program Files"
    Range("A1").Select

    'Get folder
    Set Folder = FSO.GetFolder(targetFolder)

    'Loop through folders
    For Each Folder In Folder.Subfolders
        ActiveCell.Value = Folder.Name
        ActiveCell.Offset(1, 0).Activate
    Next Folder

    Set FSO = Nothing

End Sub
```

You need to set ListFoldersHelper to accept variables when it is called. You do this by putting in the variables and their type in the empty parenthesis after ListFoldersHelper macro name.

6   Change the macro name to this:

Sub ListFoldersHelper(targetFolder As String, StartCell As Range)

Notice how the Call line order matches the variables in the ListFoldersHelper name. They must be in the same order.

Now onto changing the interior of the ListFoldersHelper macro.

```
Sub ListFoldersHelper(targetFolder As String, StartCell As Range)

    Dim FSO As Scripting.FileSystemObject
    Set FSO = New Scripting.FileSystemObject

    'Specify target folder
    targetFolder = "C:\Program Files"
    Range("A1").Select

    'Get folder
    Set Folder = FSO.GetFolder(targetFolder)

    'Loop through folders
    For Each Folder In Folder.Subfolders
        ActiveCell.Value = Folder.Name
        ActiveCell.Offset(1, 0).Activate
    Next Folder

    Set FSO = Nothing

End Sub
```

You will need to change the highlighted lines to use the variables that will be passed from Main.

7   You no longer need the targetFolder = "C:\Program Files" line (or the remarks line). Delete it.

Why don't you need it? Because it has already been received from Main. There's no need to set it again.

8   Change line:

Range("A1").Select

to

StartCell.Select

Once again, the starting point for the list has been sent by Main. There's no need to set it again.

The ListFoldersHelper macro should look like this now:

```vba
Sub ListFoldersHelper(targetFolder As String, StartCell As Range)

    Dim FSO As Scripting.FileSystemObject
    Set FSO = New Scripting.FileSystemObject

    StartCell.Select

    'Get folder
    Set Folder = FSO.GetFolder(targetFolder)

    'Loop through folders
    For Each Folder In Folder.Subfolders
        ActiveCell.Value = Folder.Name
        ActiveCell.Offset(1, 0).Activate
    Next Folder

    Set FSO = Nothing

End Sub
```

One Minor Drawback

The one thing you will notice when you pass parameters to a macro is that you will no longer be able to run the macro without running Main. Excel doesn't know what to pass to the ListFoldersHelper macro so it will not allow you to run it in isolation.

9. Run Main and then check to see if the folders were listed. You can also try stepping through the code of Main (press F8 to move from line to line) and you will see Main hand off execution to ListFoldersHelper.

Now you are going to do the same thing to ListFiles.

10. Create a new macro called ListFilesHelper.

11. Copy the interior code from ListFiles into ListFilesHelper.

12. Change ListFilesHelper so that it can accept the targetFolder and StartCell variables.

13. Delete these lines:

targetFolder = "C:\Program Files"

Range("A1").EntireColumn.Clear

14. Remove Range("A1").Select and replace with StartCell.Select

After all that, the ListFilesHelper macro looks like this:

```
Sub ListFilesHelper(targetFolder As String, StartCell As Range)

    Dim FSO As Scripting.FileSystemObject
    Set FSO = New Scripting.FileSystemObject

    StartCell.Select

    'Get folder
    Set Folder = FSO.GetFolder(targetFolder)

    'Get files
    Set AllFiles = FSO.GetFolder(targetFolder).Files

    'Loop through files
    For Each File In AllFiles
        ActiveCell.Value = File.Name
        ActiveCell.Offset(1, 0).Activate
    Next File

    Set FSO = Nothing

End Sub
```

Last step is to add the line in Main that calls the ListFilesHelper macro.

15 Add this line to Main.

Call ListFilesHelper("C:\Program Files" , ActiveCell)

Whoa! Why aren't we passing Range("A1") like we did before? Can you figure it out?

It's because after ListFoldersHelper runs in Main, you don't know where the list will end. You only know that the last cell is the first empty cell and the active cell. The last cell of ListFoldersHelper is the first cell of ListFilesHelper. It just happens to also be the active cell.

Note: You *could* call ListFilesHelper from ListFolderHelper but why create an unnecessary daisy chain of procedure calls? It is simpler and more manageable to have Main call the macros it needs.

Main should look like this now:

```
Sub Main()

    Range("A:A").ClearContents
    Range("A1").Select

    Call ListFoldersHelper("C:\Program Files", Range("A1"))
    Call ListFilesHelper("C:\Program Files", ActiveCell)

End Sub
```

The great thing about this is that now you have ListFoldersHelper and ListFilesHelper that you can copy and paste into any other workbooks that need it.

FSO Object Reference

Below is a list of the most frequently used FSO methods. Anything in brackets [] means the parameter is optional. I have added the FSO reference to remind you that you must always have an object variable of FileSystemObject type created.

FSO.CopyFile (source, destination[, overwrite])

- This copies a file from source to destination. Overwrite means the method will replace any existing files in the destination with the new one.

FSO.CopyFolder (source, destination[, overwrite])

- This copies a folder from source to destination. Overwrite means the method will replace any existing folder in the destination with the new one.

Note: You can use wildcards in CopyFile and CopyFolder source parameter. No wildcards are allowed in the destination parameter.

FSO.CreateFolder (foldername)

- Creates a folder. foldername must be the full path like this: FSO.CreateFolder ("C:\Common").

FSO.CreateTextFile (filename[, overwrite[, unicode]])

- Creates a text file. Unicode means the type of text that can be stored. Unicode text files can store non-roman alphabet characters.

FSO.DeleteFile (filespec[, force])

- Deletes a file. Filespec is the full path and name of the file.

Note: The DeleteFile deletes the file. It **does not** send it to the Recycle Bin!

FSO.DeleteFolder (folderspec[, force])

Note: The DeleteFolder deletes the folder. It **does not** send it to the Recycle Bin! This method does not distinguish between folders than have contents and folders that are empty. It will delete the folder specified.

The force parameter can be set to allow only files/folders when their attribute is set as Read Only. Most people don't mess with these attributes. It's an optional parameter. You can ignore it if you don't know about file/folder attributes.

FSO.FileExists (filespec)

- Returns TRUE if the file specified exists; FALSE if it does not.

FSO.FolderExists (folderspec)

- Returns TRUE if the folder specified exists; FALSE if it does not.

FSO.GetFile (filespec)

- Returns the file object that can then be manipulated via a macro.

FSO.GetFolder (folderspec)

- Returns the folder object that can then be manipulated via a macro.

FSO.GetParentFolderName (path)

- Returns the parent folder of the path specified.

FSO.MoveFolder (source, destination)

- Moves a folder from source to destination.

To see the full list of FSO methods/properties, go to this webpage on the Microsoft website:

https://msdn.microsoft.com/en-us/library/d6dw7aeh.aspx

Summary

This lesson extended the capabilities of Excel quite a bit. You can now use Excel to manipulate large volumes of files via a macro. When your macros start to get too large and complex, try to use the Single Responsibility Principle. In other words, break down the macros into small single-purpose units. It will help you in the long run.

I hope this lesson was helpful and that you are getting a great value from the series! I'll see you in the next one.

Lesson:9
VBA Forms and Events

This lesson focuses on building custom forms in Excel. Just to be clear, my other lesson, Mastering Excel: Forms, was about using forms on worksheets. This lesson delves deeper into forms that do not have to be placed in a worksheet, that can have macros behind them and are much more customizable than the standard Excel forms.

There's a lot of very cool stuff you are going to learn in this lesson. Let's get started.

Data Forms

There is a neat little function in Excel that you can use to get an input form built for you automatically. It used to be easy to find, but now it takes a few steps. If you have a situation where you need to input lots of data, this might help you.

Adding the Forms button to Excel

1. Open the follow-along workbook, VBA Forms.xlsm.

2. Go to the DataForms worksheet.

This is a sample of what the worksheet looks like.

3. Click the small black button to add a new button to the Quick Access Toolbar (QAT).

4. Click on More Commands.

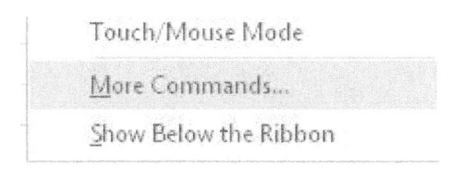

5. In the top left drop down box, select Commands not in the Ribbon.

6. Scroll down and look for the Form... button.

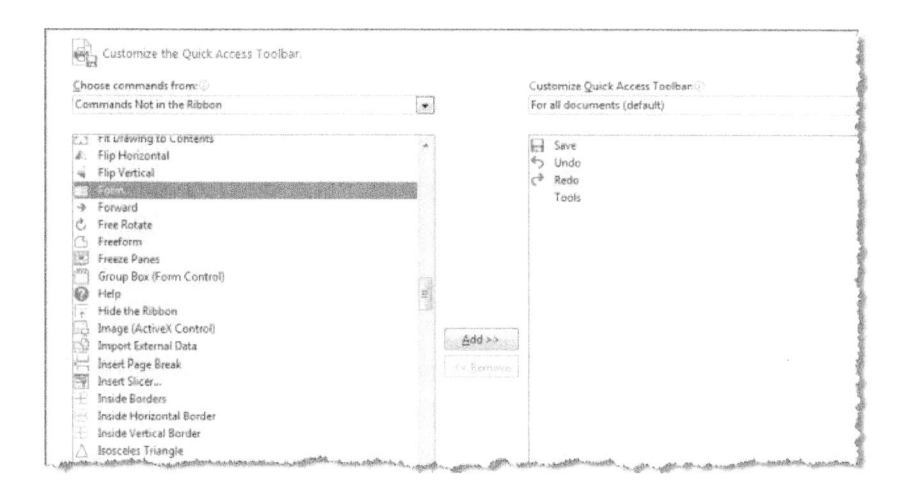

7   Select the Form... button and click the Add button.

You should now see the Form... button in the right hand pane.

As a side note, this is how you can add any button you want to the QAT. Your QAT is going to look different than mine. I have added the Save As, Strikethrough, Document Location and Camera buttons since I tend to use those features frequently.

8   Click OK.

OK, now you have the new Form... button in the QAT (Quick Access Toolbar).

9   Click in any cell of the table.

10   Click the Form button.

You will see this window appear:

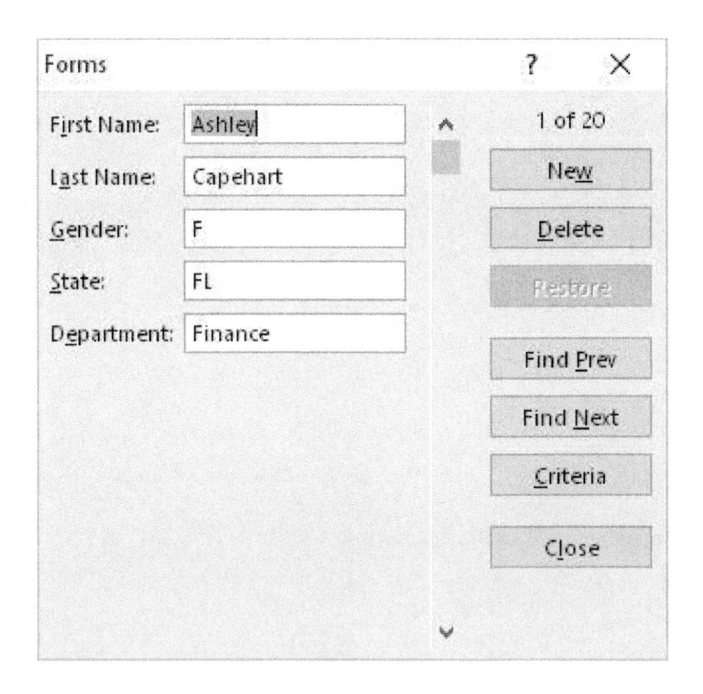

Pretty cool huh? Excel reads the column titles and creates a custom-built form that you can use to manipulate the data.

11   Change the State for Ashley (I'm changing it to HI).

12   Press Enter.

13   Look at row 2 in Excel; Ashley is now in HI.

Note: Any change you make in the form will be applied to the record as soon as you move to another record in the form.

Here is what the buttons do:

New: Creates a new record at the bottom of the table.

Delete: Deletes the displayed record. Excel will confirm that you want to delete that displayed record. (Note you cannot undo a row deletion after you confirm).

Restore: Undoes the last change you made.

Find Prev: Moves to the previous record.

Find Next: Moves to the next record.

Criteria: Finds records that meet the criteria you specify.

Using Criteria

14   Click on the Criteria button.

15   Type in ma in the First Name box.

16 Press Enter.

The form will find all the records that begin with 'ma'. The search is case insensitive. Click on Find Prev and Find Next to scroll through the found records.
Note: You can also use wildcard characters as search criteria.
? represents one character; t?m will find tim, tom and tam.
* represents any number of characters; west* will find westward, westing, western
If you are working with many columns, you might get an error that says 'Too many fields in the data form'. This happens when you have over 32 columns of data. The only workaround is to insert a blank column to break the large column set into two smaller sets, and then use one form for each.

Built-in Dialogs

There are several built-in dialog forms that you can invoke using VBA. Sometimes, these dialog boxes are enough for your project and you don't have to go through the trouble of creating a completely customized form.

MsgBox

This is the simplest dialog. It consists of a pop-up box by which you can communicate with your users.

1 In the follow-along workbook, go to the VBA editor (Developer menu).

2 Click on Insert, Module.

3 From the Tools menu, select Macros.

4 Add a new macro called MsgBoxLesson.

```
Sub MsgBoxLesson()


End Sub
```

5 Type Reply = MsgBox("Test Message")

```
Sub MsgBoxLesson()
    Reply = MsgBox("Test message")
End Sub
```

6 Click the Run button to execute the macro.

You will see the following text box appear:

You can put anything you like as the message. For example, to use the contents of cell A1 as the prompt, you would use this code:

Reply = MsgBox(Range("A1").Value)

The syntax for the MsgBox function is:

MsgBox(prompt[, buttons] [, title] [, helpfile, context])

There are several additional parameters (other than the prompt) for the msgbox function. Let's review them.

Prompt

You've already seen the prompt parameter. This is the only required parameter. The maximum length of the prompt is 1024 characters. You can set up the prompt to span multiple lines. At the end of each line you need to use either a Chr(10) or a Chr(13) command.

For example, this code shows you how to build a two line prompt:

```
Sub TwoLine()
    Reply = MsgBox("This is line 1" & Chr(13) & "This is line 2")
End Sub
```

Buttons

You can get kind of fancy with this simple box. The basic box only has an OK button; you can use the second parameter to change the buttons that are displayed.

For example, to show a message box with OK and Cancel buttons, the code would be this:

Reply = MsgBox(Range("A1").Value, vbOKCancel)

Below is a list of the most commonly-used buttons:

VBA Constant	Value	Description
vbOKOnly	0	Display OK button

vbOKCancel	1	OK and Cancel buttons
vbAbortRetryIgnore	2	Abort, Retry, Ignore buttons
vbYesNoCancel	3	Yes, No, Cancel buttons
vbYesNo	4	Yes, No buttons
vbRetryCancel	5	Retry, Cancel buttons
vbCritical	16	Critical Message icon
vbQuestion	32	Warning Query icon
vbExclamation	48	Warning Message Icon
vbInformation	64	Information message icon

To change the type of button, you can use the VBA constant or the Value. For example, if you want to show the Yes and No buttons, these lines of code would have the same effect:

Reply = MsgBox(Range("A1").Value, vbYesNo)

or

Reply = MsgBox(Range("A1").Value, 4)

Mixing Buttons

Values 0,1,2,3,4,5 are button types and values 16,32,48,64 are icon types. You can mix these groups together (use only one number from each group). For mixing buttons, you must use the values, not the constants.

Suppose you want to show the Yes and No button with a question icon. You would use this code:

Reply = MsgBox(Range("A1").Value, 36)

How do you get the last number, the 36? You add the VBQuestion number from the chart (i.e. 32) and the vbYesNo number (i.e. 4).

Responding to Buttons

Just because the message box says Cancel, that doesn't mean your macro will respect the button. You need to code in some respect. Each button has a return code (e.g. a number) that gets sent back and loaded into the reply variable in the code. You need to write out commands that respond to the value returned. Don't worry, it's easier than it sounds.

First let me show you the chart of possible returned values from buttons:

VBA Constant	Value	Description
vbOK	1	OK
vbCancel	2	Cancel
vbAbort	3	Abort
vbRetry	4	Retry
vbIgnore	5	Ignore
vbYes	6	Yes
vbNo	7	No

Now let's write a macro that will respond to the buttons appropriately.

1. In the follow-along workbook, go to the VBA editor.

2. Click on Insert, Module.

3. Add a new macro called MsgBoxButtons.

```
Sub MsgboxButtons()


End Sub
```

4. Add code that will display the Yes and No buttons with a question icon. Choose any prompt that suits your fancy. (I chose a slightly-altered famous movie line.)

Reply = MsgBox("Do you feel lucky?", 36)

Looking at the button values, I see that Yes returns a 6 and No returns a 7. Now I need to write an IF statement that evaluates those values.

5. Type in this IF statement:

```
    If Reply = 6 Then
        MsgBox "Play the lotto today."
    Else
        MsgBox "Look for a four leaf clover."
    End If
```

The complete macro will look like this:

```
Sub MsgboxButtons()

    Reply = MsgBox("Do you feel lucky?", 36)

    If Reply = 6 Then
        MsgBox "Play the lotto today."
    Else
        MsgBox "Look for a four leaf clover."
    End If

End Sub
```

Note: You don't have to use 6. Per the chart, you can use vbYes instead.

6   Run (or step through the macro by pressing F5 in the macro window) and choose a different button to see the results.

Title
You can add a title to the message box. The title is the third parameter. If you wanted to add a title to the previous prompt, you could do it like this:

> Reply = MsgBox("Do you feel lucky?", 36, "How do you feel?")

The phrase, "How do you feel?" is the title.

Helpfile/Context
I'm skipping these. Truthfully, I've never used them and I suspect you won't either. These last two optional parameters let you assign a specific help topic for a message box.

InputBox

The InputBox function displays a message box with an input field that you can use to collect information from your users.

The syntax for the InputBox is:

> InputBox(prompt[, title] [, default] [, xpos] [, ypos] [, helpfile, context])

The only required parameter is the prompt. All others are optional (whenever you see a parameter enclosed in square brackets, that means they are optional).
Prompt: The instructions for your users.
Title: Title of the pop up box.
Default: The default value for the inputbox. If blank, then the inputbox will be empty.
xpos: Used to set the precise location of the input box, along the x axis.
ypos: Used to set the precise location of the input box, along the y axis.
Helpfile/Context: Used to launch a specific help file.

1. In the follow-along workbook, go to the Inputbox worksheet.

2. Add a new macro in the previous module you have been working on. Call it InputBoxLesson.

```
Sub InputBoxLesson()


End Sub
```

3. Add these lines to the macro:

```
Sub InputBoxLesson()

    Reply = InputBox("Enter invoice amount:", "Invoice Entry")

    'Find first empty row and put input
    Cells(WorksheetFunction.CountA(Range("A:A")) + 1, 1).Value = Reply

End Sub
```

4. Run the macro (Developer tab, macros, select InputBoxLesson, click OK).

The first line captures the input from the user. The second line puts the input in the first available empty row in Column A.
How does the second line work?
"Cells" is a way to refer to a cell. The syntax is Cells(RowNumber, ColumnNumber)
RowNumber: This will be changing as new numbers are input. I used CountA. CountA counts the number of **nonblank** cells in a range. Since there will be no blanks in this column, the first empty row is: # nonblank cells in column A + 1 (i.e. one cell past the last populated cell).
ColumnNumber: This one set to 1 since I am only populating column A.
I have seen macros that in order to find the last populated cell, it physically moves the active cell down the column to find the first blank cell. That works okay but for a large amount of data, it is very slow. This method calculates where that first blank cell is and puts the value in it, without having to move the active cell at all.

GetOpenFilename

Suppose you wanted to open a file that your user specifies. You could use the InputBox method but that would force the user to type in the full path and filename...with no errors. Users will be frustrated with that. Instead you can use the GetOpenFilename method to display the standard Open dialog box.

Note that you do not *have* to open the file specified. This method simply collects the file and path so that you can use it as you see fit.

This method returns the full file path and name.

Let's review the syntax.

GetOpenFilename(FileFilter, FilterIndex, Title, ButtonText, MultiSelect)

FileFilter: This is a string that specifies which files the dialog box will show. The image below shows the FileFilter box. I'm sure you've seen it for years but you didn't know it had a name.

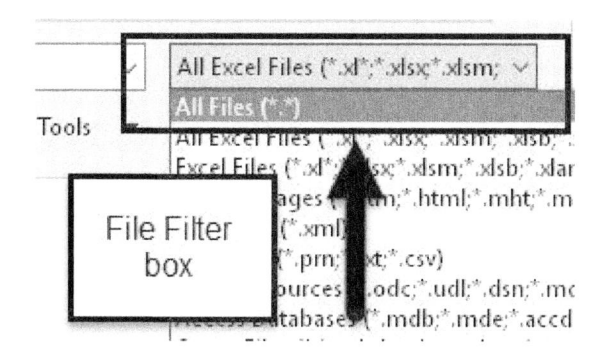

You set the FileFilter so the users can only select the files you choose. For example, if you use this:

"Excel Files (*.xl*), *.xl*"

The dialog box will show all types of Excel files. To figure out the other file filters, just look at the file filter options that you see when you open a file in Excel. If this parameter is blank, it will default to All Files (*.*)

FilterIndex: If you have multiple FileFilters set, this number will indicate which one will be the default option initially selected.

Title: The title of the dialog box.

ButtonText: This is only applicable for Macs.

MultiSelect: Set this to True to allow users to select multiple files. The default value is False and means only one file can be selected. When using MultiSelect, the filenames are returned in an array.

Let's work through an example where the macro gets the file, parses the filename and path and puts it in the worksheet.

1. In the follow-along workbook, go to the GetOpenFilename worksheet.

2. Create a new macro called GetOpenLesson.

```
Sub GetOpenLesson()


End Sub
```

3. Add a line that calls the GetOpenFilename method and stores the result in a variable.

```
Sub GetOpenLesson()
    myFile = Application.GetOpenFilename("Excel Files (*.xl*), *.xl*", , "Select a File")
End Sub
```

Test out the macro. The line filters only for Excel files, so you will need a test Excel file. Any one will do. I created a dummy file called Book1.xlsx in the C:\Common Folder on my PC.

Step through the macro (press F8 in the macro editor), select your Excel file and stop at the End Sub line. You can hover over the myFile variable to see the value or type in ?MyFile.

Do you remember how to use the immediate window? If not, go to View, Immediate Window. A ? tells the window to evaluate any math or variable in the window. Think of it as a real-time testing area.

You should see something like this. Of course, if you chose a different file, the path and name are going to be different.

```
Immediate
?myFile
C:\Common\Book1.xlsx
```

We're basically done right now. All you would do is something like Activecell.Value = myFile to put the full filename and path in a cell.

Instead, let's parse the path and filename in VBA and then put both pieces in two different cells.

Looking at the myFile variable, you can see that the last "\" is the character that separates the filename from the path. If you find the position of that last character you can separate the name from the path.

The command, Instr, finds one character in a string and returns the position of the character. Sounds good right? Nope. It won't work in this case. Look back at the path. If you ask Instr to find a "\" it will return a 3. That's the position of the first backslash. You could devise some convoluted logic to skip the first backslash but what about if you have a long, complex path with several folders and subfolders, each separated by a backslash?

What you need is to find the last backslash. Or, the first backslash starting at the end of the string. Excel has a function that does exactly that. InstrRev stands for InString Reverse.

The syntax for InstrRev is:

InStrRev (string, substring [, start [, compare]])

string: This is the string that will be searched.
substring: This is the character (or characters) that you want to find.
start: This is optional but if you did not want to start at the end you would put the starting position here.
compare: This is optional. You can specify the comparison type.

4   This formula will return the filename from myFile and assign it to the myFileName variable:

$$myFileName = Right(myFile, InStrRev(myFile, "\"))$$

Remember that InStrRev returns the position of the character. I use that position in the Right function to extract just the filename.

5   This formula will return the file path from myFile and assign it to the myFilePath variable:

$$myFilePath = Left(myFile, InStrRev(myFile, "\"))$$

Same logic as before except that I am using the Left function.

6   The last step is to put the values in a cell.

$$Range ("A1").Value = myFileName$$

$$Range("B1").Value = myFilePath$$

The complete macro should look like this:

```
Sub GetOpenLesson()
    myFile = Application.GetOpenFilename("Excel Files (*.xl*), *.xl*", , "Select a File")
    myFileName = Right(myFile, InStrRev(myFile, "\"))
    myFilePath = Left(myFile, InStrRev(myFile, "\"))
    
    Range("A1").Value = myFileName
    Range("B1").Value = myFilePath
End Sub
```

Last item in this section. What if you really do want to open the file that the user selected? This line will do that:

$$Workbooks.Open Filename:=myFile$$

GetSaveAsFilename

This method is almost identical to GetOpenFileName. The primary difference is that it displays Excel's Save As dialog box instead of the Open dialog box.

Look at the syntax:

GetSaveAsFilename(InitialFilename, FileFilter, FilterIndex, Title, ButtonText)

It is very similar to the previous command. The order is different and IntialFilename is a new parameter.

InitialFilename: This is the suggested filename to use in the dialog box. If you leave this blank, Excel will use the active workbook's name.

ActiveX Controls

What are ActiveX Controls?

ActiveX controls look exactly like the regular form objects. You can make buttons, checkboxes, etc., but these objects behave differently behind the scenes. ActiveX controls can be extensively customized either at design time or during run time (while the macro is running). These customizations cannot be done with normal controls.

The other difference is that macros aren't assigned to a button like you do in a normal control. Instead, the macro lives inside the ActiveX object.

ActiveX Controls on a Worksheet

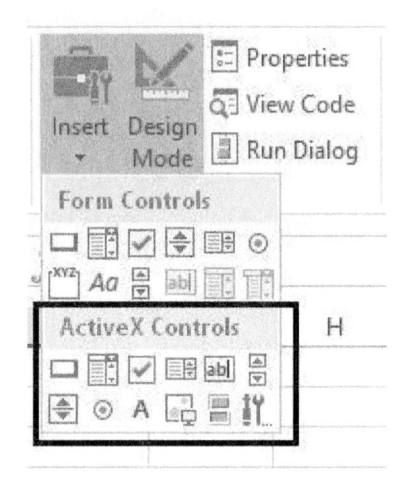

The ActiveX buttons are in the bottom half of the Insert pane.

Ok, this can get confusing. You see two panes with very similar buttons. The Form controls look like the ActiveX controls. What's the difference? The table below specifies just a few of the differences between the two.

	Forms	ActiveX
Macros	Can be linked to a macro	Macro lives inside control
Placement	Must be put on a worksheet	Can be put on a worksheet or a custom form
Types	Limited to standard types	Can be extended to include various types (YouTube videos, etc.)
Customization	Limited to control size, position and text	Extensive customization including font type, font color, etc.

When do you use Forms vs. ActiveX controls?

Of course, it all depends on what you want to do. If you want just basic form functionality, use Forms. If you want to include complex logic, customizations or want to use third party controls, definitely use ActiveX controls. Here's a list of just a few criteria to think of when deciding which to use.

If you need:

Action	Use
Extensive customization	ActiveX controls
Quick for to affect a formula	Forms
A completely customizable (colors, fonts, etc.) form	ActiveX
Additional control types	ActiveX
Do not want to put the form in a worksheet	ActiveX
Stability	Forms

READ THIS SECTION-THIS IS IMPORTANT!!!

It has been my experience that ActiveX objects can be more unstable than normal Form objects. Different users might see the buttons differently depending on their version of Excel or their screen resolution. I have also heard that some Microsoft updates will make an ActiveX object not work. When this happens, you have to rebuild the object and the code inside it.

The only workaround for this is to keep a backup of your workbook. If you have to rebuild you can recover the code from our backup workbook.

END OF SECTION

You can put ActiveX controls directly on a worksheet and have them interact with cells. Let's work through an example by adding a command bar button to a worksheet.

1. In the follow-along workbook, go to the ActiveX worksheet.

2. Click on the Developer tab.

3. Click on Insert.

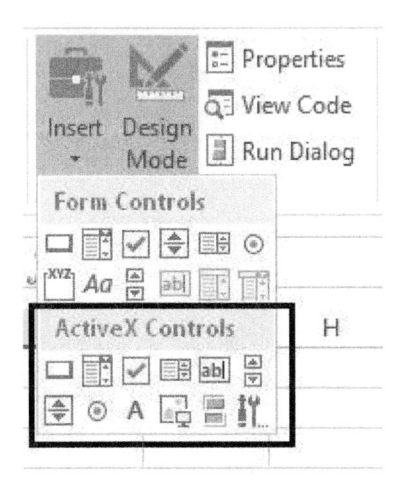

4   Click on the first button in the ActiveX Controls section to create a Command Button.

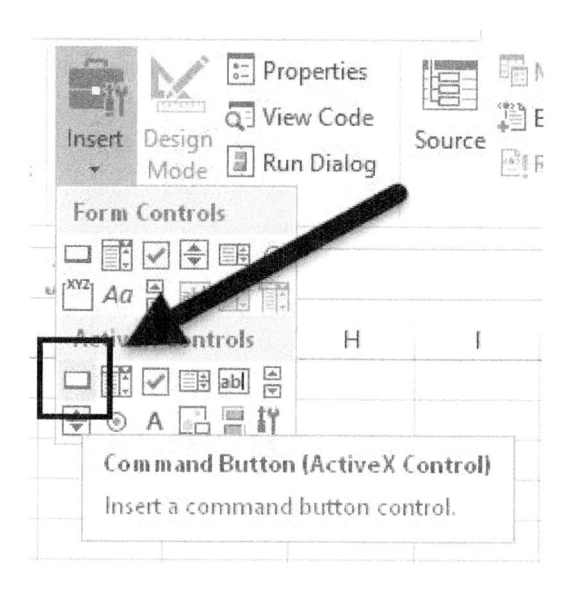

5   Click and drag your mouse on the worksheet to create a button.

Now you have created a button. However, it doesn't *do* anything. You can't link it to a macro or a cell like you can with regular Form objects. You must write a macro to tell it what to do.

6   Double-click on the button you just created.

This will open the macro editor where you can start coding in the button's functionality. Let's make this button do something simple, like put a value in a cell.

7   Add this line of code:

Range("A1").Value = "Sample Text"

Your macro should look like this:

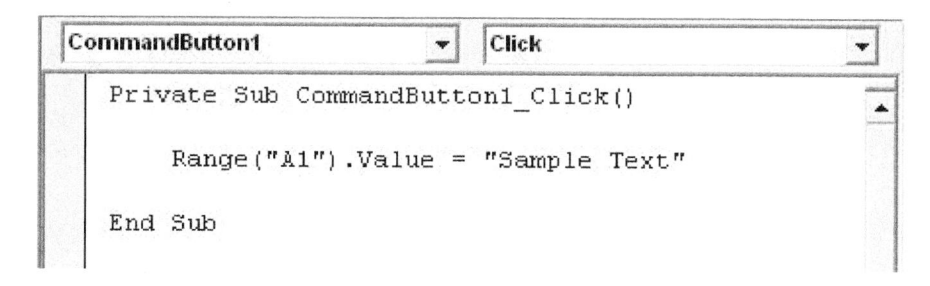

```
Private Sub CommandButton1_Click()

    Range("A1").Value = "Sample Text"

End Sub
```

8   Go back to the Excel worksheet.

Design Mode
You can't use the button yet because Excel is in Design Mode. Design mode is the mode you use to make changes to ActiveX controls. To actually run and use the controls, you need to turn Design Mode off.

9   Turn Design Mode off by clicking on the Design Mode button in the Developer tab.

10 Click the button to run the macro. The text should appear in cell A1.

This is the very basic functionality of ActiveX controls. At this point, you have only replicated what regular forms could do in Excel. Let's explore the additional features of ActiveX controls.

Actions
A Form button can respond to only one action, the click action. ActiveX controls can respond to various actions. Obviously, the click action (the actions are really called 'events') is the primary one but there are many others available.

11 Go back to the macro editor.

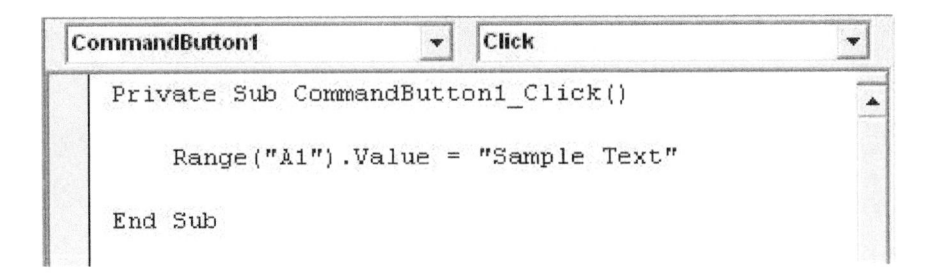

```
Private Sub CommandButton1_Click()

    Range("A1").Value = "Sample Text"

End Sub
```

Notice how the name of the macro was built in for you when you initially double-clicked the button. Don't change that name, that syntax tells Excel that the button will run that macro when the button is clicked.

12 Click the drop down button in the upper right to see the available events.

```
                    ┌─────────────────────────────┐
                    │ Click                     ▼ │
                    ├─────────────────────────────┤
                    │ BeforeDragOver          ▲   │
                  .o│ BeforeDropOrPaste           │
                    │ Click                       │
                    │ DblClick                    │
                  : │ Error                       │
                    │ GotFocus                    │
                    │ KeyDown                     │
                    │ KeyPress                    │
                    │ KeyUp                       │
                    │ LostFocus                   │
                    │ MouseDown                   │
                    │ MouseMove               ▼   │
                    └─────────────────────────────┘
```

You can write macros to execute when any of these events occur.

13 Select the DblClick event.

A new, empty macro will be created for you.

14 Input this line in the macro:

```
Private Sub CommandButton1_DblClick(ByVal Cancel As MSForms.ReturnBoolean)
    MsgBox ("click me!")
End Sub
```

15 Go back to the worksheet and double-click the button.

A message box saying 'click me!' will appear AND the value sample text will also be put in cell A1.
This is one major difference between forms and ActiveX objects. ActiveX objects are built to look for certain events and you can write different macros to execute at each event.

Customization
ActiveX objects are also much more customizable than standard Form objects.

1 In the follow-along workbook, go to the Customize worksheet.

2 Create a new command bar button.

3 Click on the Command Button in the Insert menu.

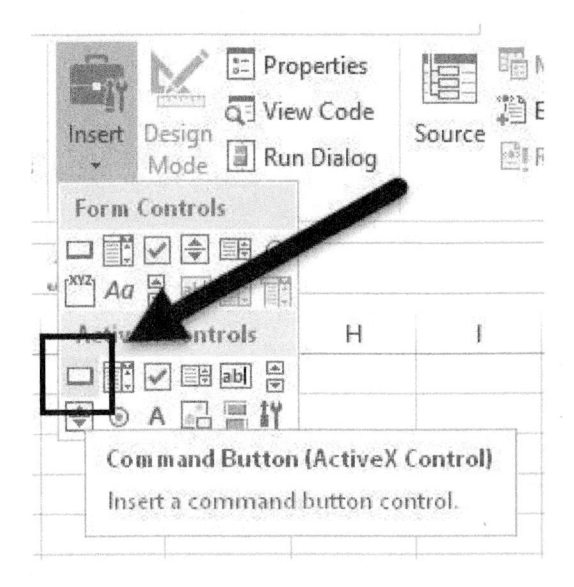

4. Click and drag your mouse to create a button.

Look at the formula bar, it will say this:

=EMBED("Forms.CommandButton.1","")

Now go back to the ActiveX worksheet and click on the button. The formula bar says the same thing. How does Excel know the difference between the two? ActiveX objects are embedded directly in the worksheet. The combination of Worksheet name and ActiveX object name helps Excel tell the difference between the two.

How do you find the macros for the ActiveX object?

5. Go to the macro editor. The Project pane looks like this.

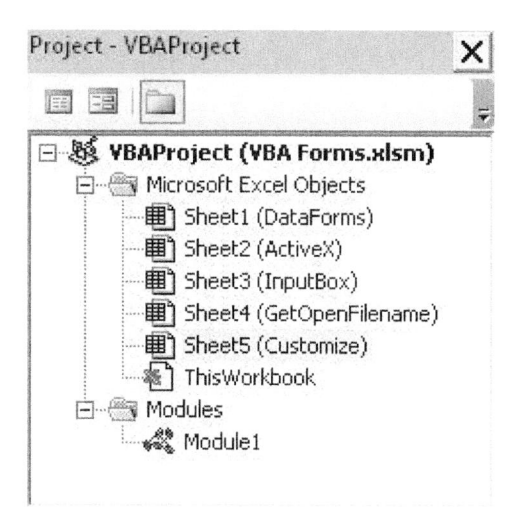

Module1 contains the code that you created for the Built-In dialog exercises. Where are the ActiveX macros? They are actually stored in the worksheet code.

6   Double-click on the Sheet2 (ActiveX) item.

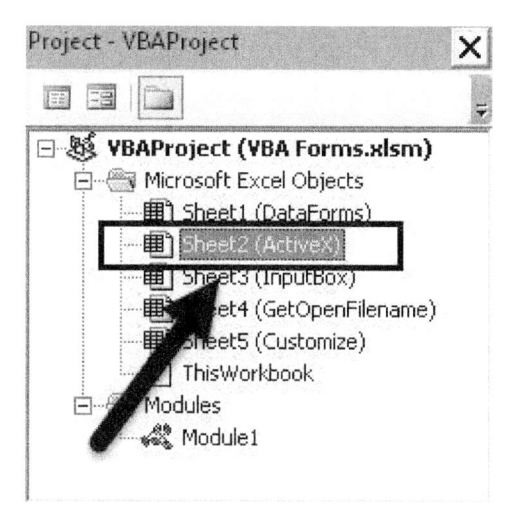

Now the macro code for the first ActiveX button you wrote will appear. You can also store macros in individual worksheets. These macros have additional functionality that macros stored in modules do not have. We will cover this additional functionality later in this lesson.

Okay, I went off on a little tangent to show you that; let's get back to customization.

7   Go back to the Customize worksheet.

8   Open the Properties dialog box. There are two ways to do this:

- Right click and select Properties.

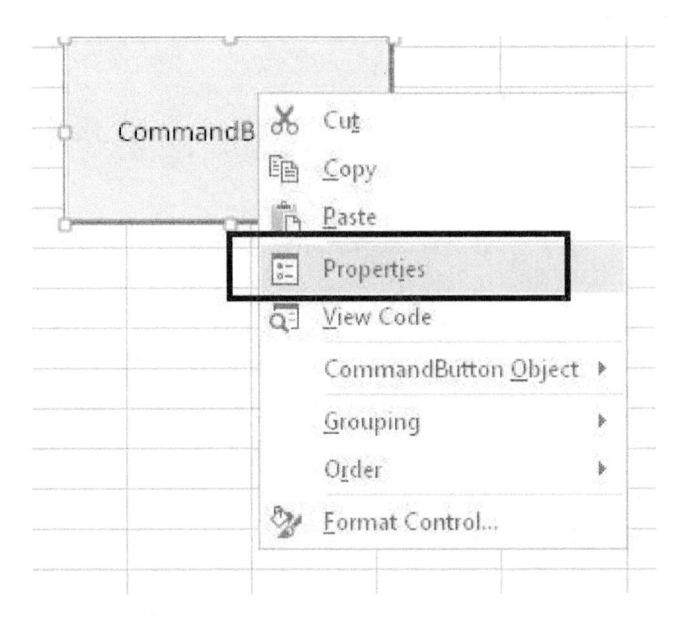

or,

- Click on the Properties button in the ribbon.

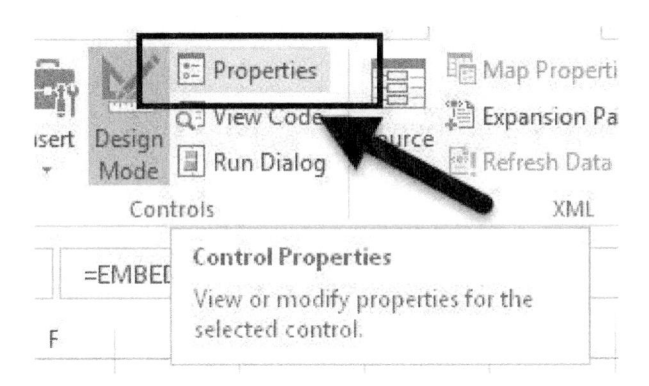

Either method will display the Properties window.

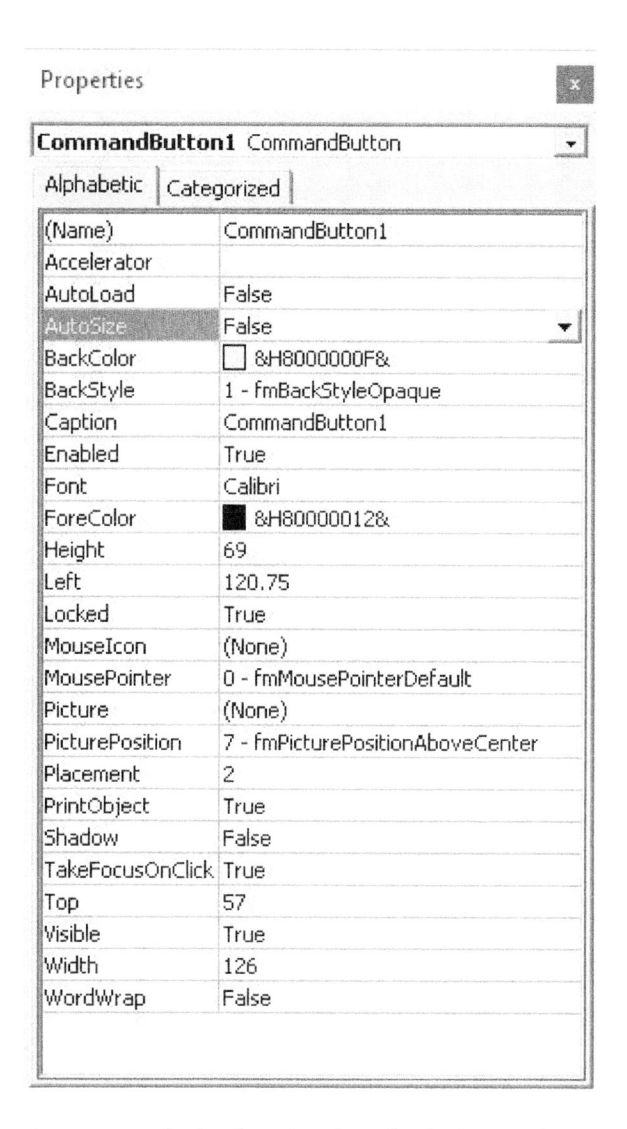

Properties	
(Name)	CommandButton1
Accelerator	
AutoLoad	False
AutoSize	False
BackColor	&H8000000F&
BackStyle	1 - fmBackStyleOpaque
Caption	CommandButton1
Enabled	True
Font	Calibri
ForeColor	&H80000012&
Height	69
Left	120.75
Locked	True
MouseIcon	(None)
MousePointer	0 - fmMousePointerDefault
Picture	(None)
PicturePosition	7 - fmPicturePositionAboveCenter
Placement	2
PrintObject	True
Shadow	False
TakeFocusOnClick	True
Top	57
Visible	True
Width	126
WordWrap	False

You can manually change these properties by changing the value in the panel.

9. Click in the Caption box.

10. Change the text to my Button. This will change the caption of the button.

11 Click in the Font box.

12 Change the font to any other one of your liking. The button font will update accordingly.

Customizing via a Macro

You can also customize the properties of an ActiveX control by using a macro. Let's work through an exercise on this.

Go to the Customize worksheet (if you aren't on it already). You are going to add macros to this button.

13 Close the Properties dialog box, if it is still visible.

14 Double-click on the button to open the button's click macro.

15 Add a line to change the macro so the caption will change on a click.

```
Private Sub CommandButton1_Click()

    CommandButton1.Caption = "You clicked me."

End Sub
```

16 Click on the event box to select the double-click event.

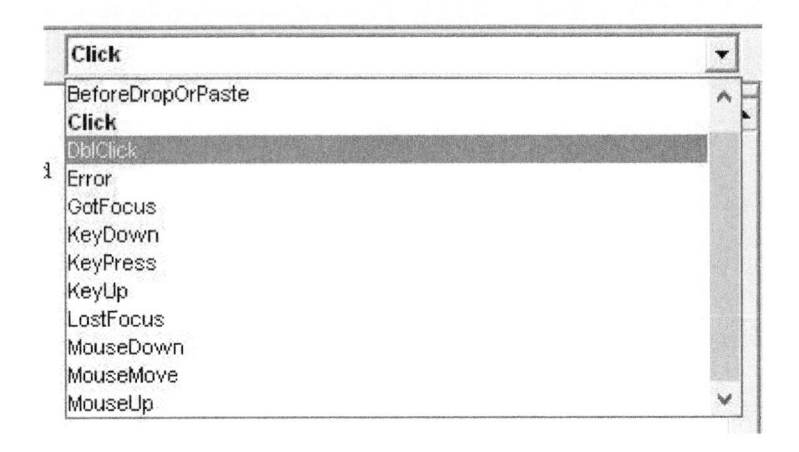

```
Click
BeforeDropOrPaste
Click
DblClick
Error
GotFocus
KeyDown
KeyPress
KeyUp
LostFocus
MouseDown
MouseMove
MouseUp
```

17 Change the macro so it looks like this:

```
Private Sub CommandButton1_DblClick(ByVal Cancel As MSForms.ReturnBoolean)

    CommandButton1.Caption = "You double clicked me."

End Sub
```

18 Go back to the Customize worksheet and click, then double-click the button (You might have to turn off Design mode).

Note: In the macro editor, you can see the Properties window. Go to View > Properties window to show it (if it is not visible).

There's a little trick to this though. If you do not have the ActiveX object selected, you will not see its properties. In other words, if you have a cell selected, you will see the worksheet properties. You must be in Design Mode, select the button and then go to the macro editor.

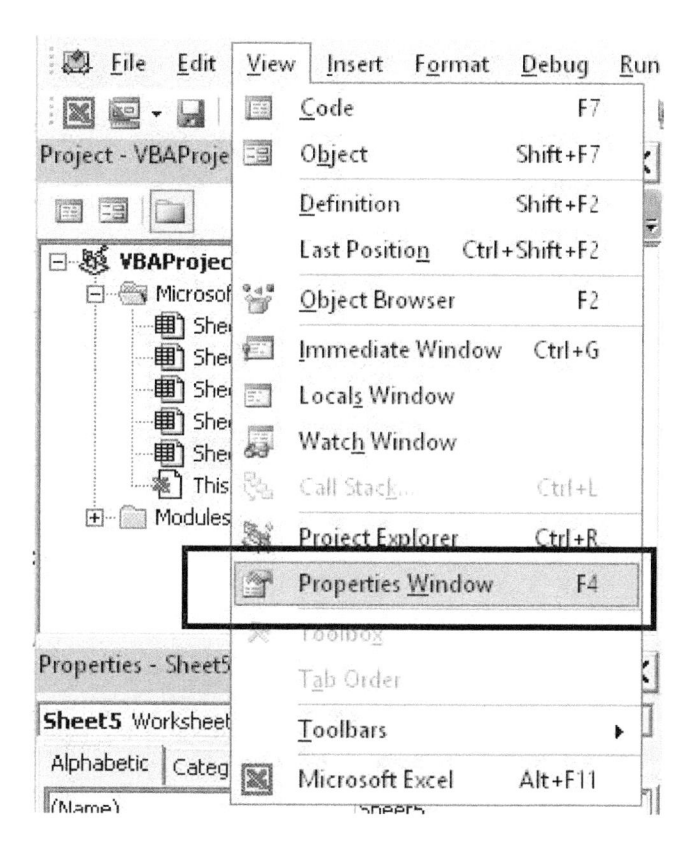

Look at this example that I cooked up. Instead of changing the caption, clicking and double-clicking change the buttons colors.

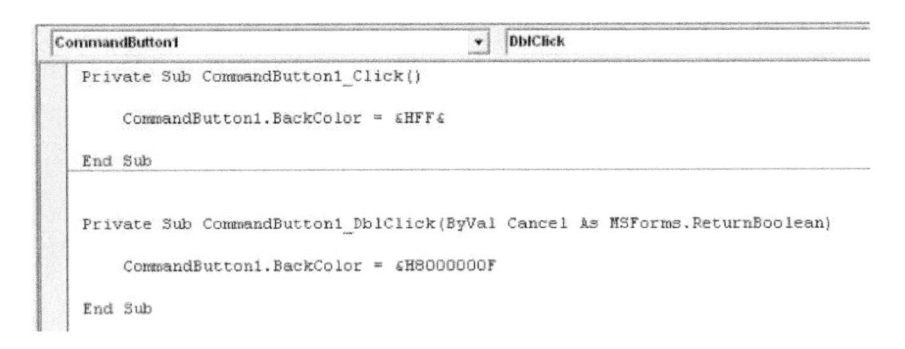

```
CommandButton1                          ▼   DblClick
    Private Sub CommandButton1_Click()

        CommandButton1.BackColor = &HFF&

    End Sub


    Private Sub CommandButton1_DblClick(ByVal Cancel As MSForms.ReturnBoolean)

        CommandButton1.BackColor = &H8000000F

    End Sub
```

What are those values? Those are the numerical representation of the colors. However, they are expressed in a hexadecimal notation (it's a different numbering system). I didn't bother researching nor memorizing which number goes with which color. Instead, I just let Excel tell me.

In the Properties window, when I click on the BackColor box, Excel tells what the number is, I just copy it from the box and paste it into the macro.

There are two tabs in this mini-window. You can select the System colors or use the Palette to select any colors you like.

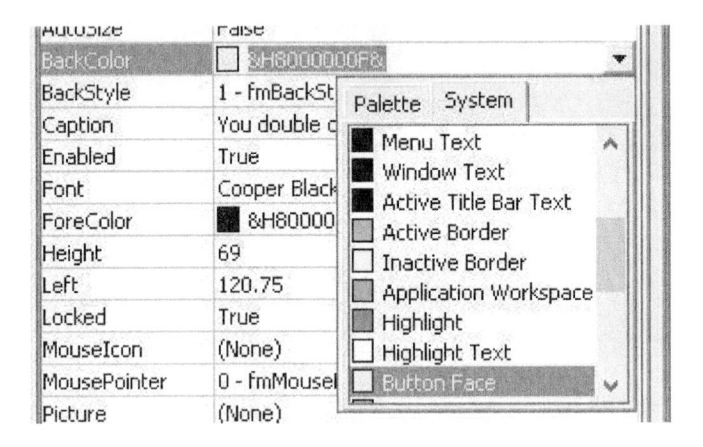

Also notice that there are no quotations around the numbers in the macro. Putting quotations around them would make them the text representation of a number; you don't want that, you want the number itself. Yeah, I know it's weird having a number that has letters in it. I just work here, okay? That's how hex numbers are written.

You can take some time and play around with changing properties of the button, if you like. If you mess up, just delete it and create a new one.

Toggle Button

This ActiveX control does not exist in the standard Form toolbar. This button is a toggle; it works like a light switch. It stays clicked when you click it and un-clicked when you click it again. Other than that, it works like the other controls.

The button example you have been working on will give you the basic knowledge needed to work with ActiveX controls. I'm not going to explain how to use every other ActiveX object like checkboxes, drop down boxes, etc., because they function the same way. You create them, add code and change their properties.

VBA Forms

Here is where you can get super creative. In this section I will teach you how to build completely customizable forms with many new types of ActiveX controls. Many of these controls cannot be inserted into a worksheet; they can only be used in a Form object.

Let's just start working and learn through hands-on exercises.

1. Select the VBAUserForm worksheet in the follow-along workbook.

2. Go to the macro editor.

3. In the VBAProject pane editor, right click any object; select Insert, and then choose UserForm.

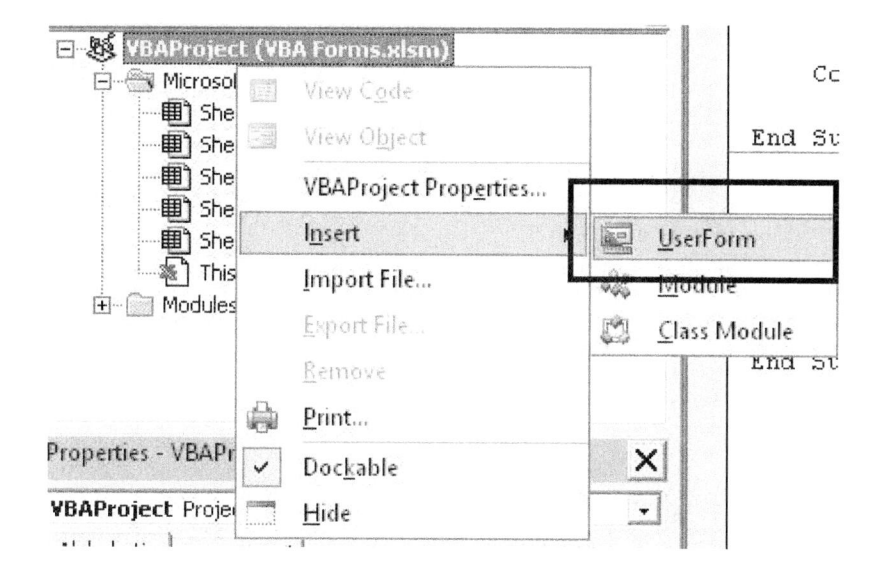

A blank user form will be created.

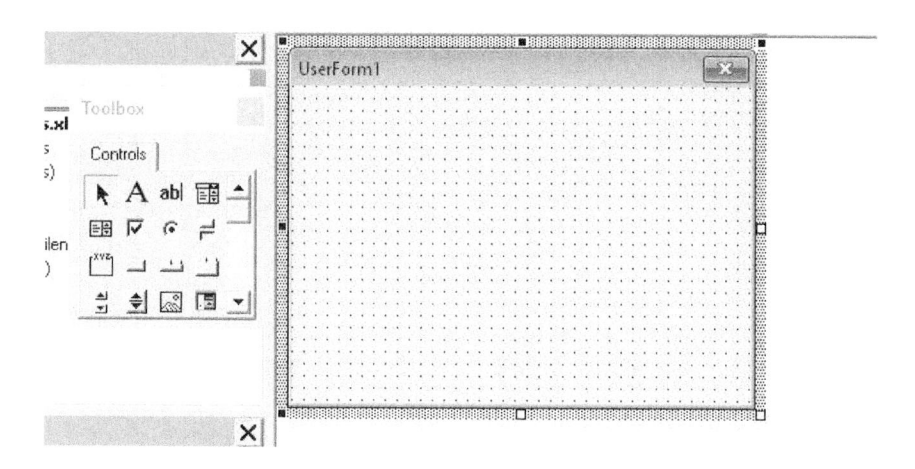

The UserForm is also an ActiveX control. Notice how it also has a Property pane where you can alter its appearance? The difference is that the UserForm ActiveX control is a container for other ActiveX controls. Everything you just learned about using ActiveX controls on a worksheet still applies, just that now the controls live in a UserForm instead of a spreadsheet.

4. Click on the caption box to rename the form. Name it Data Entry.

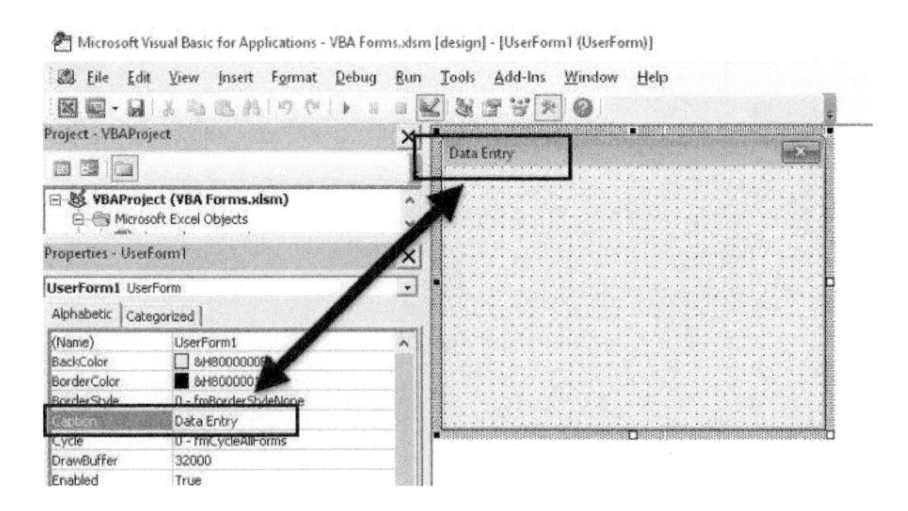

5. Add a command button to the UserForm.

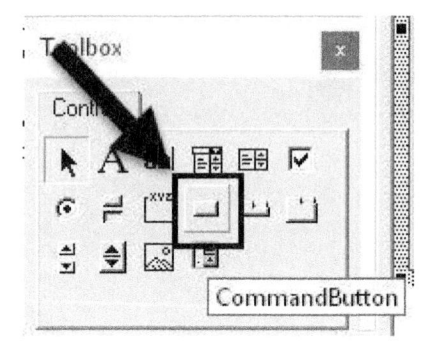

6. Change the name of the button to btnClose.

Tip: As you start to build forms, it is a best practice to rename the controls to something meaningful. btn is shorthand for button and Close indicates what the control will do. This makes it easier to refer to objects in the macro code.

7. Following best practices, rename the form to frmDataEntry.

You can switch the Properties pane to other objects by using the drop down box at the top of the pane.

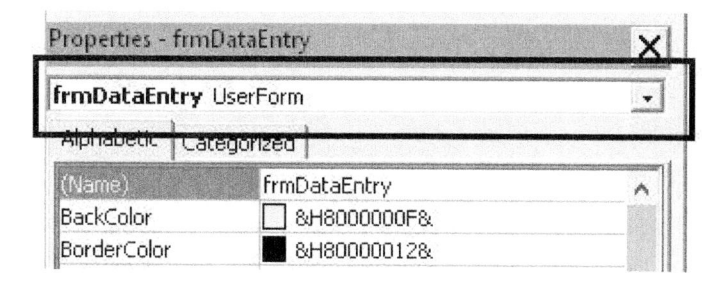

8. Change the caption of btnClose to Close

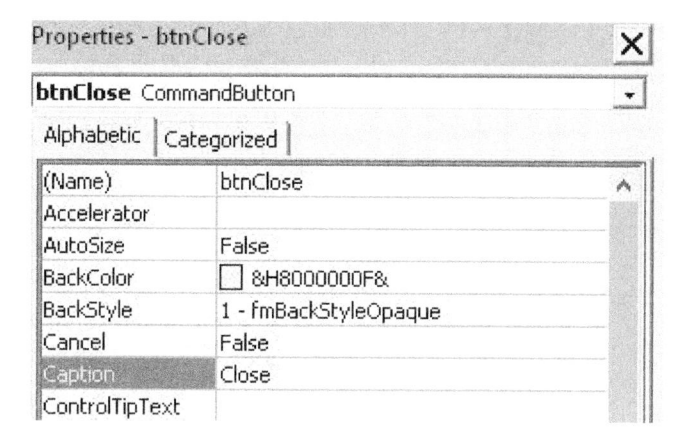

9. Change the Cancel property to True. This property does what many users take for granted; it clicks the button when the ESC key is pressed.

10. Double-click the btnClose control to open the click macro for the control

11. Insert code to close the UserForm. I added an alternate method in the comments. You can use whichever method appeals to you.

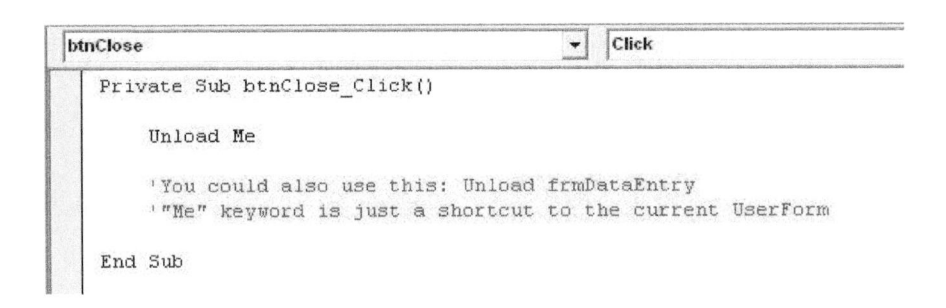

```
btnClose                                      ▼    Click

    Private Sub btnClose_Click()

        Unload Me

        'You could also use this: Unload frmDataEntry
        '"Me" keyword is just a shortcut to the current UserForm

    End Sub
```

Unload vs. Hide

Unloading a form will remove it from Excel's memory. When you display the form again, it will be recreated. Hiding a form will only remove it from display and keep it in memory. Showing it will re-display it. Any information in the form will still be available when you Hide/Show a form. All data in the form will be lost when you Unload it.

Okay, now you have a user form. You have a button and a way to remove the UserForm. How do you show it to the user? You are going to use a Form button to display the UserForm.

12 Go to the VBAUserform worksheet.

13 Add a Form control to the worksheet (not an ActiveX control, a normal button).

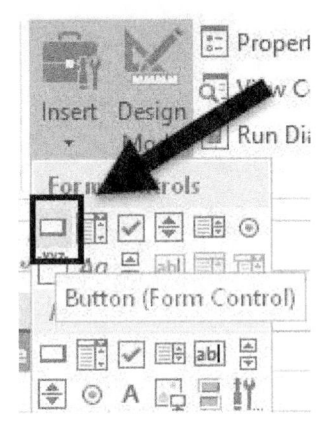

14 Click Cancel on the Assign Macro window.

15 In the macro editor, open Module1.

16 Add a new macro at the bottom of the existing macros, called OpenfrmDataEntry.

```
Sub OpenfrmDataEntry()

End Sub
```

17. Add this line to load and display frmDataEntry:

$$\text{frmDataEntry.Show}$$

The macro will look like this:

```
Sub OpenfrmDataEntry()
    frmDataEntry.Show
End Sub
```

That's it. It just takes one line to show the UserForm.

18. Go back to Excel and right click on the Form button.

19. Select Assign Macro.

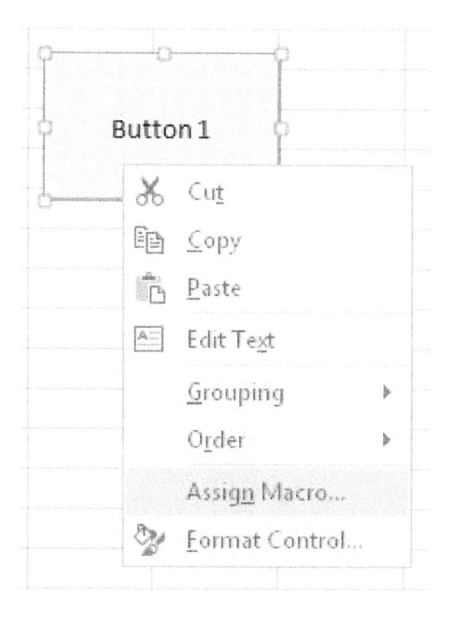

20. Select the OpenfrmDataEntry macro you just wrote.

21. Click OK.

22. Change the caption in the button to read Enter Data (this is optional).

Time to test!

23 Click the button and see if the UserForm appears.

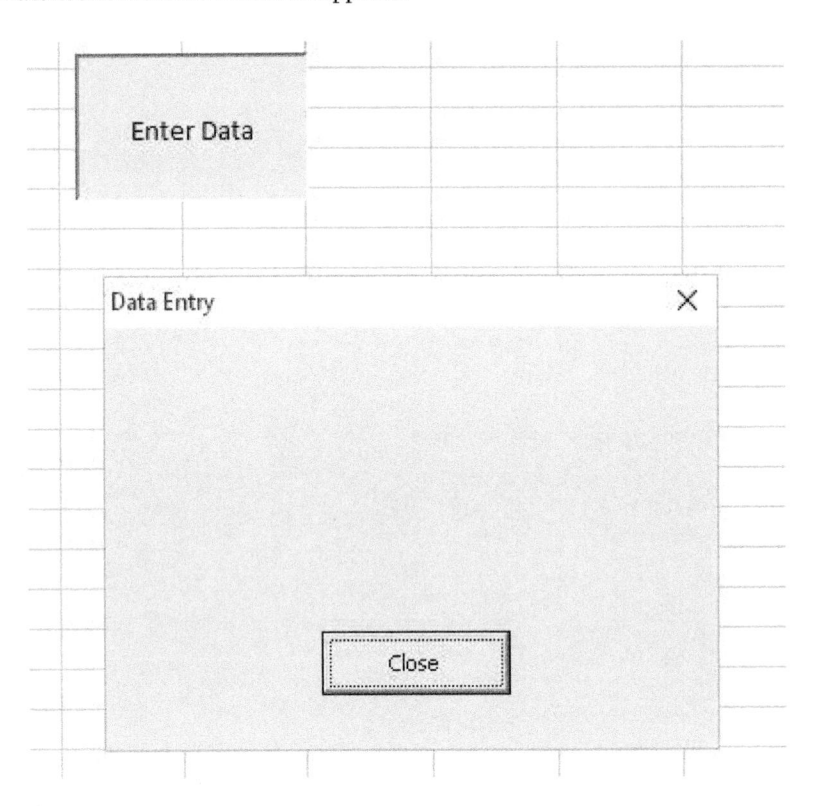

24 Click Close to remove the form.

Now does it make a bit more sense when I told you in the beginning of this lesson that the form does not 'live' in the worksheet like the normal controls? The form object is saved in Excel but you do not have to use a worksheet to store the form. Excel will load the form into memory when needed and remove it based on your code.

You are now going to build a custom form to allow users to input data in the table in the VBAUser Form worksheet.

1 Go to the macro editor; double-click frmDataEntry to edit it.

2. Add two labels, two text boxes. These will store the First Name and the Last Name. Name the objects per best practices. I am using txtFName and txtLName as names.

My form looks like this now:

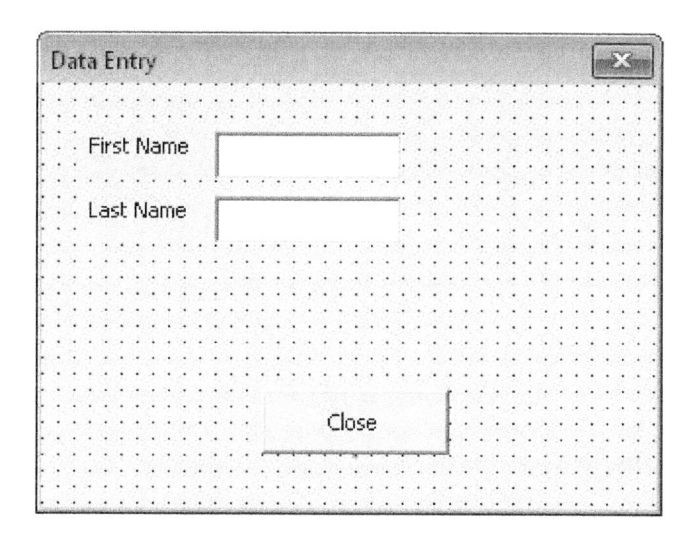

Users will input either M(ale) or F(emale) for gender and they will be mutually-exclusive. For mutually-exclusive options you can use option buttons. However, the option buttons must be included in a frame. Both options buttons and their labels must be entirely enclosed in the frame. Make the frame wide enough to accommodate them.

3. Add a Frame and two Options buttons.

4. Change the Frame caption to Gender.
5. Name one Option Button optMale; change caption to Male.
6. Name one Option Button optFemale; change caption to Female.

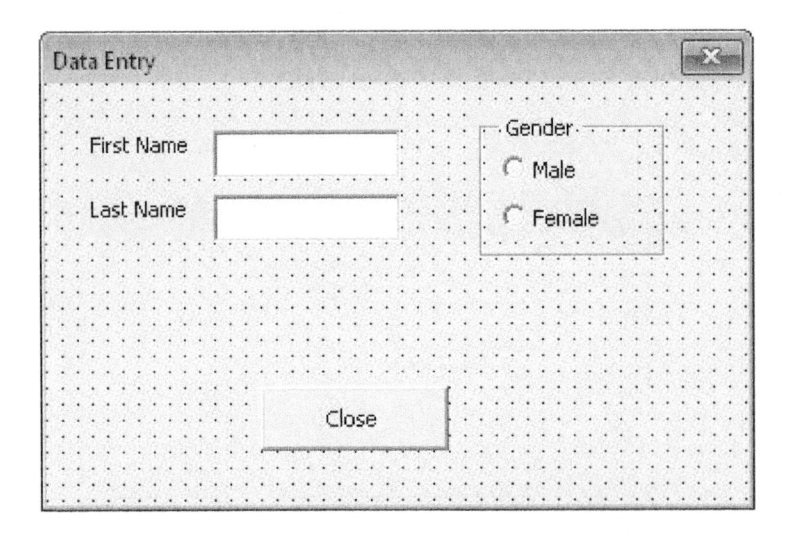

[Screenshot of Data Entry form with First Name, Last Name text boxes, Gender group with Male/Female radio buttons, and Close button]

7   Add another label and text box to store the State. Name the object txtState.

Note: I am not naming the labels because I am not going to do manipulate them via a macro; they are there to help guide the user.

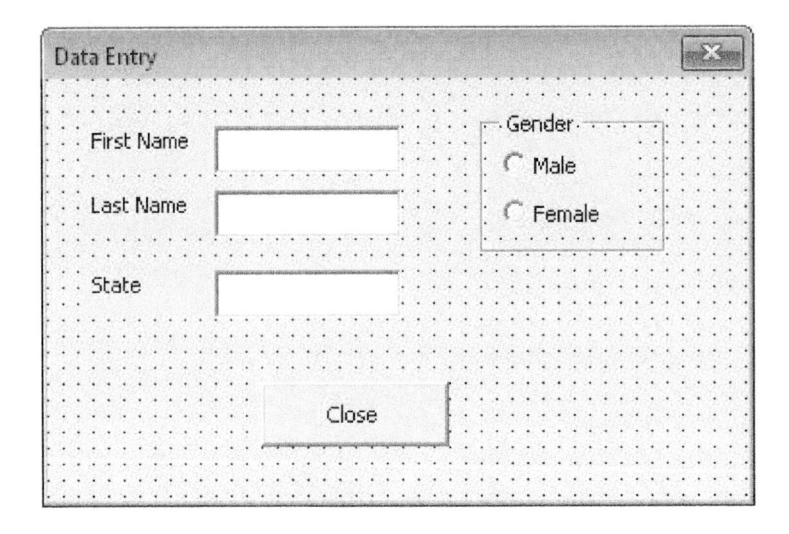

[Screenshot of Data Entry form with First Name, Last Name, State text boxes, Gender group with Male/Female radio buttons, and Close button]

There are a limited number of departments that the users can input. Additionally, you want to prevent typos. To keep data integrity in the department column, you are going to use a list box.

ListBox vs. ComboBox

When there is a small list of options, use a ListBox because it will show all the options. If there is a large list of items to choose from, use a ComboBox because it has a drop down that can show the list when needed. Users can also type in the box to search.

8   Add a label and a list box control.

9   Name the list box lstDepartment.

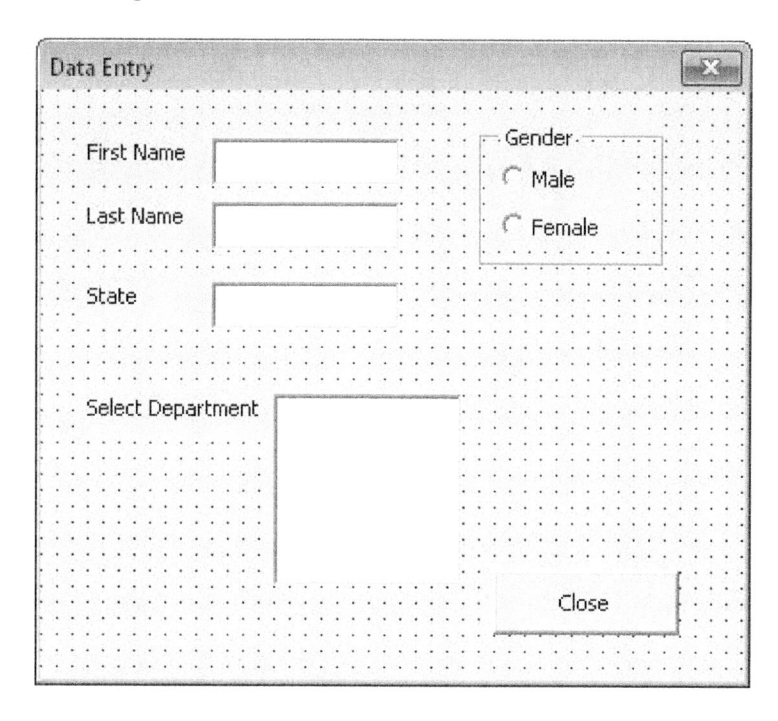

[Form mockup: Data Entry form with First Name, Last Name, State text boxes; Gender frame with Male and Female radio buttons; Select Department list box; Close button.]

We need to populate the list box with valid values. You are going to do that with a macro that will run after the user clicks the button on the worksheet but before it is displayed to the user. Before anything is displayed to a user it is loaded into memory and values populated (if required). This loading is called Initialization.

You are going to populate the list box when the form is initialized.

10   Go to the macro editor.

11   Right-click on frmDataEntry and select View Code.

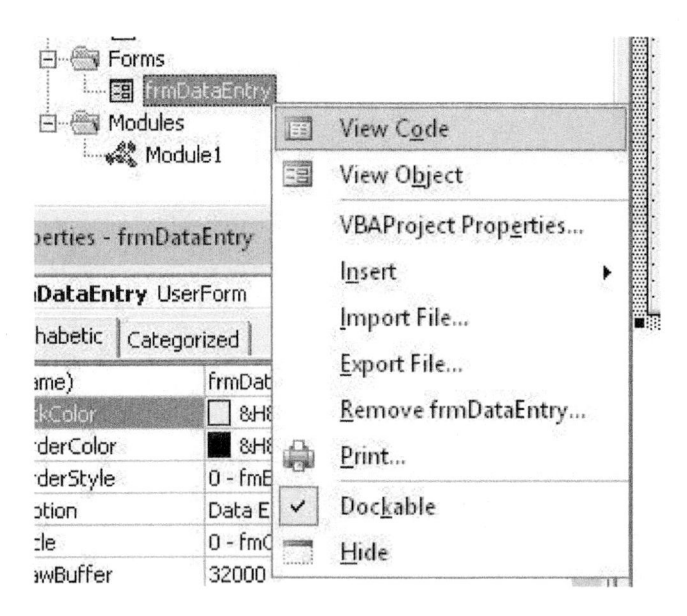

12 Click the Event drop down and select Initialize.

Note: You must select UserForm in the left pane, then select Initialize.

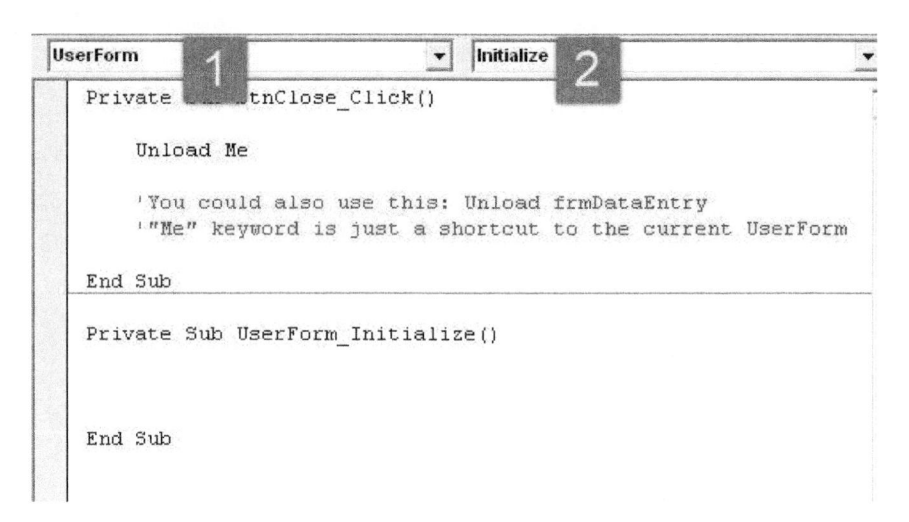

13 Add this code to the Initialize macro.

```
Private Sub UserForm_Initialize()

    With lstDepartment
        .AddItem "Finance"
        .AddItem "Operations"
        .AddItem "Marketing"
        .AddItem "Sales"
        .AddItem "Human Resources"
        .AddItem "Public Relations"
        .AddItem "IT"
        .AddItem "Legal"
    End With

End Sub
```

14 Test out the form. Click the button in Excel to load it. If you don't like the looks of it, go to the editor and adjust size and/or position as needed.

As you can see, I had to readjust my list box.

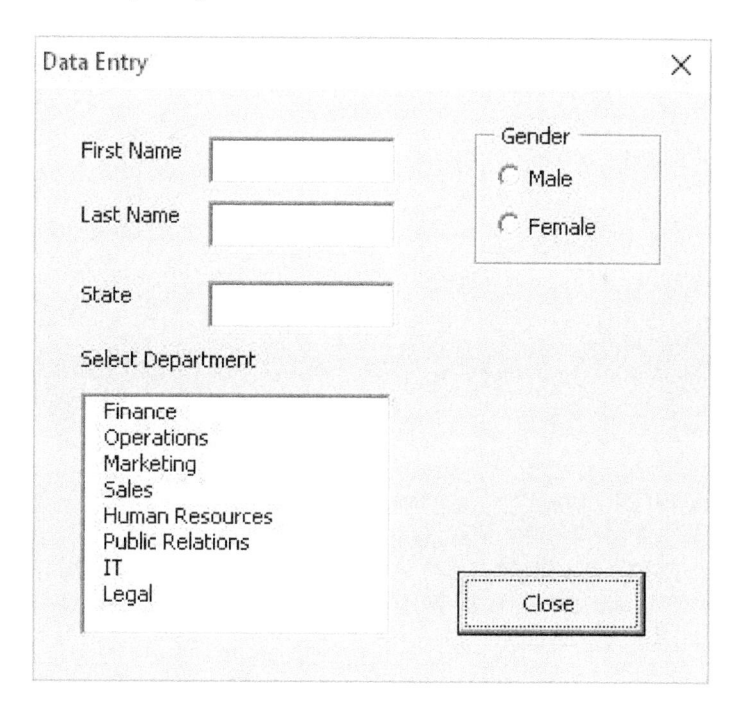

Ok, you are almost done.

You built the UserForm, displayed it, and collected the information. Now you just have to add an OK button and put the data from the form into the first empty row in the worksheet.

15 In the macro editor, add a second Command Button.

16. Change the caption to Ok; change the name to btnOk.

17. Double-click the Ok button.

Now you need to find the first empty row in the worksheet, then put the values from the form in the worksheet. I'm not going to bore you by going through every single line of the code. Instead, I'm going to paste the completed macro below and when you see it, it will make sense.

```
Private Sub btnOk_Click()

    'Find first empty row
    EmptyRow = WorksheetFunction.CountA(Range("A:A"))
    
    'Select first empty row
    Cells(EmptyRow + 1, 1).Select
    
    'Populate name
    ActiveCell.Value = txtFName.Value
    ActiveCell.Offset(0, 1).Value = txtLName.Value
    
    'Populate gender
    If optMale = True Then
        ActiveCell.Offset(0, 2).Value = "M"
    Else
        ActiveCell.Offset(0, 2).Value = "F"
    End If
    
    'Populate State
    ActiveCell.Offset(0, 3).Value = txtState
    
    'Populate Department
    ActiveCell.Offset(0, 4).Value = lstDepartment.Value

End Sub
```

18. Test the macro and input data. When you click Ok, the data will be loaded into the worksheet.

Now you have built a custom form that you can use to capture data from your users. It takes more work to get this set up compared to the Data Form at the beginning of the lesson, but this method gives you extensive customization options and layout control.

Worksheet Events

This is going to be a very short section; the hard part is over.

In every macro you have written, you always give users a method to execute the macro. The most common way to do this is to add a button the user can click. With ActiveX objects, you learned that objects can respond to different events (i.e. double-click, mouse move, etc.).

MASTERING EXCEL MACROS

Excel is an object (not an ActiveX object though) and of course it looks for events. You click a button, Excel does something. Everything in Excel is also an object. These objects also look for events and act accordingly.

I am going to show you how to put your macros in a worksheet so that the macro will listen to the worksheet events.

1. Go to the WorksheetEvents worksheet in the follow-along workbook.

2. Go to the macro editor.

3. In the VBAProject editor, double-click Sheet8 (WorksheetEvents).

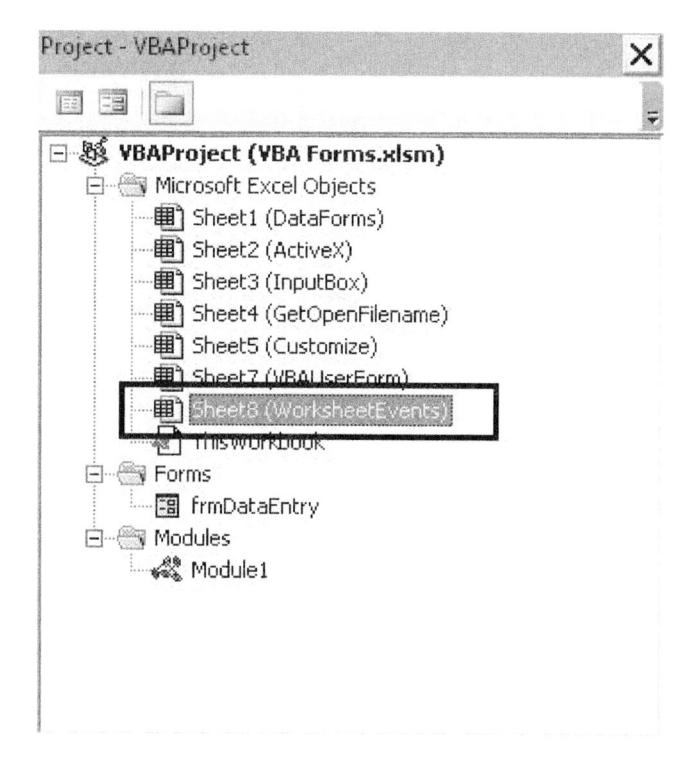

The macro sheet that opened is not in a module. This is in the WorksheetEvents worksheet. You can write macros here that will execute based on worksheet events. Look at the event drop down:

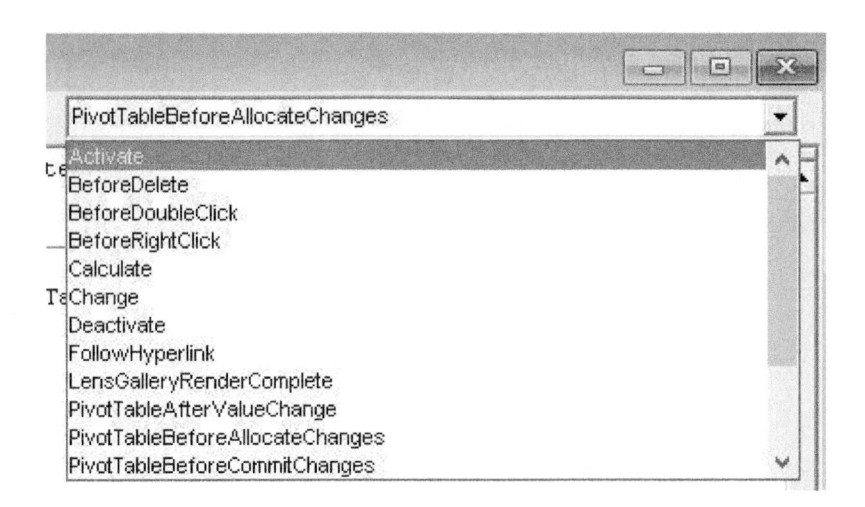

This works just like when you wrote a macro for the button click event except that you can write macros for the worksheet activate event. Or the Calculate event, or the Change event, etc. In other words, you can have your macro run automatically whenever the indicated events occur (e.g. on calculate, when worksheet is activated, before worksheet is deleted, etc.).

A few comments on this:

•   If you put a macro in the Change event, **the macro will run every time the user changes anything on the worksheet**. Depending on the macro, this might slow down your file considerably.

•   Do not load a form automatically when a user activates a worksheet. They might not need the form every time.

•   Keep macros here small and fast. You don't want the file to be slow because large macros are running all the time.

•   Usually the macros that run here are for data validation. Use them when you must be certain that mission-critical data has been checked and re-checked.

•   The macros will only execute when the worksheet has the events listed. Since you clicked WorksheetEvent, that is the worksheet that will execute the macros. If you want a macro to run for another worksheet, you will need to create new macros for the other sheets.

Lesson:10
Arrays

Introduction

Welcome to another Mastering Excel lesson. If you have previous lessons, thanks for sticking around. If you are new, I hope you enjoy the lesson. The lessons are an easy-going, relaxed, no-nonsense easy to understand. I try my best to explain complex topics in a simple and entertaining way. My goal is that you will finish reading each lesson and have immediately applicable skills you can use at work or home.

Suppose you have thousands of data points in a worksheet that need to be processed. You could populate a single variable with each cell value, process it, then put the new value back in the cell. This would work but it is very, very slow. Alternatively, you could create thousands of variables in your macros (i.e. Item1, Item2, Item3, etc.), populate them, process them, then put them back in the worksheet. This is marginally better. However, do you really want to be managing thousands of variables? Of course not.

VBA has special types of variables that let you manage large amounts of data easily. They are Arrays, Collections and the Dictionary. This lesson will focus on how to use these objects to greatly speed up your macros.

As an example, let's look at the follow-along workbook, Speed.xlsx. This workbook has about 5,000 data points in column A. I need to calculate the sum of squares for column A. In other words, I need to raise the number to the power of 2 and then take the sum of all the squares.

There are two macros in the workbook. They each take the value from a cell in column A, square it and store the value. One macro does this cell by cell, the second macro does it by using an array.

Look at the performance improvement just by using arrays! It took 14 seconds to process the data cell by cell but just milliseconds to use an array.

If you don't believe me, go ahead and run the macros to see for yourself.

Sum of Squares		Start Time	End Time	Processing Time
165,936,250,011.00	Cell by Cell:	9:07:20 PM	9:07:34 PM	0:00:14
165,936,250,011.00	Array:	9:07:38 PM	9:07:38 PM	0:00:00

Process Data Cell by Cell

Process Data by Array

Why is the improvement so drastic? Because arrays are stored in the computer's memory. It is exponentially faster for a computer to use memory space for calculations versus having to constantly go back and read the data cell by cell.

If you are dealing with large amounts of data and calculations, you are better off using arrays, collections or dictionaries.

Arrays

An array is a variable that can store multiple values of the same type. You can think of an array as a shoe rack. Each pair of shoes has a location where you can store the shoes until you need them. An array is similar except that instead of shoes you are storing data **of the same type**. Shoe racks are only for shoes; you can't stick a coat in there (well you could, but it would get all wrinkled). In an array, you have to declare the data type and then put data in it that matches the data type. For example, if you create an array to store integers, you can't store text in it.

Arrays are excellent for when you need to:

- Store many numbers and use them in calculations

- Change the numbers in the array to other numbers

Arrays are not great when you need to:

- Find one particular number

- Sort the numbers

I want to set the expectations for these exercises before I start. These exercises are designed to be simple on purpose. Almost everything you are going to do in this lesson can be done using formulas. The goal here is not to show you the best way to perform a calculation in Excel, the goal is to show you how to do it in VBA.

If you find yourself thinking, 'Why would I do this task this way when a simple formula would work?' then suppose you are working on a very large, complex workbook that takes 10 or more minutes to calculate. Now the convenience of doing the calculation in a macro versus waiting for 10 minutes becomes apparent.

Types of Arrays

Arrays can be *static* or *dynamic*. Static arrays are fixed in size; you know exactly how many items you are going to store. Dynamic arrays are variable and can be resized as needed.

Array Dimensionality

Arrays have the concept of a dimension. You can think of a dimension as a field. A one-dimensional array will have one field available to store data. A two-dimensional array will have two fields to store data. You can have as many dimensions as you like in an array, but anything past two dimensions get really tricky to work with. This lesson will not go into the topic of arrays with more than two dimensions.

Let's begin with a hands-on exercise. I will explain new topics as you work through the exercise.

The goal of this first exercise is to create a one-dimensional array, calculate the average score of all the students, and put the average score in a cell in the worksheet.

1   Open the follow-along workbook, One-dimensional Array.xlsm.

This is an image of the sample data you will be working with.

	A	B	C	D	E	F	G
1	Student Name	Test Score					
2	Ji Kratz	86			Average:		
3	Anderson Fentress	92					
4	Terina Milholland	98					
5	Leila Allyn	53					
6	Leonarda Scruggs	70					
7	Shawnta Barbeau	79					
8	Adelaide Mccalla	82					

2   Insert a new VBA module (Developer>Visual Basic).

3   Create a new macro called CalcAverage.

```
Sub CalcAverage()



End Sub
```

Declaring Arrays

The first thing you have to do when using array is to declare (i.e. create) it. When you declare an array, Excel sets apart a portion of memory to handle that data.

The data has 50 students. You are going to create a 50-item static array to process the data.

Data Types

I've covered data types before, but let's have a quick refresher. Specifying the exact type of data that the array will store will make the array more efficient. Excel will store just enough memory to handle the data. You can use a 'bigger' data type that is needed and it won't break anything. Honestly, you might never see any performance improvements depending on how complex your code or calculations are.

VBA also has a data type called Variant. This is a catch-all data type that can store both text and numbers. However, it is not as efficient as the other data types.

For your reference, here are the various data types you can use:

Data Type	Range of Values
Boolean	True or False
Integer	-32,768 to 32767
Long	-2,147,483,648 to 2,147,483,647
Single	-3.402823E38 to 1.401298E45
Double (negative)	-1.79769313486232E308 to -4.94065645841247E-324
Double (positive)	4.94065645841247E-324 to 1.79769313486232E308
Currency	-922,337,203,685,477.5808 to 922,337,203,685,477.5807
Date	1/1/100 to 12/31/9999
String	Varies
Object	Any defined object
Variant	Any data type

4 Declare a new 50-item static array of type Integer. Name the array Scores.

```
Sub CalcAverage()
    Dim Scores(1 To 50) As Integer


End Sub
```

A one-dimensional array is really just a list of numbers. That's it. In this case, you created a 50-item list of numbers. This array starts a 1 and extends up to 50 items. As you get exposed to arrays, you will notice that some arrays start at 0, not 1. The default behavior is for an array to start at 0. It's not that big of a deal, just remember that if you start at 0, you will need one less item. For example, if I started at 0, the array would be 0 to 49, since the first score would be in the 0 spot.

The 'As Integer' tells Excel that each one of those 50 spots will store an integer. I hope that now it makes sense when I initially told you that arrays store data of the same type. If you must mix and match data types, then use the Variant data type. That one can store both types but then you will have to write more code to test which data type is currently being processed.

Populating the Array

Now you have to get the data from Excel into the array. I'm going to show you two ways to do this.

Populating by Looping

The first method of populating an array is by writing a loop. You know there are 50 students, the array is 50 items large, therefore the loop has to process 50 cells.

5   Write code to select cell A1.

6   Write a 50 item For Each loop.

```
Sub CalcAverage()
    Dim Scores(1 To 50) As Integer

    'Select cell A1
    Range("A1").Select

    ' Loop 50 times
    For i = 1 To 50

    Next i


End Sub
```

To get the data from Excel into the array, you're probably thinking, "I'm going to move to the first cell, load that data, move to the second cell, load that data and do that 50 times." Yes, that would work but it is way slow. Imagine you have 1 million rows, moving from cell to cell will take several hours!

Excel knows where the cells are. You don't have to move to the cell to get the data. I am going to show you one way to get the data in without having to move the Active Cell from A1.

Loading data into an array is done by position. For example, Scores(1) = 86 will load 86 into the first spot in the array. Scores(1) = ActiveCell.Value will load the contents of the active cell into spot 1 of the array.

You are not going to use the active cell property to load data, that would be the equivalent of moving from cell to cell. Instead you are going to use the OFFSET function.

7   Load data into the array using the OFFSET function.

```
Sub CalcAverage()
    Dim Scores(1 To 50) As Integer

    'Select cell A1
    Range("A1").Select

    ' Loop 50 times
    For i = 1 To 50
        Scores(i) = ActiveCell.Offset(i, 0).Value
    Next i

End Sub
```

i is the variable that I used to count from 1 to 50.

The i variable is doing double duty, I'm also using it to move from spot to spot in the array.

The OFFSET function returns data from a cell that is x rows and y columns away from the active cell. I'm making the i variable do triple duty by using it as the offset to return data from the cell that is i rows and 0 columns away. i rows and 0 columns away means down the same column as the active cell (column A in this case).

8   Run the macro

What happened? Did you get this error?

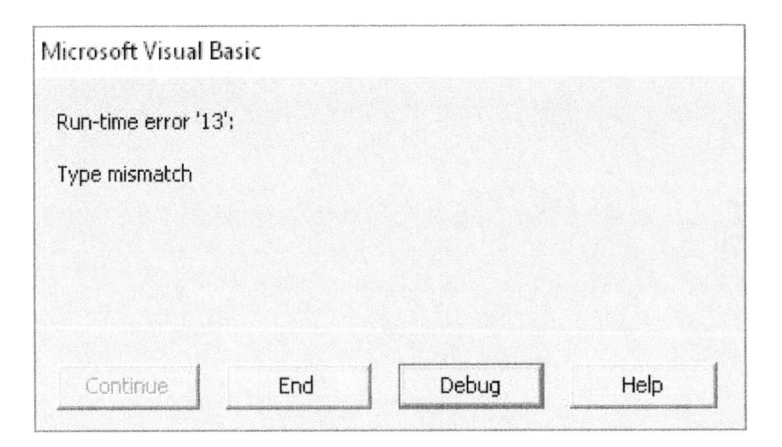

Microsoft Visual Basic

Run-time error '13':

Type mismatch

[Continue] [End] [Debug] [Help]

Although the error message is not that descriptive, looking at the data you can figure out what is wrong. You selected the start point as A1. Column A has the names of the students as text, the array is expecting integers since we are trying to load the numbers.

It's an easy fix. Instead of selecting cell A1, select cell B1. That's the column where the numbers are.

```
Sub CalcAverage()
    Dim Scores(1 To 50) As Integer
    
    'Select cell A1
    Range("B1").Select
    
    ' Loop 50 times
    For i = 1 To 50
        Scores(i) = ActiveCell.Offset(i, 0).Value
    Next i


End Sub
```

You can run the macro now and there should be no errors. However, it doesn't 'do' anything other than load the array. You can't even see if it did it correctly.

Show Specific Values of an Array

Once the macro finishes running, the array is destroyed. You need to create a breakpoint in the code and then use the Immediate window to see the individual values. Let's do that now.

9   Click on the row header at End Sub to create a breakpoint in the code.

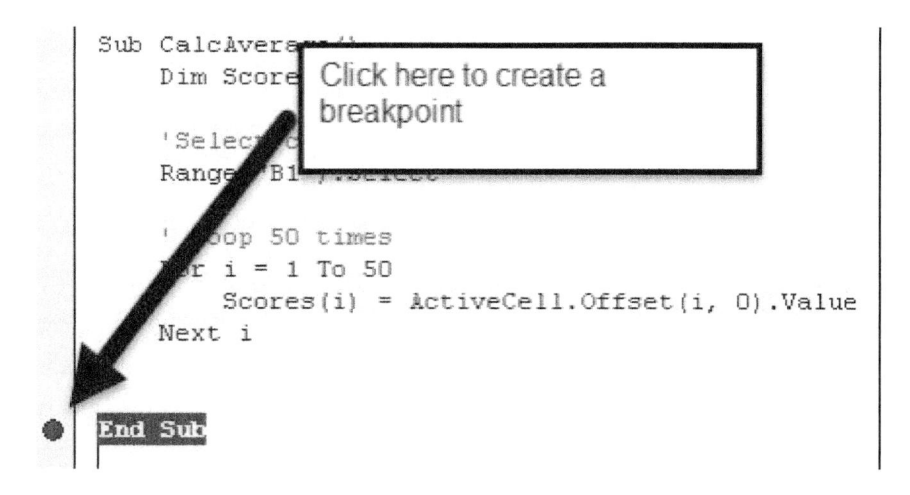

```
Sub CalcAvera
    Dim Score    Click here to create a
                 breakpoint
    'Selec
    Range   B1
    
    '   op 50 times
       r i = 1 To 50
        Scores(i) = ActiveCell.Offset(i, 0).Value
    Next i

● End Sub
```

Now when you run the macro, the code will stop right before the macro ends. At this point, the array has been completely loaded.

10 Show the Immediate window.

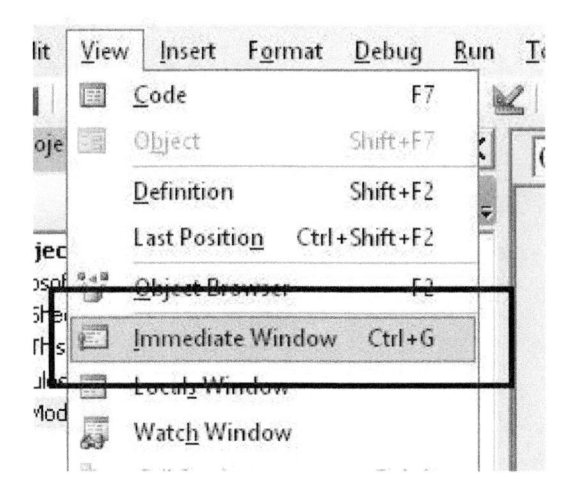

11 Run the macro.

```
Sub CalcAverage()
    Dim Scores(1 To 50) As Integer
    
    'Select cell A1
    Range("B1").Select
    
    ' Loop 50 times
    For i = 1 To 50
        Scores(i) = ActiveCell.Offset(i, 0).Value
    Next i

End Sub
```

The yellow means the macro has paused at the breakpoint line.

12 Type this in the immediate window to see the value of Scores(1).

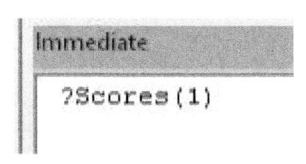

```
Immediate
?Scores(1)
```

13 Press Enter to evaluate the expression.

```
Immediate
?Scores(1)
   86
```

You can change the number in the parenthesis to check a few numbers, if you'd like.

Keep in mind that the order of the numbers is irrelevant. Also note that you cannot write code that retrieves the data for a specific student; this array is just a list of numbers.

14. Click stop to stop the macro.

Now you just have to finish the macro by adding lines that calculate the average. Unfortunately, there is no built-in formula to calculate the average of an array, you will have to do it yourself. The average of a set of numbers is calculated as the sum of all the numbers divided by the count of the numbers. In this case it would be the sum of all the numbers / 50.

After loading the data to the array, you can create a new variable to aggregate the new values. After the loop is finished, you will put the result into cell F2. It will make much more sense when you see the example.

15. Click the red dot in the breakpoint line to remove the breakpoint.

16. Add lines to calculate the average and put the result in cell F2.

```
Sub CalcAverage()
    Dim Scores(1 To 50) As Integer

    'Select cell A1
    Range("B1").Select

    ' Loop 50 times
    For i = 1 To 50
        Scores(i) = ActiveCell.Offset(i, 0).Value
        Total = Total + Scores(i)
    Next i
    Range("F2").Value = Total / 50

End Sub
```

When you run the macro, the array will be populated; the average will then be calculated and put in cell F2.

Populate by Range

Now, I'm going to show you another way to load data into an array where you don't have to process or point to each cell. As long as the source data size matches the array size, you can load a range into an array. Excel is intelligent enough to know that each cell corresponds to a lot in the array.

For example, you can use this line to populate the array:

Scores = Range("B2:B51").Value

The above line would replace the Scores(i) = ActiveCell.Offset(i,0).Value and it would go outside the loop. You would still need to loop through each item to calculate the average.
The trick to this method is that the data type of the array must be Variant. You will get an error if you use another data type.

Dynamic Arrays

What about if you don't know how many students are going to be in the worksheet? For this scenario, a static array won't work. Instead you need to use a dynamic array. Dynamic arrays work just like static arrays except you have the additional task of writing a few extra lines of code telling Excel how large the array is going to be.

1. Create a new macro called CalcAverageDynamic

```
Sub CalcAverageDynamic()


End Sub
```

To declare a dynamic array, you don't put a size in between the parentheses. For example, Scores () as Integer.

2. Declare the Scores array as a dynamic array.

```
Sub CalcAverageDynamic()
    Dim Scores() As Variant

End Sub
```

3. Add the line to select cell B1.

```
Sub CalcAverageDynamic()
    Dim Scores() As Variant

    'Select cell B1
    Range("B1").Select

End Sub
```

How many items are going to be in the loop? You need to figure that out. In a worksheet you would use the COUNTA function to count the number of non-blank cells in column B. Guess what? You can use Excel formulas in a macro. You just have to use them by using the WorksheetFunction.

To count the number of non-blank cells in column B the macro code would be:

```
        arrSize = WorksheetFunction.CountA(Range("B:B"))
```

4. Add the line that calculates the number of data rows (which is equal to the array size).

```
Sub CalcAverageDynamic()
    Dim Scores() As Variant

    'Select cell B1
    Range("B1").Select

    'Calculate array size
    arrSize = WorksheetFunction.CountA(Range("B:B"))

End Sub
```

The ReDim statement resizes an array. The syntax is the same as the Dim statement. In this example you are resizing the array once, however, you can resize the array as many times as necessary.

5. Resize the array to 50.

```
Sub CalcAverageDynamic()
    Dim Scores() As Variant

    'Select cell B1
    Range("B1").Select

    'Calculate array size
    ArrSize = WorksheetFunction.CountA(Range("B:B"))

    'resize the array
    ReDim Scores(1 To ArrSize)

End Sub
```

6. Populate the array (use the shortcut way with the range).

```
Sub CalcAverageDynamic()
    Dim Scores() As Variant
    
    'Select cell B1
    Range("B1").Select
    
    'Calculate array size
    ArrSize = WorksheetFunction.CountA(Range("B:B"))
    
    'Resize the array
    ReDim Scores(1 To ArrSize)
    
    'Populate array
    Scores = Range("B2:B51").Value

End Sub
```

Now you have a choice, you need to loop through the array and calculate the average. You could do something like:

For i = 1 to arrSize

Next i

That would work fine. However, let me show you another way. Instead of using a For Loop, you can use a For Each loop. The For Each loop will cycle through all objects in a collection. An array can be thought of as a collection; it is a grouping of similar items, and the For Each loop is well suited for the task.

7   Use a For Each loop to loop through each item in the array.

```
Sub CalcAverageDynamic()
    Dim Scores() As Variant
    
    'Select cell B1
    Range("B1").Select
    
    'Calculate array size
    ArrSize = WorksheetFunction.CountA(Range("B:B"))
    
    'Resize the array
    ReDim Scores(1 To ArrSize)
    
    'Populate array
    Scores = Range("B2:B51").Value
    
    'Loop through each item
    For Each c In Scores
        Total = Total + c
    Next c
    
End Sub
```

Note: In case you forgot, the c in the loop is a variable I created. It doesn't have to be c. You can call it b, Bobby, Santa, etc.

For Each Loop Benefits

You don't need to know how large the array is. The loop will process every element in the array.

For Each Loop Drawbacks

It is read only. You cannot change the elements in the array in this loop.(You CAN change the elements in the For Loop).

This last point is important. I want to make sure you understand it.

This loop will process and change the values that are stored in the array. In this example, I am taking the value, dividing it by 2 and putting it back into the array.

```
Sub ForSample()
    Dim arrSample(1 To 2) As Variant
    
    arrSample(1) = 100
    arrSample(2) = 300
    
    'This will work
    'Inside a For loop, I can change the values inside the array
    For i = 1 To 2
        arrSample(i) = arrSample(i) / 2
    Next i

End Sub
```

The next example WILL NOT WORK. Look at the image below to see how tricky this is. Variable d did get divided by 2 but the value in the array, arrSample(1) did not get changed. In a For Each loop, the variable (in my case, d) is a copy of the value in the array. I can do whatever I want with variable d but I cannot change the value of the actual item inside the array.

```
Sub ForEachSample()
    Dim arrSample(1 To 2) As Variant
    
    arrSample(1) = 100
    arrSample(2) = 300
    
    'This will work
    'Inside a For loop, I can change the values inside the array
    For Each d In arrSample
        d = d / 2
    Ne d = 50

    End Sub
```

```
Immediate
?arrsample(1)
 100
```

In summary, if you need to change the values inside the array, use a For Loop.

8   Finish the macro by calculating the average and putting it in cell F2.

```
Sub CalcAverageDynamic()
    Dim Scores() As Variant
    
    'Select cell B1
    Range("B1").Select
    
    'Calculate array size
    ArrSize = WorksheetFunction.CountA(Range("B:B"))
    
    'Resize the array
    ReDim Scores(1 To ArrSize)
    
    'Populate array
    Scores = Range("B2:B51").Value
    
    'Loop through each item
    For Each c In Scores
        Total = Total + c
    Next c
    
    Range("F2").Value = Total / 50
    
End Sub
```

Yet Another Way to Loop

Ok, now that you have the basics of looping, I'm going to show you another way to use array functions to loop. Excel has a few functions that are designed to be used with arrays. I'm going to show you two of them now.

UBound() - Ubound returns the largest subscript of the array.

LBound() - LBound returns the smallest subscript of the array.

Subscript refers to the slot number of the array. In essence, UBound tells you how large the array is. You can use UBound and LBound as a way to ensure that your loop will always start at the lowest slot, end in the highest slot, and you will have the ability to edit the values in the array.

Look at this example:

```
Sub UsingBounds()
    Dim arrSample(1 To 5) As Variant
    
    For i = LBound(arrSample) To UBound(arrSample)
        'do stuff here
    Next i
    
End Sub
```

This code will work regardless of the size of the array. You will never have to change your looping code to accommodate the array.

SPLIT Function

The SPLIT function is a very useful function that splits a text string by a delimiter into a zero-based, one-dimensional string array. Sounds complicated right? Not really. You already know all this stuff.

Zero based - The array starts at 0 not 1.

One-dimensional array - An array of one dimension. Just like the student scores you have been working with.

String array - an array of string data type.

So, what the SPLIT function does is split the text you give it, at the delimiter you specify and puts each part in its own array slot.

The syntax for the SPLIT function is:

SPLIT (String, Delimiter, Limit, Compare)

String - The text to be processed.
Delimiter - The character that determines the substring.
Limit - The maximum number of times the string should be split. This is optional.
Compare - Numeric value indicating which type of compare to use. This is optional.
You will mostly use only the first two parameters.

This example will help you understand. I am just going to show you the example, you are not going to build it here. The example is in the follow-along workbook. SPLIT is a fantastic way to parse text that you get from other systems or long text values in Excel.

```
Sub UsingSplit()
    Dim Fruits() As String

    strText = "Orange, Banana, Apple, Kiwi, Grape"
    Fruits = Split(strText, ",")

    For i = LBound(Fruits) To UBound(Fruits)
        MsgBox Fruits(i)
    Next i
End Sub
```

This example parses the string of fruits by each comma. The text in between each comma gets loaded into the Fruits array. The For loop displays a message box with each individual fruit.

Erasing an Array

If you want to remove all the items from an array you use the Erase command. Using the example above, to erase the Fruits array the command would be:

Erase Fruits

Using Erase on a static array will remove all the items and the array will still exist. Using Erase on a dynamic array will delete the array. You will need to use ReDim to recreate and resize the array.

Two-Dimensional Arrays

A two-dimensional array can be thought of as having rows and columns, much like a spreadsheet. To loop through a two-dimensional array, you need to use two nested loops; one to loop through the row and a second one to loop through the columns.

The loops always go through the rows. In other words, the loop will get to row 1, loop through all the columns in row 1, move to row 2, loop through all the columns in row 2, etc.

1   Open the workbook Two Dimensional Array.xlsm.

This is the data you will be working with:

	A	B	C
1	Student Name	Test Score 1	Test Score 2
2	Ji Kratz	86	48
3	Anderson Fentress	92	45
4	Terina Milholland	98	40
5	Leila Allyn	53	38
6	Leonarda Scruggs	70	55
7	Shawnta Barbeau	79	74
8	Adelaide Mccalla	82	44
9	Tambra Beaty	99	73
10	Henriette Dillard	88	72

You are going to declare a two-dimensional array, populate it and then print out the values in the immediate window.

2   Create a new macro name it TwoDim.

```
Sub TwoDim()


End Sub
```

When you declare a two-dimensional array, you need to specify how many rows and how many columns in this format (1 to 10, 1 to 2). The next image will show you how to write the declaration statement.

3   Declare a dynamic array of Variant data type called arrScores.

```vba
Sub TwoDim()
    Dim arrScores() As Variant


End Sub
```

You can use the shortcut range method to populate the array.

4. Populate the array with this line: arrScores = Range("B2:C10").Value.

```vba
Sub TwoDim()
    Dim arrScores() As Variant

    'Populate array
    arrScores() = Range("B2:C10").Value

End Sub
```

Now you are going to write two nested loops to print out the results to the Immediate window. Why the Immediate window? Because when you are developing code, you don't need to write to the worksheet. The Immediate window can serve as a scratchpad to see your results without interfering with the Excel file.

```vba
Sub TwoDim()
    Dim arrScores() As Variant

    'Populate array
    arrScores() = Range("B2:C10").Value

    'Print headers
    Debug.Print "Row", "Column", "Value"

    'Loop through each row
    For i = LBound(arrScores) To UBound(arrScores)
        'loop through each column
        'the 2 indicates the second dimension
        For k = LBound(arrScores, 2) To UBound(arrScores, 2)
            Debug.Print i, k, arrScores(i, k)
        Next k
    Next i

End Sub
```

5. Run the macro.

6. Display the Immediate window (if it is not visible) to see your results.

```
Immediate
  Row              Column           Value
   1                 1                86
   1                 2                48
   2                 1                92
   2                 2                45
   3                 1                98
   3                 2                40
   4                 1                53
   4                 2                38
   5                 1                70
   5                 2                55
   6                 1                79
   6                 2                74
   7                 1                82
   7                 2                44
   8                 1                99
   8                 2                73
   9                 1                88
   9                 2                72
```

This ends the section on arrays. This has not been an exhaustive and complete lesson on arrays. There are many, many more things you can do with arrays but this information will give you a solid foundation to start using this feature that you can build upon on your own.

Now, we move on to Collections...

Collections

Collections are similar to arrays in that they store data of the same type. Arrays get all the glory (because arrays exist in almost all programming languages), but collections are actually easier to use than arrays.

Many of the skills you just practiced with arrays (For Each loops, For Loops, etc.) are also applicable to collections. In fact, you use them the same way. You need to use the loops to cycle through each element. One BIG difference between collections and arrays is that **you cannot change the item in a collection. Collections are read only.** If you need to change the item in the collection, then you need to use an array instead.

Ok, let's write a macro so you can see how collections are easier to work with than arrays.

1   Open the follow-along workbook Collections.xlsm.

This has a small data set of students.

	A	B
1	Student Name	Test Score
2	Ji Kratz	86
3	Anderson Fentress	92
4	Terina Milholland	98
5	Leila Allyn	53
6	Leonarda Scruggs	70
7	Shawnta Barbeau	79
8	Adelaide Mccalla	82
9	Tambra Beaty	99
10	Henriette Dillard	88
11		

2. Insert a new macro. Call it myCollection.

```
Sub myCollection()

End Sub
```

You can create the collection in one line with the Dim keyword. You can add the collection to Excel with the New keyword.

3. Create a new collection called Students.

```
Sub myCollection()
    Dim Students As New Collection

End Sub
```

Notice that unlike arrays, there is no sizing parameters needed with collections. **Notice that no data type is needed.**

Before you start writing loops to load the collection, let's work through a few simple exercises that will show you how convenient collections are. You have an empty collection. You need to add a few items to it.

You can add individual items to a collection by using the Add method. The syntax is [collection name].Add "value to add"

4. Add the student Susie Tink to the collection.

```
Sub myCollection()
    Dim Students As New Collection

    Students.Add "Susie Tink"

End Sub
```

5   Add a new line that displays item #1 in the Immediate window.

```
Sub myCollection()
    Dim Students As New Collection

    Students.Add "Susie Tink"
    Debug.Print Students(1)

End Sub
```

6   Run the macro and confirm that Susie Tink appears in the Immediate window (you might have to display the window if it is not visible).

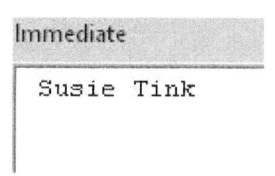

```
Immediate
Susie Tink
```

Remember a few steps ago, I told you that you did not need to declare a data type when creating a collection? In collections, you can mix data types! Add a new item that is numeric.

7   Add this line: Students.Add 42.

8   Change the Print line to display the second item.

9   Run the macro to see the second item.

```
Sub myCollection()
    Dim Students As New Collection

    Students.Add "Susie Tink"
    Students.Add 42
    Debug.Print Students(2)

End Sub
```

Immediate
```
42
```

Wait. Maybe you messed up and in this case, order matters. You need to add a new student before Susie. In an array, you would be out of luck. Thankfully, you are working with a collection. In a collection, it is easy to add an items in a specific spot in the collection.

10   Add this line to add item James Polk before Susie Tink: Students.Add "James Polk", Before:=1.

11   Change the order of the macro code to match the image below. This will let you check that James is really the first item in the collection.

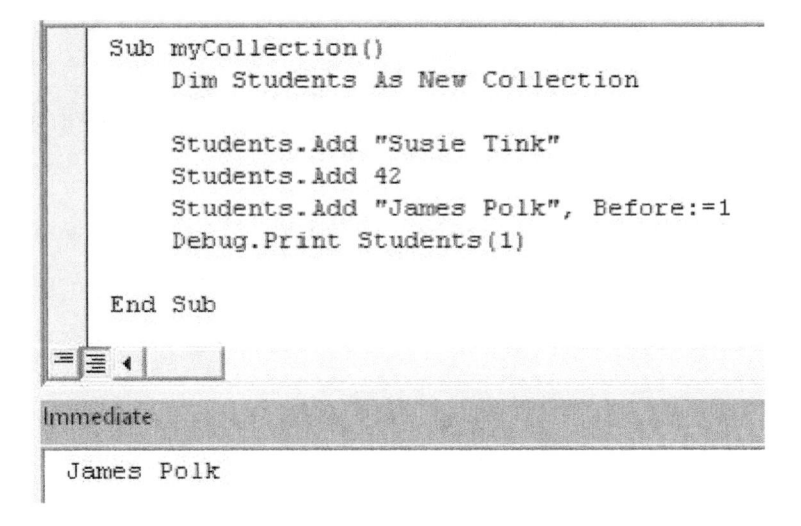

```
Sub myCollection()
    Dim Students As New Collection

    Students.Add "Susie Tink"
    Students.Add 42
    Students.Add "James Polk", Before:=1
    Debug.Print Students(1)

End Sub
```

Immediate
```
James Polk
```

Ok, we made a mistake. That 42 should not be in there. You need to get rid of it. Unfortunately, the code has moved items around and you aren't sure where the 42 is in the collection.

Similarly to what you did for arrays, you are going to write a For loop to display the item number and the item for each item in the collection. Arrays had the issue where you had to calculate the size of the array and use that in the For i = 1 to x line in the macro (where x was the size of the array). Collections are easier. The Count property returns the number of items. Students.Count is what you will use.

12   Add a For loop to display each item and its index.

If the Immediate window has previous values in there, you can highlight them and press the DELETE key to clean it up.

```
Sub myCollection()
    Dim Students As New Collection

    Students.Add "Susie Tink"
    Students.Add 42
    Students.Add "James Polk", Before:=1
    'Debug.Print Students(1)

    For i = 1 To Students.Count
        Debug.Print i, Students(i)
    Next i

End Sub
```

```
Immediate
  1            James Polk
  2            Susie Tink
  3               42
```

Which one of those items is not like the others? 42. In this case, 42 is not the answer. You need to remove that item. You know that it is item 3 from the code you just ran. You need to use the collection's remove method.
Students.Remove 3

13   Add the remove method to remove item #3.

Note: Put the remove method before the loop so you can see that 42 is actually removed.

```
Sub myCollection()
    Dim Students As New Collection
    
    Students.Add "Susie Tink"
    Students.Add 42
    Students.Add "James Polk", Before:=1
    'Debug.Print Students(1)
    
    Students.Remove 3
    
    For i = 1 To Students.Count
        Debug.Print i, Students(i)
    Next i
    
End Sub
```

```
Immediate
    1           James Polk
    2           Susie Tink
```

In cases where you need to delete all the items from a collection, you would set the collection to Nothing, like this:

Set Students = Nothing

Using Keys in Collections

I put the heading for this section in big blue letter because (in my humble opinion) keys are a MAJOR advantage of collections over arrays and I wanted you to pay attention to it.

When you add an item to a collection, you can assign it a key and then retrieve it using the key. **The one condition is that the key must be unique.**

For example, if you wanted to add a key value pair, you could use this line:

Students.Add Item:=42, Key:="James"

Then when you want to retrieve the value, you would use:

Debug.Print Students("James")

Let's work with this feature so you can see how great it is. You are going to load the data in the worksheet into a new collection.

1   Create a new macro called UsingKeys.

MASTERING EXCEL MACROS

```
Sub UsingKeys()


End Sub
```

2. Create a new collection named StudentScores.

```
Sub UsingKeys()
    Dim StudentScores As New Collection

End Sub
```

3. Add a line to select cell A1.

4. This time you are going to use a Do Until loop to process each row. (You could use a For loop, a While loop, or anything you like. There are many ways to do the same thing in a macro.)

```
Sub UsingKeys()
    Dim StudentScores As New Collection

    Range("A1").Select
    i = 1
    Do Until ActiveCell.Offset(i, 0).Value = ""

    Loop

End Sub
```

5. Inside the Do loop, you are going to populate the StudentScores collection with data by keys.

```
Sub UsingKeys()
    Dim StudentScores As New Collection

    Range("A1").Select
    i = 1
    Do Until ActiveCell.Offset(i, 0).Value = ""
        StudentScores.Add Item:=ActiveCell.Offset(i, 1).Value, Key:=ActiveCell.Offset(i, 0).Value
        i = i + 1
    Loop
End Sub
```

That line in the middle looks intimidating huh? It isn't if you have been following with all the other lessons, you know all this stuff. It's just that when you put it all together it looks complicated. Let's figure it out.

OFFSET: The active cell is not moving around. For large data sets, moving the active cell is inefficient and very slow. Instead of moving the active cell, you are going to point to it using the active cell as **a base of reference**. OFFSET basically says: Give me a cell that is x rows away and y columns away from the current cell.

OFFSET ([Rows away from current cell], [Columns away from current cell])

	A	B
1	Student Name	Test Score
2	Ji Kratz	86
3	Anderson Fentress	92
4	Terina Milholland	98
5	Leila Allyn	53

Ok, now pretend i = 1 and the current cell is A1.

The item is 1 row down and 1 column to the right of A1 (the active cell). 1 row down, 1 column left of A1 is B2. 86 is the first item.

The key is 1 row down and 0 columns to the left of A1 (the active cell). 1 row down and 0 columns away (the same column) from A1 is A2. Ji Kratz is the first key.

Then you follow the same procedure for i = 2.

Does that make sense? You can refer to any cell in a worksheet by figuring out how many rows and columns it is away from the current cell. You don't have to move to it to use it. One drawback is that it might be hard to debug this. Why? You can't see what is going on. The workaround is to use something like OFFSET(x,y).Select to move the cell to the location you want. When you are sure the correct cell is being referenced, remove the line with OFFSET(x,y).Select.

1. Add a debug.Print statement to show a student's score. (I chose Leila Allyn).

```
Sub UsingKeys()
    Dim StudentScores As New Collection
    
    Range("A1").Select
    i = 1
    Do Until ActiveCell.Offset(i, 0).Value = ""
        StudentScores.Add Item:=ActiveCell.Offset(i, 1).Value, Key:=ActiveCell.Offset(i, 0).Value
        i = i + 1
    Loop
    Debug.Print StudentScores("Leila Allyn")
End Sub
```

Immediate
53

Keys make retrieving data much simpler and are more intuitive than arrays. However, there are certain drawbacks to using keys.

- You cannot retrieve or list the keys in a collection

- The keys must be unique

- You cannot check to see if the key already exists

- You cannot change the key

- You cannot change the value of an existing item (remember that collections are Read Only)

If you like the idea of working with keys, then you are going to love the next section...

Dictionary

The dictionary object behaves similarly to the collection object, but it can do a few things the collection object can't:

•You can change an item in the dictionary

•You can test to see if a key already exists

One very important item you must be aware of before you continue learning about dictionaries: **Case matters!** If you add a key 'orange' and then add another key with 'Orange' the dictionary will add both.

If you want to use the dictionary, you need to add it to Excel. The library that contains it is installed, just not activated. There are two ways to add the dictionary to Excel: Early Binding and Late Binding.

Early Binding

When you use Early Binding, you are explicitly telling Excel that you are going to use an extra programming object, in this case, the dictionary.

Note: If you already added the 'Microsoft Scripting Runtime' in a previous lesson, you do not have to re-add it. Just follow the steps to make sure it is still there.

To set up Early Binding:

1 Open Excel.

2 Go to the Developer tab.

3 Click on Visual Basic to open the VBA environment.

4 Click on Tools, References.

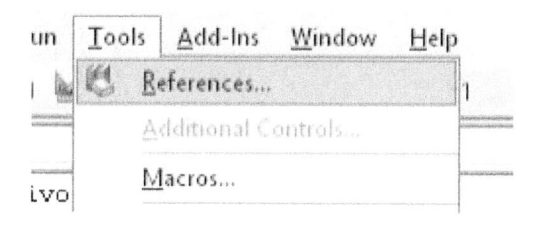

5 Scroll down until you find the Microsoft Scripting Runtime library.

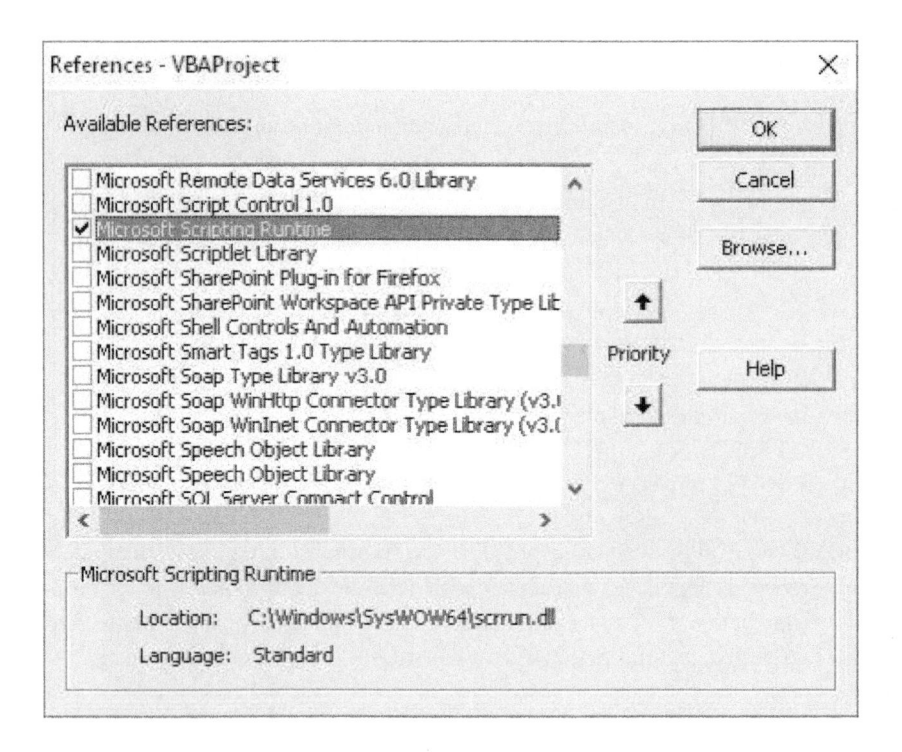

6   Select Microsoft Scripting Runtime.

7   Click OK.

Now, Excel knows that you are going to be using the dictionary object. One immediate benefit of this is that you now have Intellisense ready to help you out with the dictionary object. Intellisense is the feature that displays pop ups when you use the dot notation to access a property or method.

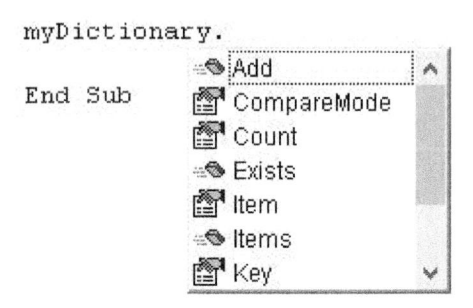

One drawback to using Early Binding is that you might have to add the library reference to users that run your macro.

Late Binding

When using Late Binding, you don't have to add a reference to the library beforehand, instead you add a reference right in the code.

The code below shows you an example of using Late Binding:

```
Sub DictionarySample()
    Dim myDictionary As Object

    Set myDictionary = CreateObject("Scripting.Dictionary")

End Sub
```

Now you can use the myDictionary object as you would any other object.
The drawback with Late Binding is that you lose the availability of Intellisense.
Most of the previous skills you learned in this lesson (For Loops, For Each Loops, etc.) also apply to dictionaries. Let's work through an example to show you the new features of dictionaries.

1. Open the Dictionary.xlsm workbook.

2. Create a new macro called DictLesson.

```
Sub DictLesson()


End Sub
```

3. Create a new dictionary using Late Binding.

```
Sub DictLesson()
    Dim myDictionary As Object

    Set myDictionary = CreateObject("Scripting.Dictionary")

End Sub
```

Case and Keys

Excel can use one of two methods to find keys: TextCompare or BinaryCompare.
TextCompare is case insensitive. That is, lower case and upper case are treated the same.
BinaryCompare is case sensitive. "Orange" will be different than "orange". This is the default method.
You can force Excel to use one method by using the CompareMode method.

4. Use the TextCompare method in your code.

```
Sub DictLesson()
    Dim myDictionary As Object

    Set myDictionary = CreateObject("Scripting.Dictionary")

    'Make key matches case insensitive
    myDictionary.CompareMode = TextCompare


End Sub
```

Adding items to a dictionary

When you add an item to the dictionary, you **must** add the item key and the item value. Each key must be unique. One feature of the dictionary is that you can retrieve values based on the key. The key must be unique for this lookup feature to be able to work.

Keys don't have to be numbers. They can be anything you like. Items can be text or numbers; you can mix data types in dictionaries.

Adding items to the dictionary is done using the Add method. Below are a few ways to add items to the dictionary:

myDictionary.Add Key:="Paul Revere", Item:=42
myDictionary.Add "John Adams", 56
myDictionary.Add 2, 3.14
myDictionary.Add "6/21/2016", "Mike"

5   Add the students to the myDictionary dictionary using a For Loop.

```
Sub DictLesson()
    Dim myDictionary As Object

    Set myDictionary = CreateObject("Scripting.Dictionary")

    'Make key matches case insensitive
    myDictionary.CompareMode = TextCompare

    'Populate the dictionary
    Range("A1").Select
    For i = 1 To WorksheetFunction.CountA(Range("A:A"))
        myDictionary.Add Key:=ActiveCell.Offset(i, 0).Value, Item:=ActiveCell.Offset(i, 1).Value
    Next i

End Sub
```

Retrieving a value from the dictionary

Getting a value from a dictionary is pretty straightforward. You use the dictionary name followed by the key in parentheses. For example, to retrieve the score for Tambra Beaty you would use this code:

myDictionary("Tambra Beaty")

Try using this code in the Immediate window to see it in action.

```
Immediate
?myDictionary("Tambra Beaty")
 99
```

Removing an item from the dictionary

Also pretty straightforward.

myDictionary.Remove "Tambra Beaty"

This will remove all the items in a dictionary:

myDictionary.RemoveAll

Changing the value in a dictionary

This is where collections differ from dictionaries. Collections are read only. Dictionaries aren't; you can easily change the value in the dictionary. This line would change Tabra's score to 89.

myDictionary("Tambra Beaty") = 89

6   Add a line in the loop to decrease everyone's score by 10%.

```
Sub DictLesson()
    Dim myDictionary As Object

    Set myDictionary = CreateObject("Scripting.Dictionary")

    'Make key matches case insensitive
    myDictionary.CompareMode = TextCompare

    'Populate the dictionary
    Range("A1").Select
    For i = 1 To WorksheetFunction.CountA(Range("A:A"))
        myDictionary.Add Key:=ActiveCell.Offset(i, 0).Value, Item:=ActiveCell.Offset(i, 1).Value

        'ActiveCell.Offset(i, 0).Value is each cell in column A
        'ActiveCell.Offset(i, 1).Value is one column to the right of column A
        myDictionary(ActiveCell.Offset(i, 0).Value) = ActiveCell.Offset(i, 1).Value * 0.9
    Next i

End Sub
```

Sneaky Trick

This line:

myDictionary("Paul Revere") = 79

not only changes Paul's score but if Paul does not exist in the dictionary, it will add him and his value to the dictionary. **This is another way to add items to the dictionary.**

Keys must be unique.

If you try to add a key that already exists you will get this error:

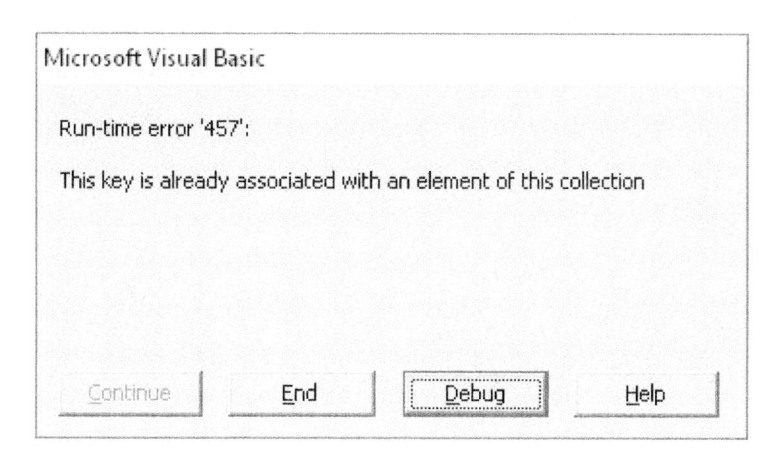

Microsoft Visual Basic

Run-time error '457':

This key is already associated with an element of this collection

Continue   End   Debug   Help

You can avoid this error by using the Exists method before adding a key.

```
'Check key before adding student
If myDictionary.Exists("Tambra Beaty") Then
    MsgBox ("Tambra Beaty has already been added")
Else
    myDictionary.Add "Tambra Beaty", 54
End If
```

Lesson Summary

This lesson dealt exclusively with tools that you can use to manage large amounts of data in a macro. When you are just starting out, knowing when to use which tool gets kind of confusing. Let me summarize the reasons here:

Arrays: You use arrays when you have a ton of numbers that you need to change. You change them in the array and then put the answer wherever you like (a message box, a cell in a worksheet, etc.). All Items in the array must be the same data type.

Collections: Use collections when you need to process items but not change them; collections are read-only. Adding items is easy and you can use keys with collections. You cannot access the key once created in a collection. You can mix data types in collections.

Dictionary: Use dictionaries when you have a list of unique items and you need to retrieve values by each item key.

Other Lessons

I have many other lessons covering various Excel topics.

You can find all of them on my website at:

http://markmoorebooks.com/excel-lessons/

If this lesson has helped you, please take a few minutes and leave a review on Amazon. The more reviews the lesson gets, the easier other students will be able to find it.

Thank you!

Mark

Printed in Great Britain
by Amazon